THE STRANGER IN THE MIRROR

The Stranger in the Mirror

A Memoir of Middle Age

JANE SHILLING

Chatto & Windus
LONDON

Published by Chatto & Windus 2011

2 4 6 8 10 9 7 5 3 1

Copyright © Jane Shilling 2011

Jane Shilling has asserted her right under the Copyright, Designs
and Patents Act 1988 to be identified as the author of this work

Extract on p. 47 from 'The Djinn in the Nightingale's Eye' by A.S. Byatt, published
by Chatto & Windus. Reprinted by permission of The Random House Group Ltd.
Lines on p. 228 taken from 'One Art' from *The Complete Poems 1927–1979* by
Elizabeth Bishop. Copyright © 1979, 1983 by Alice Helen Methfessel. Reprinted by
permission of Farrar, Straus and Giroux, LLC.

Every effort has been made to trace and contact all copyright holders, and the
publishers would be pleased to rectify any omissions brought to their notice at
the earliest opportunity.

First published in Great Britain in 2011 by
Chatto & Windus
Random House, 20 Vauxhall Bridge Road,
London SW1V 2SA
www.rbooks.co.uk

Addresses for companies within The Random House Group Limited can be found at:
www.randomhouse.co.uk/offices.htm

The Random House Group Limited Reg. No. 954009

A CIP catalogue record for this book
is available from the British Library

ISBN 9780701181000

The Random House Group Limited supports The Forest Stewardship
Council (FSC), the leading international forest certification organisation. All our titles
that are printed on Greenpeace approved FSC certified paper carry the FSC logo. Our
paper procurement policy can be found at www.rbooks.co.uk/environment

Mixed Sources
Product group from well-managed
forests and other controlled sources
www.fsc.org Cert no. TT-COC-2139
© 1996 Forest Stewardship Council
FSC

Typeset by SX Composing DTP, Rayleigh, Essex
Printed and bound in Great Britain by
Clays Ltd, St Ives Plc

For Sarah L and Sarah C

And in memory of Nora and Bobby Lock

With love

Lord, are we as old as all that? I feel about six and a half.
                    Virginia Woolf, letter to Vanessa Bell

Je n'ai pas plus fait mon livre que mon livre ne m'a fait.
                    Montaigne, *Essais*

What's gone and what's past help
Should be past grief.
                    Shakespeare, *The Winter's Tale*

Contents

Preface

So, what are you working on at the moment? they would ask politely. A book about middle age, I would say. And whoever I was speaking to would give a terrible sort of roguish bridle, or squirm, and say, 'Not that you'd know anything about *that*, of course.'

Without exception, they said it. Men and women, young, old and middle-aged themselves. A beautiful young writer at a Notting Hill party said it sweetly; a red-faced old farmer at a point-to-point said it with creaking flirtatiousness. Everyone seemed to think it their duty to reassure me that I was exempt from what they obviously thought of as a kind of bad spell. Which was odd, for I was 47 when I began writing this book; not a borderline case, but as unambiguous an example of female middle age as you could possibly imagine.

The other thing they all wanted to know was, 'How are you defining middle age?' I wasn't convinced that defining middle age was a useful exercise. For women (and it is female middle age that concerns me here. Male middle age is certainly a very interesting subject, but not one about which I feel qualified to write) the menopause is the unequivocal marker of the boundary between youth and what is left of life. Cross that frontier and you are in no doubt that you are middle aged. But middle age and the menopause are not precisely the same thing. Fashion journalists and doctors would place the onset of middle age well before the end of fertility, at the point at which one's rate of egg production and cellular renewal begins to slow, and one's ability to wear hot pants and biker jackets with conviction to diminish.

I was more interested in describing than defining this passage of female experience, in particular because, although middle-aged people now predominate in the UK population (in 2009 the average age was 39.5 years, with the graph showing a large peak of baby boomers in their forties and fifties), as I approached middle age myself I could find no contemporary model of it that interested me.

Throughout my adult life I had been accustomed to find my own experience as a woman reflected in the culture. Magazines and newspapers contained pictures of women of more or less my age, dressed in clothes that I might also like to wear, describing experiences that were familiar to me. Programmes on the television and radio took as their raw material the lives of my contemporaries. In bookshops, the female experience appeared in a myriad narrative forms. Until the onset of middle age, when, all of a sudden, there was apparently no one like me at all. Like the children of Hamelin led away into the mountain cavern, we had all vanished.

I exaggerate. There were, if you looked for them, some traces of middle-aged experience to be found. In newspapers and magazines these generally took a sternly prohibitive form. In my twenties and thirties, I read magazines in which the features and fashion shoots described a world of possibility and fantasy. But at 40 and beyond there were no fashion shoots, only grim lists of the garments one could (apparently) no longer wear without appearing grotesque, together with much shorter lists of suitable alternatives, all designed to conceal or restrain the imperfections of the ageing body.

The features, too, tended to dwell on the indignity of middle-aged experience; its lamentable divergence from the youthful norm, with an outrageous catalogue of reckless post-menopausal love affairs, heroically late pregnancies, marital humiliation, extremities of cosmetic surgery, the alarming side effects of HRT. The repulsiveness of the middle-aged female body and the constant vigilance required to suppress its determination to sag, bloat, flab, sprout, droop and wrinkle was a prevailing theme.

On television, where the rate of attrition among middle-aged female presenters is tremendous, the alternative voice of middle age was represented by the Grumpy Old Women, and their anodyne daytime cousins, the coy kaffeeklatsch of Loose Women. The prevailing tone among the Grumpies is rage and disappointment, artfully tweaked into a simulacrum of comedy. The brilliance of the concept is that in the complicit guise of telling middle age like it really is – sluttish, surly, rueful, defeated – it reinforces the caricature and so keeps everyone happy. Middle-aged women can feel the Grumpies have given them an authentic voice, while everyone else is confirmed in their comfortable prejudices about the battiness of women of a certain age. My teenage son adores them.

I, on the other hand, as I passed 40 and began to head for 50, wondered whether there might be more to the narratives of middle age than hot flushes, absent-minded shoplifting and an overwhelming sense of having been cheated by life.

'I don't believe in ageing,' wrote Virginia Woolf at 50. 'I believe in forever altering one's aspect to the sun.' Altering one's aspect to the sun struck me as a more interesting approach to ageing than sticking a patch on my bottom and knocking a decade off my age, but I wondered how one went about it. Since my thirties had been, on the whole, happier than my twenties, and my forties happier than my thirties, there seemed some grounds for cautious optimism about the future.

At 47 I thought that a steady nerve, a good haircut and an enquiring mind would be sufficient protection against most of the outrages that middle age might inflict. By 50 I knew better. But although the experience was (and is) harder and more painful than I thought; more full of confusion and loss, it is also more interesting than I had imagined. As it goes on, the process of ageing seems to me to be less about what is lost, and more about what remains.

This is not a manual of advice on how to cope with the menopause. There is no shortage of those. It is, rather, what Henry James in his Preface to the 1908 New York edition of *The Portrait of a Lady*, called an 'ado'. 'Millions of presumptuous girls, intelligent or not intelligent, daily affront their destiny, and what is it open to their destiny to be, at the most, that we should make an ado about it?' wrote James, adding, 'The novel is of its very nature an "ado" . . . about something.'

By middle age, of course, one has a fair idea of what one's destiny is to be. Nevertheless, one must continue to affront it, and it seems to me that the struggle is worthy of an 'ado'. This is not a novel, but it is a story – my story – and, like all stories, it is shaped by omission as well as inclusion. Every woman's experience of middle age is both universal and particular, and the particularity of my own experience contains some significant omissions. I have never, for example, been married and so I cannot write from experience about the joys and chagrins of middle-aged marriage. What I can do is, as Montaigne put it, 'tell the truth, as much as I dare – and as I grow older I dare a little more'.

I
Message in a Bottle

Around the inexorable checkpoint of the menopause a debatable land extends, in which one's experience of middle age is determined not by this or that arbitrary boundary of years, but by individual sensibility. One becomes, in short, middle aged when one feels oneself to be middle aged, and not before.

'When I'm grown up . . .' children say to one another. But grown-upness, like middle age, is an infinitely receding quality. 'How old do you feel inside?' I ask my mother and grandmother as we sit podding peas in the garden one sunny day thirty-five years ago. Thirty-five, says my grandmother, quick as a flash, slitting the pods with her fingernails, sending the peas skipping into the colander with a musical bounce, plink, plink, like a fairy xylophone. She is 71. Twenty-seven, says my mother, who is 44 and wears big glasses for short sight and has short pale eyelashes and her brown hair coiled up into a bun which she skewers to the back of her head with brown wire hairpins like a handful of pine needles.

I have seen pictures in the family photograph album of my mother as a child, kneeling in the wavelets on a Cornish beach, with a halo of white-blonde hair and angel's wings borrowed from a seagull that flew behind her just as the shutter snapped. I have clocked the photo of her doing a showy-off splits in the sand on the same holiday, dressed in a knitted swimsuit with a swimming-ring around her waist. And I have noted the later pictures of her, a few years older, still with the wavy silver-gilt hair but now with bosoms and long, long legs and a heavy-lidded regard like that of Bette Davis, photographed with her equally pretty (but dark-haired) French penfriend, Françoise, in an assortment of the beauty spots they visited on their exchange trips, or clasping a menagerie of animals that died before I was born, but whose names I have grown up knowing: Trixie, the terrier bitch; Diogenes, the dockyard cat with austere views on interior design, who used to pace along the mantelshelf, fastidiously pushing to the floor any knick-knack that stood in his way.

Though my imagination continues to reject the notion, there is irrefutable evidence in these pictures that my middle-aged mother was once both a child and a teenager. In the later shots she is 16 – a year younger than I am now. Although arithmetic is mainly beneath me, I have done sums. I have worked out that in the year 2000 I shall be 42, or two years younger than my mother is as we sit in the sunshine, podding peas. The maths is undeniable – which is one of the many things I have against mathematics. On the one hand I am in no position to disbelieve the calculations showing that in twenty-five years' time I shall be 42 and nearly as old as my mother (and she, in turn, will be 69, or nearly as old as her mother). On the other, the fact is that I do disbelieve them.

I peer under my 17-year-old eyelashes at my mother, sitting on the plaid rug on the grass with those long legs tucked up under her sensible skirt. The tender coltishness of the early photographs has vanished. The legs are heavy now, their skimmed-milk pallor etched with a tracery of bluish-purple veins; the toenails sticking out of her flat navy sandals are ridged like limpet shells, the skin of the heels is cracked like old cheese. The muscular calves of someone used to trudging up and down suburban streets encumbered with prams and shopping baskets are covered in a springing growth of cobwebby hairs.

It looks (I think, getting up to pick some mint to go with the peas) as though some sort of bad spell was cast over the golden-haired teenager with the kitten and terrier and the pretty French penfriend in the album pictures. As though a spiteful magician had come along and shut her up in a carapace of thickened limbs and mottled skin, from which only her heavy-lidded Bette Davis eyes peer out, myopic but still recognisable, behind the big lenses of her spectacles.

Whatever the sums say, whatever the photographic evidence, I am quite certain that the same spell is not going to be cast over me. I wonder, briefly, if my mother is secretly harbouring a similar disbelief at the idea that time will turn her into an old woman like my grandmother, and conclude that she can't be. She seems bizarrely unaware of the way she occupies space, of the body she inhabits. Minutely aware as I am of the pores on my adolescent nose, the precise state of development of every tiny blemish, of every minuscule change in the size of my almost non-existent bosom, of the position of each hair in the arch of my eyebrows, I find it hard to understand how someone can get up in the mornings, contemplate their reflection in the mirror, even draw breath, looking as my mother does.

Perhaps, I speculate, once you reach a particular age – 25, perhaps (a quarter of a century has a certain knell-like resonance), or 30, or 35, the halfway mark of the biblical three score and ten – some kind of grown-up phenomenon ensures that you just stick right there. Some trick of perception means that when you look in the mirror, the reflection you see there isn't you as everyone else sees you, not the ridged, veined, hirsute husk that has accumulated over the years like some old caddis fly's dwelling of sticks and stones and bits of weed, but the person you were when you got stuck.

As I formulate this hypothesis, I can see that it contains some significant lacunae. I'm not entirely clear, for a start, whether the gap between yourself as you are and the person you feel yourself to be is a process of active self-delusion – whether you decide at 27 or 35 that this is the face you will henceforth see in the mirror, or whether the self-deception mechanism simply kicks in automatically one day. A passage in Nancy Mitford's *Love in a Cold Climate* confirms the phenomenon without altogether clarifying it.

'What was she like when she was young?' (asks the teenaged narrator, Fanny, about a terrifying old battleaxe, Lady Montdore, who is in her sixties and looks like a Grenadier guardsman in drag).

'Exactly the same as she is now,' replies Fanny's fiftysomething uncle, Davey. 'I've known her ever since I was a little tiny boy and she hasn't changed one scrap.'

'I left it at that' (writes Fanny). 'It's no good, I thought, you always come up against this blank wall with old people, they always say about each other that they have never looked any different, and how can it be true?'

This seems to suggest that the peculiar not-seeing of themselves by grown-ups – their preposterous conviction in the teeth of the evidence that they're still in the prime of life – is just another of the arbitrary tricks that nature every so often plays on the unsuspecting person. At 17, I have not yet emerged from the grip of late adolescence and so I am quite used to these. At 13, 14 and 15, the rest of my year at my girls' grammar school were turning into women. One moment they were galloping up and down the playground, pretending to be horses and playing jacks on the music-room steps. The next, they had acquired the appendages of our teachers and mothers – bulging chests contained within hammocky bras; a tendency to conduct interminable conversations in complicit undertones, a mysterious smell of iris mixed with cat pee when they put their hands up to answer a question in class, and something else, a sort of self-important languor that distanced them irrevocably from the world of pretend horses and jacks in which I was left behind.

At last, at nearly 16, it happened to me, too: the disturbing sprouting and reshaping of the body and the feelings; the messiness of womanhood with its complicated secret paraphernalia – the sordid elastic rigging of training bras and sanitary belts and half-slips, their utilitarian function rather emphasised than disguised with coy embellishments of scratchy nylon lace and little ribbon bows; the half-smug, half-rueful expressions of the handful of girls excused each week from swimming lessons, the sinister pains in one's joints and abdomen, the greasy, lumpy ruin of one's childish skin, the giggling and swooning over pop stars, make-up and boys.

At 17, I am still at the graceless, half-fledged stage of the transition from child to woman. The training bra slips about uselessly on my flat chest and is spitefully remarked on by the bosomy girls when we get changed for PE. I am interested in clothes and make-up and being allowed to wear high-heeled shoes (these are forbidden in our house). I am fascinated by the exotic emotional dilemmas of girls my age, who write in to Cathy and Claire, the agony aunts of a teen magazine called *Jackie* (also on the domestic Index of proscribed items). I can't see the point of Donny Osmond or David Cassidy, who look to me, with their polite smiles, pastel trouser suits and mid-length bouffants, a bit like some of my friends' mothers – distinctly low on sexual allure, at any rate.

I harbour a passionate, unreciprocated attachment to a boy from my old primary school, but that's been going on since we were both five years old, so it's hard to know whether it belongs among the vague feelings of nameless discontent and unspecified longing that have been troubling me this summer.

At the moment, my erotic imagination is more engaged by girls than boys. The pictures on my bedroom wall, the objects of my narcissistic daydreams, are of the wayward *jolies laides* I would like to become when my chrysalis of suburban adolescence eventually ruptures to let me out: Janis Joplin in her tattered peacock finery; Patti Smith and her dandyish androgyny. But between dreams of becoming a Rimbaudesque *âme damnée* with kohl-rimmed eyes, I still quite often play with my doll's house. And along with those instruction manuals of female adolescence, *Wuthering Heights*, *The Bell Jar* and *Claudine at School*, from time to time I secretly reread a book from my early childhood called *The Very Little Girl*.

This is a book by an American author, Phyllis Krasilovsky, with delicate, Frenchified illustrations by Ninon in a palette of four colours – black, white, powder pink and a vivid spring green – that seems somehow both innocent and vicious. The story is a simple version of that most basic of fairy-tale archetypes, the transformation narrative.

'Once there was a little girl,' it begins, 'who was very very very little.' There follows a list of all the things she was smaller than – rose bush, kitchen stool, mother's work basket, all her friends – and a description of the privileges attached to her diminutive size: 'A special little chair to sit on and a special little table to eat on and a special little bed to sleep on.' Very desirable, they are, the pictures of tiny furniture, especially the special little bed – a white four-poster strewn with rosebuds and covered with a frilly pink counterpane.

At the halfway point of the story, the transformation sets in. One day the very little girl finds the proportions of the world have shifted. She is bigger than her dog; she can lift up her cat and see over the garden fence. Insects, lizards and rabbits are smaller than she, as are her special little table, chair and bed. The illustration, a night scene sombrely shaded in dark grey, shows her uneasily crammed into the dwarfish four-poster with her feet sticking out at the end, looking cold and uncomfortable.

On the next page, the night-time crisis is over. There follows a list of the advantages of being a big girl: a new bed – just as frilly as the old one, but roomier – meals eaten at the big table with her parents, games with the other big girls. Best of all, 'Now she was big enough to be a big sister to her brand new baby brother who was very very very little!' As a narrative for a young child facing the prospect of a new baby in the family, the message could hardly be more reassuring – Change is exciting! Growing up is good! – were it not for the tendency of the illustrations delicately but devastatingly to subvert the text.

In the early images, the very little girl trots about barefoot and unoccupied, marvelling at the bigness of the world with a toddler's intent absorption. There follows the *noirish* crisis of her growing bigger, after which there comes a subtle change, not just in her appearance, but in the quality of her engagement with the world. She no longer runs about barefoot, but is shod in flirtatious pink mules. She wears a frilled apron with a bib and is shown performing a series of housewifely tasks – picking fruit, taking a packet of something out of a cupboard, testing her baby brother's milk by squirting a few drops from the warmed bottle on to her wrist and finally feeding him the bottle with a maternal air as he reclines like a little emperor on a pink cushion.

Growing bigger has given her a mastery over the world that she lacked when she was small. She can reach the door handle, she can see over the fence: to this extent her transformation has given her power to explore a universe beyond the tiny strangenesses of her domestic boundaries. But her vanished littleness has taken with it a kind of liberty. The world shrinks as the child grows, pressing her into shape as it contracts. In the feathery pink and green pictures of her testing her brother's bottle and feeding him, there is an edge of melancholy that disturbs me. It is as though the little girl's fate has hardened as she has grown into the age of responsibility. In the sweetly maternal pictures of her caring for her baby brother, there is an ominous prefiguring of the housewife she is destined to become.

Though I have been mocked at school for being the last person in my class to cross the frontier between childhood and womanhood, privately I cling to what remains of my tenacious littleness. Smallness gives me, like the Very Little Girl, the illusion of floating in a world of infinite possibility. It seems a kind of refuge. Small and overlooked, you can inhabit a world of your own imagining. But once you grow large and bosomy, it strikes me that your opportunities start closing down at a hectic rate.

Already I know I will never be a ballerina, a musician, a gymnast or a vet. Like every teenage girl of my generation, I have been captivated by the performance of Olga Korbut in the 1972 Olympics. Her effortless, sinewy, child-woman charm was so potent as to persuade us all that we, too, could be Olgas. I am physically maladroit. Even so, I manage to convince myself that the force of my imagination will be enough to propel me from the ground in an antic series of leaps and turns and scything airborne twists like hers, until a crushing series of experiments with gravity on our back lawn proves me wrong.

The details of Olga's brutal training regime are not yet public knowledge. They will emerge a couple of decades later, when she has thickened from the enchanting Olympic waif into a sturdy American housewife with a story to tell. But already I have discerned that the power of wishing, which seems so potent and – sometimes – so effective when you are a child, is ineffectual when it comes to the bleak business of being grown up.

Willpower has failed to make me execute a flip-flop like Olga Korbut. It has failed to take me beyond grade 5 at the piano, or grade C in O-level sciences. It has failed even to allow me to do the splits like my mother could when she was a little girl on a beach in Cornwall. Life, I am beginning to apprehend, is not simply a matter of wishing for things to happen, but some much more chancy combination of opportunity and fate. Which is all very well, if you feel certain of seizing the right opportunity when it presents itself. Unnerving if you don't.

I have no confidence in my ability to seize an opportunity. I imagine them as hard, glittering objects; golden apples that hurtle unexpectedly towards you, like the ball in school rounders games that looms out of the air and inflicts a sharp, insulting blow when you are standing in the outfield thinking about something else. In rounders, I invariably fumble the catch. I look again at my mother and wonder with a sudden chill if this is what happens to teenagers who fail to catch the right opportunity: life contracts around them, squeezing them out of shape until one day they find themselves sitting on a tartan rug in a suburban back garden with cracked heels and mottled legs and all the showy-off-ness, all the lusciousness and spirit and infinite possibility of their younger selves squashed out of them, and ahead of them the prospect of what, exactly? Of an inexorable decline into an even more squashed and mottled old age?

Here my train of thought takes a detour, for I am much less troubled by the idea that one day I shall be an old woman, like my grandmother, than I am by the prospect of middle age. It's not that old age is further off: from the perspective of 17, 70 seems no more remote than 40. More that my two grandmothers have a focus about them, a sense of who they are and what they are for, that I don't see in my mother. When I look at her, it is as though the winged child on the beach, the long-legged teenager and the shapeless 40-year-old are separate people, ghosts of each other, double exposures. I don't really know who she is; I don't think she knows herself, and it is unsettling.

My grandmothers, on the other hand, seem quite clear about who they are. Mrs Shilling and Mrs Charlton, they still call each other, though their children – my parents – have been married for twenty years. Grandma Shilling is small and severe and elegantly dressed. She lives in a house of hot and muffled richness, where red velvet curtains hang at the windows, and even over some of the doors. Four white cherry trees stand in a row in her garden, at the bottom of which is a goldfish pond surrounded by tuffets of purple thyme, humming with bees in summer, and a rockery on which blue gentians and an edelweiss are displayed like rare jewels. This grandmother is fond of real jewels also. In the dimness of her pink velvet-curtained boudoir she gets down the jewel box from the top shelf of her wardrobe and opens it to show rows of pearls, a necklace and earrings of silver-gilt and blue enamel like shards of blue and silver light, a butterfly brooch of rubies and sapphires.

Once in a while, she picks up a trinket – a narrow gold bar brooch with a frosting of diamond chips, a necklace of gilt and enamel forget-me-nots – puts it into the palm of my hand and closes my fingers over it. 'Don't tell anyone,' she whispers. From her I learn the rudiments of the secret and complicit grammar of self-adornment. This grandmother is famous for her hats (a different one every time she visits, which she does on Sunday mornings after church, driven by my grandfather in his stately, gunmetal Rover), and for the shameless lies she tells about clothes. 'Is that a new hat, Grandma?' 'Oh, this old thing,' she says, her gaze as candid as the little shepherdess she once was (well, she grew up on a sheep farm). 'Had it for years.'

If this grandmother represents the mystery of the grown-up world: jewels, secrets, rare flowers, unfamiliar flavours (it is at her table that I first encounter – with chagrin, since I thought it was a bit of chicken when I put it in my mouth – an anchovy), my Charlton grandmother is the guardian of my childhood. Gentler, more diffident and funnier than her formidable Shilling counterpart, over whom she towers awkwardly on the rare occasions when they meet, like a mild, bemused sheep over a fierce little vixen, she is the thirteenth and youngest child of a north London publican and has led a rackety, hand-to-mouth life as a sailor's wife. Perhaps it is the insecurity of moving from port to port, of never having a home of her own, not knowing for long stretches quite where her husband is or even, in wartime, whether she will see him again, that has taught her a hard-won sweetness.

When I was small she used to do a lot of baking. Her house smelt sugary, of cherry cake and rhubarb-and-ginger jam, and when she wasn't cooking, she knitted: intricate, cable-patterned jumpers with stitches as regular as if a machine had made them. Then she got Parkinson's disease, and the tremor in her hands brought the cooking and knitting to an end. I was 12 when she made me my last jumpers, one in a tawny squirrel colour and another, the same pattern with a cabled front, in wool of a tender dusty pink.

My grandmother's knitting was indestructible. Outgrown garments were handed down to smaller and ever more distant relations. (Somewhere in the world, I am sure of it, the child of some unknown cousin many times removed is still wearing my squirrel-coloured jumper.) At 17, I could still just about cram myself into the tawny jumper and the pink, and sometimes did, when I suddenly felt a panicky sense of having travelled too fast down the road that led towards the unknown territory inhabited by Janis Joplin and Patti Smith, and a need to retreat to the safer realm of cherry cake and cable knit.

As a child and then a teenager, I do not analyse what it is that makes me feel so close to my grandmothers. I feel safe and happy with them because I know it is the job of grandmothers to make their grandchildren feel safe and happy. I don't think myself lucky to be showered with love and approval and trinkets and beautifully knitted jumpers. I consider it my due, and I accept their tributes with the magnificent assurance of a little princess.

But from the perspective of middle age it seems to me that the secret ingredient of our cloudless relationship was their composure. That, and a certain frivolity. Both these old women had plenty to be anxious about. They were born Victorians and grew up with the turbulent twentieth century. Both had husbands who went to war, one as a soldier in 1914, one as a sailor in 1939; both were separated by war from their young children; neither led a perfectly secure life; both suffered disappointment, pain and grief.

Though their characters were very different each seemed to me, growing up, to have the steady calm of someone perfectly in command of her own domain and with it an insouciance, a lightness, a capacity almost for silliness unexpected in someone officially old; at any rate, a readiness to take pleasure in small details – a cake, a flower, a hat, a jewel, a robin on the windowsill, a new kitten – that was absent from my own anxious, careworn and heavily hormonal household.

'Remember,' said Gloria Steinem, interviewed at 60, 'when you were nine or ten or 11, and maybe you were this tree-climbing, shit-free little girl who said, "It's not fair," and then at 12 or 13 you suddenly turned into a female impersonator who said, "How clever of you to know what time it is!" and all that stuff? Well, what happens is that when you get to be 60, and the role is over, you go back to that clear-eyed, shit-free, I-know-what-I-want, I-know-what-I-think, nine- or ten-year-old girl. Only now – you have your own apartment.'

This is a very American account of ageing, with its sweet Panglossian optimism and its eccentric retrospective character-isation of women from menarche to menopause as 'female impersonators'. But although there are good reasons to be upbeat about growing old, it is a mistake to think that life's journey is circular. Getting old does not involve a return to anywhere. It is an onward passage to an unknown destination. The 'last scene of all' in Shakespeare's seven ages of man is 'second childishness': not clear-eyed, assertive or even 'shit-free', but dwindling towards infantile helplessness and an eventual vanishing into the void from which we were first conjured.

Embedded within the fantasy confection that is Steinem's take on old womanhood as second girlitude there is this much of truth: that if the old and the young, the pre- and post-fertile, have a special understanding, it is because their perspectives on the world are the mirror image one of the other. The twenty-first-century vogue for pressing very small children into formal education, and encouraging the old to beguile post-retirement boredom and loneliness with constant activity, has meant a blurring of the contrast in texture between the lightness at either end of life and the heavy duties of the middle. But it is still just true that the old and the young have more time to remark the strangeness of the world.

If the limits of your world are small and the time available to examine it either infinite or almost run out, its particularity is bound to engage your close attention. If you have never seen a bee, a marigold, a fire engine before, these things are astonishing, as they are if you are conscious that not much time is left in which to admire them.

'Sir,' wrote Colette's mother, Sido, aged 77, to her daughter's second husband, Henri de Jouvenal. 'You ask me to come and spend a week with you, which means I would be near my daughter, whom I adore . . . All the same I'm not going to accept your kind invitation. The reason is that my pink cactus is probably going to flower . . . I'm told that in our climate it flowers only once every four years. Now, I am already a very old woman and if I went away when my pink cactus is about to flower, I am certain I shouldn't see it in flower again . . .'

At 17 I am untroubled by a sense of mortality. Infinite quantities of time stretch out into the distance ahead of me. So much of it that its unendingness seems almost boring, like the very beginning of the school holidays with the whole interminable summer ahead. No need for me to mourn the falling of the cherry blossom, nor to see the corn vanishing beneath the scything blades of the combine harvester and think of the blades sweeping away yet another of my diminishing store of years.

All the same, I feel a sense of something passing. It is my childhood. I am no longer a very little girl. My time of waiting in astonishment for a pink flower to open is almost over. By the time it comes again, I shall be an old woman. For now, everything is changing fast.

This autumn I shall sit the Oxford entrance examination, and pass it. By this time next summer I shall have left home, having become an intolerable nuisance to my exasperated parents who predict (correctly, as it turns out, though their prediction doesn't come true for another decade and a half) that I will end up an Unmarried Mother. By the autumn, I shall no longer be standing on tiptoe to peer over the garden fence at the distant hills and villages beyond, but out there, exploring the approaches to the life of busyness and preoccupation, work and love and sex and child-rearing that will keep me occupied for three decades before it all suddenly changes again.

This change is what is happening to my mother as we sit in the garden podding peas. I don't realise it, because I am much too preoccupied with my own metamorphosis, and even if I did, I shouldn't care to think about it: my own awkward, struggling, reluctant emergence from the safe egg of childhood makes me an intolerant spectator of anyone else's struggle. Graceless myself, I am sharply critical of my mother's lack of physical grace.

There is a word I have come across in my French reading, which seems to express more exactly the quality of my life at the moment than any approximately equivalent English term. The word is *flou*, meaning loose, fluid, vague, hazy, mutable, blurred. As I traverse the debatable land that stretches between childhood and womanhood, I can feel that my mother has embarked on an equivalent journey, from the fertility that I have just arrived at, to whatever lies beyond. I sense an uncertainty, a tentative searching for who she is, and who she might become, and I really don't want to know. Between us, we are bracketing what Gloria Steinem called the 'long familiar plateau' of womanhood and each of us, I think, is impatient with the other's reluctance to make the leap into the future.

The cherry blossom has come and gone thirty times since my grandmother, my mother and I sat together in the garden, talking about age. My grandmother is dead, buried somewhere in the village churchyard, her grave, as far as I know, unmarked and unvisited. My mother is the old lady now, and I the middle-aged woman, and we don't sit together in the garden with my daughter, shelling peas, for I interrupted the tidal ebb and flow of female experience across the generations by having an only son. And besides, the impatience that my mother and I felt for one another when I was adolescent and she perimenopausal hardened eventually into estrangement, so that I breasted those risky adventures of adult female life, childbirth and the end of fertility, without a guide. Not alone, exactly, but in the company of friends as baffled and uncertain as I.

For twenty years and more we were all so busy – building our careers, having our babies, growing into ourselves, dodging between work and motherhood like a fielder beneath a relentless series of tumbling balls, hands spread to catch whatever crisis came curving towards us out of the air – so intent on surviving to the next day, and the next, and the one after that, that the very idea of a life that is *flou*, of vagueness or mutability, of an absence of the rigid shell of duty and demand that work and family imperceptibly encrust upon the character, became a fugitive memory, as hard to recapture as a dream at the moment of waking. As easy to imagine being a circus acrobat, a soldier on the field of battle, an airline pilot seated in front of a bank of winking lights and dials, carving cloudy trails across the sky, as to grasp again the vanished languor of the years between childhood and womanhood.

Until one day in the mid-forties, it comes again: that vague stirring within the body of something about to happen, of cells on the change, of an imminent, catastrophic transformation from one state to another; of leaving behind an accustomed state which, if not precisely comfortable (all that dodging about, all those hard-flung balls, barely fielded, some of them and others ruinously dropped), had at least the virtue of familiarity. And more virtue than that, when you come to think of it. For the intimation of change brings with it a powerful nostalgia.

While I am sitting at my desk among a litter of notebooks and pens, passing the weed-sown gasworks on the upper deck of the bus, grappling the laden supermarket trolley around the tricky chicane of Tinned Vegetables and Foods from Other Lands beneath the arctic blast of the air conditioning, memories flash, vivid as hauntings. Here, for the space of a fraction of a second, I am 18 again, leaning out of a great sash window of a room on the first floor of a quadrangle of honey stone. Behind me a tea party is going on – has been going on for some time, for it began in the late afternoon and it is evening now; the gold light tarnishing, the shadows lengthening, the sky darkening from limpid eggshell blue to lavender. There are bed-sheets on the floor by way of tablecloths; the brown liquid in the teapots is not tea but whisky, the teacups clatter, the voices gabble and above them rises the crystalline soprano of Elisabeth Schwarzkopf, singing Richard Strauss's *Four Last Songs*.

I have not heard Strauss before. My musical education has consisted of ladylike tinklings among the easier piano sonatas of Mozart and Clementi. Twice a year my school has combined with the matching boys' school down the road to render, in a frenzy of adolescent yearning, performances of the light operas of Gilbert and Sullivan (in the summer term) and choral masses at Easter (we turn in a sprightly Vivaldi *Gloria,* but our *St Matthew Passion* is distinctly ragged). The terrible melancholy and compromised harmonies of the *Four Last Songs* are disturbing – as is the presence, at the other side of the sash window, of the under-graduate owner of the rooms, the teapots, the whisky, the sheets and the record of the *Four Last Songs*: a balding, beak-nosed, 20-year-old mathematician with an intractable stammer.

I know this man doesn't care for me. He is part of a series of overlapping sets, all clever, oblique, obscurely talented, incompre-hensible: musicians, philosophers, classicists; tweed-jacketed Catholics with long, virginity-preserving beards sprouting from their milky, post-adolescent chops. A single girl is the object of their approval, privy to their complicated dry multilingual ironies and tweedy mathematical longings. She has long brown hair, grey-blue eyes, a matt skin of cream flushed with palest rose, a large bosom, shapeless clothing in modest shades of slate, mouse and taupe, a manner of enigmatic calm. She is, as even I, a non-Catholic, can see, a madonna.

It is clear to me that if I have a place at all in this very male realm of ideas and whisky, it is that of quite another biblical Mary. The mathematician has already pointed out – at length, with protracted pauses to accommodate his stammer, during which I wait patiently for the next staccato burst of disapproval – that my skirts are too short, my heels too high, my lipstick too bright, my ideas worthless, my looks negligible, my princessy airs risible. At this moment, I am only in his rooms because I consider myself in love with one of his improbable circle of friends, a noisy Irishman with a straw boater, a navy-and-white blazer striped like a pyjama jacket in the buttonhole of which he wears a pink carnation, and an immense collection of Grateful Dead albums.

Behind me in the room, Schwarzkopf's soaring vocal line quarrels with the yelping view-halloos of the Irishman brandishing the whisky-filled teapot. The mathematician and I lean on the windowsill, saying nothing, and for an instant I feel that I have been absorbed by all this, that I have merged into, been obliterated by the ancient stone, the fading sunlight, the darkening sky, the song, the babble of words, the reek of spilt whisky, the moment itself.

The song ends, the setting sun plunges the quadrangle into grey shadow, the chatter in the room turns valedictory as people scatter to supper and essays, the moment of suspension vanishes, a bubble in the mind; a translucent sphere with this little scene – the window, the light, the stone, the song, the apprehension of love – trapped inside it and the troubling power to replay itself in my mind at random, inappropriate moments.

There are other bubbles, other scenes. (Why these? It disturbs me that I have no power over the workings of my memory; a memory, it seems to me, ought to function like a library. You fill in a slip indicating the volume you want to consult, put it in a wooden tray from which the mental librarian takes it away into the dim inaccessible recesses of the mental stacks, returning after an interval with whatever was required. The notion that I have a past consisting only of what chaotic, uncatalogued fragments of recollection my subconscious has thought fit to preserve, strikes me as an affront.)

In the park at Greenwich the switch trips again. It is an unseasonably hot day in April. The buds are just breaking on the horse chestnut trees, but the sun beats down hard and brazen as July. Scattered over the grass like patches of daisies are small encampments of mothers and children: within a protective wagon-circle of buggies, sunhatted babies occupy an annexed territory of rumpled rugs, advancing at a crawl across a landscape punctuated with tinkly balls, teddies worn threadbare by exigent loving and plastic pots of mashed banana. The mothers lie strewn on the warm grass, basking like beached seals.

Fifteen years ago my baby son used to tumble here in the shade of these cedar trees, beside these pungent plantings of French marigolds and begonia, mapping his new world, inch by inch, blade of grass by snail shell, in a slow unfolding of protracted astonishment, while I lay on the grass and observed him with the same watchful languor as I see now in these seal-mothers: marvelling at the intricacy of him, the nacreous, cushiony limbs, the round white-pink knees tender as field mushrooms, the intense concentration as he moved from pine cone to worm cast to dismantling a daisy (and all without a word of language in which to form his intentions or report his discoveries).

I am the mother of a teenager now: sinewy, ironical, his knees patinated with scars and grime, his brain a cabinet of curiously assorted facts: times tables, the Holocaust, the Gormenghast architecture of the Bluewater shopping centre, verbs that form the perfect tense with *être*, the season's football fixtures, the periodic table of elements, the Dungeness lighthouse, major scales and their relative minors, the brass frogs around the fountain in St-Florent spewing jets of water from their metal throats. He is four inches taller than me. Under his bed are magazines in which girls with football breasts compete for space with news of Premiership transfers. A week ago he was mugged for his phone and his travel card under the budding chestnut trees in this park, by two boys who said they'd kill him if he grassed on them. The balance between us is shifting subtly: my arc of energy and authority just past its apex, curving imperceptibly towards a descent while his crosses it, rising.

Ten years ago – even five – I used to feel a longing, urgent as desire, to be free of the clinging drag anchor of a child; to reclaim the scornful, swift persona of my real self, my unencumbered, undivided pre-baby self. But as I stride past the large and small bodies on the grass in their milky collusion, their muddle of teddies and squashed banana, sharp as a stab of anguish in a phantom limb I sense the absent heft of a baby on my hip, the rebalancing, precise as sculpture, of the large skeleton with the small which I'll never feel again, or not the same, recapture it as I fleetingly may with borrowed babies or future grandchildren.

What else is gone, I wonder, or going, in this counter-adolescence, this shedding of most of the things that have made me myself for the past thirty years? If the momentary hauntings are a reliable guide, the list includes not just babies and the sudden apprehension of love, but a certain gaiety; a mocking confidence. I have a flashback of myself buying big bunches of lilac in the street market on the boulevard Richard-Lenoir in Paris and thinking myself queen of the world as I carried them home. It is a long time since I have felt like the queen of the world. For a decade and a half I've been too busy for that sort of reverie, and now the moment for it is long past.

Il a foutu le camp, le temps du lilas, sang the French chanteuse, Barbara. Lilac time has buggered off. Which is pretty much the conclusion that I have reached, but leaves unanswered the question of what might replace it. My father's mother was twice my present age when she died. If I have inherited her longevity along with her small hands and feet and her raptor's profile, it means that I shall emerge from this second metamorphosis on which I am just embarking, rough-hewn into the essential lineaments of the shape in which I may survive for a further half-century or so.

I wish now that I'd asked her more, when she was alive, about what the second half of life was like. Quite early on she took to exaggerating her age: 'Now I'm nearly 80,' she began to say once she passed her sixty-fifth birthday. 'Now I'm almost 90 . . .' Beyond noticing that unexpected inversion of the small vanity of lying about one's age, I have only the sketchiest idea of what the other side of youth may be like. The messages that filter through from the other side of the frontier seem vague and fragmentary, inconclusive as badly tuned radio transmissions.

I wonder if this is less a reflection of the fact that the state of middle age and what follows is less beautiful, potent and fascinating – and thus less well reported – than youth, and more an accurate representation of the condition of growing older: that life itself grows vague, fragmentary and inconclusive. I try to imagine spending the next fifty years haunted by obscure trepidation as to the ravages of the future and poignant flashbacks to a past in which (I begin to feel) I squandered the luck and promise of the first forty years in most reckless fashion. It is not an alluring prospect. I hope alternatives will present themselves as time goes on.

Meanwhile I notice that my contemporaries have gone quiet. The bold candour with which we always used to report to each other from the front lines of our lives has been replaced with a muffled discretion. Once upon a time we couldn't wait to tell the next episode. The vagaries of our lovers, our employers, our parents, our shopping habits, our looks – all became part of a rolling comic monologue.

With pregnancy and childbirth, a rich new vein of material emerged: the preposterous indignities of pregnancy, from the moment your navel pops inside out, mutating overnight from a sexy hollow to a ludicrous fleshy bobble, to the weary realisation, towards the end of gestation, that you'd pull down your knickers and offer your underparts for examination to almost anyone who demanded it with sufficiently crisp authority; the outrageous shock of labour, the unexpected catastrophe of raw feeling – rage, exhaustion, terror, boredom, love – with which the passionate intensity of motherhood is compounded.

Time passed, the children began to grow up, but still the conversation continued: more fractured now, and at longer intervals, reduced by the rending demands of work and family; the savage battle to secure some scraps of time in which to remind oneself of who one used to be, from a daily soap opera to erratic messages in bottles, brief bulletins flung into the overwhelming tides of domesticity, often saying little more than, 'I am still here. Are you?'

And then, towards the late mid-forties, even the messages in bottles seemed to dwindle to near silence. It took a while to notice, so long were the spaces of time between them, so uncommunicative the contents when they came – little more informative, mostly, than the births, deaths and marriages columns of the newspapers. It was as though the well of discourse had dried up. No intimacy, before, had been too secret to anatomise. But now the vanishing of youth – even the prospect of its loss – seemed to provoke a collective late crisis of discretion.

Perhaps it was less modesty than uncertainty that tied our tongues. Early one summer morning, I suddenly caught sight of my three-quarter profile in the bathroom mirror with its harsh side light, and noticed that my whole eye seemed to have sunk into its orbit, so that you could clearly see the bony lineaments of the eye socket beneath the skin. Face-on, the violet under-eye smudges which had been there since adolescence – a flaw so familiar that, like my crooked incisors, or the dent on the side of my nose where I walked into a lamp post while reading a book, I scarcely registered them – seemed to have migrated.

Instead of a faint mauvish tinge extending from the inner corner of the eye to just below the pupil – a look whose overtones of romantic exhaustion I relished so much in my teens that I used to emphasise it with purple eyeshadow – there was a livid indigo streak extending in a semicircle along the lower border of my eye socket. Above it, the skin was lighter – a greenish-bronze that lent the whole under-eye a pouched, bruised look from which my eyes (were they more hooded, too, than formerly, the upper lids?) gazed back like those of a dismayed tortoise.

Appalled, I gave up alcohol altogether, took to drinking two litres of water a day, mixed with drops of cleansing and energising tincture from brown glass bottles, went to bed each night as the 10 o'clock news began and spent £100 on a cream guaranteed (said the advertisements) to banish severe under-eye circles. The results of this regime were dramatic. I felt magnificent: far more vigorous and engaged with life than I had in my wretched and emotionally unstable twenties and early thirties. Every morning that summer I woke at first light and sprang out of bed with a feeling almost of bliss, avid for the day to come. But every morning from the bathroom mirror there gazed back the same ruined, saurian regard.

Eventually, 'I think my looks have gone,' I hazarded to one of my oldest friends; one of several with whom I'd grown up, talked my way through love and its failures, pregnancy, madness, bereavement, disaster of all sorts, turning catastrophe into stories and making it manageable in the process. If I was hoping for reassurance, it didn't come. 'It happens very quickly,' she said, and shut up with a snap, so abruptly that I understood (at last) that there was a kind of superstition at work; a contrary magic: if you don't speak about the loss of youth and beauty, of charm, of sexual allure and the power to beguile, to order the world into a form that suits you – then by not acknowledging it, for a while you can conjure away, abjure the terrible thing.

There is a difference between the dramas of early adulthood and the accumulated small losses of middle age. The former, however wrenching, conceal somewhere within themselves a tiny grain of excitement; a minute satisfaction at being the star of whatever scene is unfolding. Even while suffering, one is captivated, because eager to know how this bit of the story will turn out. But the outcome of middle age is not in doubt. The only ambiguity is the speed of the process, not its conclusion. It is (and this, for women accustomed to use words as the implements with which to hew and chip and carve their destiny into shape, is almost the most alarming thing about it) impervious to the power of conversation.

And so one advances towards it, moving towards the uncertain future as though through dense woods or across fogbound marshes, not quite alone, but unable to see clearly how one's companions are getting on. You know they are there; can hear their distant cries of warning or encouragement; but they remain hidden: wrapped, as you are, in a cloak of double invisibility whose effect is that you can see, for the moment, only the enveloping cloud of mist or dark leaves that parts before you as you advance, and closes again behind you.

At any moment, you think, you may cleave through the damp vapour, the clawing twigs, and emerge into a sunlit clearing with hills and fields spread out before you; or on to the bright shoreline with a view of the distant horizon. At that moment your destination will become clear, and the route you must take to reach it. But for the moment, all you can do is move gropingly towards the clarity that lies (you hope) on the other side of the mist.

2

Stopping the Clock

However stealthy the advance of middle age, there is inevitably an instant of moral drama when you understand that it has caught up with you. You catch sight of a careworn hag approaching you in a clothes shop and find she is your own reflection; your child implores you to wear something more conventional to parents' evening; you miss a period and panic that you might be pregnant before realising with stupefaction that your days of worrying about (or longing for) pregnancy are past. For me the moment of drama came with a fall from a horse on a luscious morning in early summer.

Falling off a horse was something I did with bruising frequency in my middle years – though as I got older, I began to harbour a certain pride in my ability to bounce. At least, I used to say to myself as I got up – winded, stunned, battered, but not badly hurt – from flying through the air and landing with a grievous thump . . . At least I haven't got osteoporosis – yet.

The act of falling, vehemently disapproved of by good riders, for whom a physical fall has the same dire overtones of shame and moral disorder as the original biblical Fall, held for me a perverse romance: a mixture of the human longing to fly and the cheating of fate. Standing by the final fence at a point-to-point on a fine spring day I saw a jockey hurled from the saddle as though from a catapult. He flew a long, beautiful arc through the bright air, curled up like a hedgehog on the turf, hands clasped over the fragile nape of his neck among the melee of metal-shod hooves, and once the thunderous field of galloping horses had passed he rose, furious, humiliated, marvellously alive. Then he stamped back to the paddock to find his next ride and do the same thing all over again.

Falling, falling, in love, out of love, the vertigo of emotional abandonment was something that I had relinquished as too risky before rediscovering it, on the cusp of middle age, in this less complicated physical form. There was something almost voluptuous, I thought, about the instant at which your point of balance hovered for a fraction of a second between disaster and recovery before tipping inexorably towards the earthwards tumble, the ground rising fast and implacable to meet you, the swift airborne seconds before the hard outrageous collision, and the relentless iteration of the experience. For this was the really shocking revelation about falling off a horse: if you fell and survived without serious injury, the inevitable consequence was that you had to get back on and do it again. Until you got it right.

Several years before, I had been overtaken by a feeling of restlessness and discontent – the sort of feeling that might drive a person to move house, change job or begin a love affair, but instead sent me on a journey to Kent, back to the landscapes of my childhood. There, among places I thought I knew well, I came upon a stableyard, went in and found on the other side of the gate an unknown world hidden in the familiar terrain.

When I discovered the stables my son was six years old. Our life had grown into a rhythm more formal and regular than the languid, inchoate drift of existence as a mother-and-baby pair. My son was a separate person now. He wore a uniform of grey trousers and a blue sweatshirt to go to school, passing through the gates into a world quite distinct from mine. After school he went with his nanny to the houses of people I did not know, to pursue friendships with children I had not met.

This seemed to give me licence to resume a private life of my own; even to take risks, of a cautious and limited kind. And so I strode into the stables and demanded to be taught to ride. I thought I might have a chance to capture, even at this late stage, some of the grace and physical assurance that had escaped me as a child. After the dreamy muddle of early motherhood, the notion of dash and precision, of acquiring the neat, hard body of an expert horsewoman seemed very desirable.

I thought my imagination would be occupied by the enchantment of taking up a new discipline so late. And so it was. But it soon became clear that this absurd and sometimes mortifying enterprise wasn't really about having a hobby, or taking some exercise, or a change of scene. Every 45-minute lesson exposed some disturbing new flaw: not just physical, but fault lines and fissures in the structure of my personality as well.

I didn't describe this unexpectedly trying process to myself as a midlife crisis. Not yet 40, I thought myself too young for such a thing. But that is what it was. The apprehension of my teacher's contempt was painful, but not as scalding as my own dismay at my regular failures of courage and patience – the two hard-won virtues I had thought were my only estimable character traits. To have the fragility of my composure so exposed felt like having my personality pried open and its crevices probed with sharp instruments. I felt like a soft-boiled egg, a dissected frog, a jellied blob of sea anemone pecked by the cruel beaks of seabirds.

It might have been sensible at this point to admit defeat and find some occupation better suited to my talents – a book group, amateur choir or dramatic society would have offered distraction without dismantling my psyche once a week. But I couldn't quite make up my mind to it. The acquisition of this elementary skill had become a metaphor for mastery of my life.

'I would give all my profound Greek to dance really well,' wrote the young Virginia Woolf to a friend. I felt this about riding. The grace, strength and self control required for the sport seemed necessary attributes for the conduct of my whole existence. To relinquish them in one area, I felt confusedly, might be to pre-cipitate their total fugue. And then what? Back to the disorder of abandonment and rumbling portent of breakdown that had blighted my teens, twenties and early thirties?

Less melodramatically, it struck me that the regular emotional deconstruction was not, after all, a pointless devastation but actually character-forming: the repeated experience of failure building, particle by tiny particle, a kind of moral reef of tenacity and strength of purpose that might eventually provide the foundation for the person I longed to become.

Clinging to this notion, I eventually made sufficient progress to take the next step and buy a horse of my own. For this a trip to Ireland was apparently necessary. There, in a farmyard infested with kittens, we found a slate-grey mare with a haunting, dark-eyed gaze that seemed to ask (but aloofly, I thought, with the expectation of rejection) to be taken home. I bought her. And having owned her for a while, found that I had inadvertently purchased myself in equine form. She was highly strung, savage-tempered and given to brooding lengthily on failure. My mistakes made her resentful; her own sent her into a panic; correction made her hysterical. Now I had two versions of myself to grapple with when riding: the one I inhabited, and the one I was sitting on.

Time passed. The dark-eyed mare and I moved a few miles up the road to a different yard where Matt, the owner, took a fancy to her and she to him. Trained by him she flew over huge, ramshackle obstacles of poles and barrels like the bold lady's hunter she was alleged, in Ireland, to have been. She'd always liked men better than women, flirting even with the knackerman when he scratched behind her ears with his great reeking hands. By degrees an unaccustomed element of frivolity crept into my riding, and a curious, unfamiliar quality that I identified, at last, as fun.

So here I was, this fine May morning, having driven through lanes heavy with meadowsweet and blossom towards a yard springing with new life. There were lambs in the orchard, a terrier puppy in the kitchen, a pair of ferrets sleeping in furry coils in a cage by the garden shed, two kittens, one black, one silver tabby, in the scullery and a swallow's nest with four bald shrilling hatchlings on the beam in Molly's stable. And here we were in the middle of all this lovely vitality, me and my grey mare, jumping for fun.

Once round the arena we went, and again. Then waited while Matt built the jumps higher and round once more over a cross-poles, a double, then left-handed towards a spread which, now I came to look at it, he really had built very large indeed. I kicked on, but my heart misgave me and the mare felt it at once, half took off, thought better of it and slammed into the middle of the jump while I, ahead of the movement, flew over her shoulder into an unyielding tangle of fallen poles and jump wings.

It was a fast, crashing fall and I was winded. I lay still for a moment, feeling a pole just under the point of my left hip. 'Are you all right?' said Matt – a rhetorical question, to which the required response is 'Yes', unless you are dead or dying. I wasn't, so I gave it. Strophe and antistrophe, there followed inexorably the command to get up and do it again.

'Hang on a minute,' said I, still lying in my nest of poles, 'I'm not that bloody all right. Just give me a minute.' A minute passed. I got up. Matt legged me back up on to the mare and we did it again, twice, while he stood by the jump with an enormous whip, in case of backsliding.

Then I got off, brushed the mare down and put her back in her stable, marvelling at the hideous voracity of the swallow chicks – all voice and appetite – and their elegant parents, swooping in economical arcs under the eaves to stuff their offspring's yelling gullets with bristly food packages of twitching insect leg and wing. I stroked the kittens, patted the puppy, admired the ferrets, watched the lambs racing under the apple trees, and at last got back in the car and turned towards London.

A few miles down the road, I began to think that I wasn't all right at all. There was a vivid, unpleasant sensation in my left hip where I had landed on the pole – a hot, hard pain, like the feeling you get if you turn your neck awkwardly, but much worse, as though something had burst or ruptured inside. I drove back to London gnawing my lip and trying not to cry.

Once home I considered briefly going to casualty, weighed up the certainty of an interminable wait against the almost equal certainty that after several dull and painful hours of sitting about they'd tell me to go away and rest, decided not to bother and crept up to bed where I slept fitfully, waking at intervals to swallow more painkillers, and dreaming again and again of falling headfirst into the log-pile of poles.

The next day I had an appointment with a particularly formidable newspaper editor: not the sort of woman to take a sympathetic interest in a prospective contributor's low back pain. Walking, I found, was tolerable as long as I moved at a sort of stately glide, like a slow march. But moving from standing to sitting, or vice versa, and sitting down itself were terrible.

The editor was busy when I arrived. Declining her secretary's offer of a chair, I propped myself against a wall to wait, uneasily aware that I was making the place – all chrome and glass and spindly indoor trees – look untidy. Quarter of an hour passed, and I was shown into an office where the editor sat behind a considerable expanse of desk. In front of the desk was a low metal chair upholstered in squashy leather. Even a large man, sitting in this, would find himself peering up at the person behind the desk like a delinquent child brought into the awful presence of the headmistress. It wasn't the status issue that bothered me, so much as the question of how I was going to sit down on this piece of furniture without shrieking aloud.

Gripping the metal arms with both hands, I lowered myself

into it in slow motion, as though doing bicep-strengthening exercises. The cushions felt as though stuffed with marshmallow. Impossible to find anything rigid against which to brace my back. I clenched my teeth and concentrated on sitting bolt upright.

The editor's expression of polite professional interest remained unchanged throughout this manoeuvre. Once I had come to rest she began a rapid volley of questions: who was my favourite member of the Cabinet? What did I think of the performance of the Conservatives in Opposition? Who should be the next Mayor of London? What would be the effect of the coming Olympics on the capital's economy? Where was my son at school?

I knew the answer to this last question. On all the others I put up a very limp performance. There was no fight in me, really. All my reserves of ingenuity were concentrated on not moving. After five minutes of efficient humiliation, the editor smiled a close-lipped smile of dismissal. My cue to leave.

I tried getting out of the chair as I'd got in, with the bicep press, but it was too low. Unless I slid out of it feet-first into a recumbent position on the floor (even in my extremity, I didn't think I could abandon convention to that extent) there was no way of getting up without a bit of a pelvic thrust. At any rate, I couldn't hang about any longer. The editor's eyebrows had started to creep enquiringly up her forehead. I'd better just go for it.

With a heave, I emerged from the chair. It was dazzlingly painful. Through my clenched teeth there emerged a small but clearly audible scream. 'Riding accident,' I mumbled apologetically. 'Bad back . . .' The editor waved this away impatiently – I had ceased to exist – and I shuffled from the building. On the bright side, at least the cauterising pain of the hot stone in my hip meant that I scarcely felt the shame of having failed to come up with a convincing mayoral candidate.

Rattling homewards on the District Line, the thought suddenly came to me that this was the injury from which I'd never quite recover. It would heal, in time, and it wouldn't always hurt as much. But from now until the day I died, it would creak a bit every time I got out of bed in the mornings, it would probably ache when rain was forecast, and whenever I sat down or got up from a chair, I would utter a little, involuntary 'Ouf!' – one of those treacherous mannerisms of age.

In an instant, strap-hanging among chattering Japanese girls on their way to the museums, and young men in sharp off-the-peg suits and executive briefcases on their way to business appointments, I was flooded with an overwhelming sense of my own mortality, of the brevity of existence, of the fact that half my life was over and what lay ahead of me was a long or short expanse of decline with my death at the end of it.

'*Le réveil mortel*,' Julian Barnes calls this moment of fatal apprehension in his book on death, *Nothing to be Frightened of*. Barnes's mortal wake-up call came early, he writes, when he was 13 or 14. My own sense of mortality came earlier than that, fostered by a series of hapless pets – frail hamsters, doomed guinea pigs, a cat whose highly developed hunting instinct was marked by rows of trophies laid out on the back doorstep in the early mornings: mice and shrews with tender pink noses and pathetic cold clenched paws, songbirds with feathered eyelids lowered over dulled eyes – and an early familiarity with the *Book of Common Prayer*, chunks of which, dwelling grimly on Last Things and the Valley of the Shadow of Death, I knew by heart before I could read.

Death seemed to me in childhood a familiar figure: both sinister and comic, like the orcs and goblins with whom my storybooks were populated. When, in his early twenties, a boyfriend was suddenly gripped by the horror of his own inevitable dissolution and succumbed to a sense of violent, inconsolable panic, I found it hard to sympathise. I found the prospect of an alternative to life rather comforting, if anything. I was inclined to think that when the Grim Reaper came calling, I would go with him willingly enough.

So I was unprepared for this vision on the District Line of my life – both the years that I had already lived and the uncertain expanse of years to come – as a failure. My youth was gone, I thought – and what had I done with it? I had made neither myself nor anyone else happy; done no particular good and some real harm, squandered my chances of love, left my friendships untended, wasted time and opportunities. I had drifted aimlessly through the decades of my prime. And now I was halfway through my time on earth; more than halfway, probably, with nothing behind me but mistakes and disappointments, and nothing ahead but the prospect of a series of small and large betrayals by the body that I had inhabited so insouciantly until now, until the moment of final, catastrophic betrayal.

I had not contrived to reach the age of 47 without acknowledging the fact that I was drawing nearer and nearer to – and then all of a sudden the tide was in and I was actually engulfed by – middle age. After my thirtieth birthday, I thought often of the Marschallin in Strauss's opera *Der Rosenkavalier* who, in a fit of melancholy over the passing of the years, admits that sometimes she gets up at night to roam her silent rooms, stilling the clocks whose ticking marks the relentless passage of time.

For a long time, it wasn't the fear of physical decay that made me want to stop the clocks, so much as the feeling that time was passing more swiftly than I could stumble after it. Each decade – twenties, thirties, forties – seemed to have its own particular flavour, ripening like fruit, but always too quickly, so that the season was over: the astringent gooseberry bite of 20, the greengage summer of 30, the apricot warmth of 40, all finished before one had had anything like enough of them.

I arrived at 29 and 39 and the end of my forties with the flustered, disorderly sense of someone embarking on a journey who hasn't allowed enough time to pack. It couldn't be time to move on already. I'd only just settled into 20, 30 or 40: arranged the rooms as I liked them, got on terms with the neighbours, understood the routines, the argot and the complicated dress codes of the district, learned about the movement of the tides and the direction of the prevailing wind, found out which were the best places to pick up a bargain or hear the latest news – when suddenly there was the voice of the station announcer bawling that the train was standing at the platform, it was time to embark, get on, get on now, please, stand away from the doors, the train is ready to depart. And with a lurch and a rattle one was off again on the next leg of the journey.

Growing older is not, of course, a purely private matter. Other people are keen to encourage you to keep up, if it looks as though you might be dawdling on the way. In my early thirties, a younger woman asked me whether I wanted eventually to marry and have children and, when I said that I did, gave me an assessing look and said, 'Then hadn't you better get on with it?' Some years later, having got on with having a child (though not with getting married), I fell into conversation at a party with the wife of a well-known novelist, who had just been on a long journey of self-discovery to India. 'I've always wanted to visit India,' said I, artlessly. 'When I'm middle-aged and my son is off my hands, I really want to go.'

'But Jane,' said the novelist's literary agent, looming behind me, 'you *are* middle-aged.' I looked at him, with his grey hair and patrician manner, and at the novelist's wife, who was, perhaps, fifteen years older than I, with her graceful, wrinkled elegance, her air of bony fragility and her ethnic draperies, and I thought, sensing my flesh still firm around me, my sense of my own allure still as intact as it had ever been, that he didn't know what he was talking about.

It is easier than you might think to ignore the passage of time if you have an untroubled relationship with your corporeal person. Time etches everyone's life story on their bodies, but my history, until my fall, had been quite lightly carved. I suffered a single broken collarbone in my early twenties. Soon afterwards, both my retinas became detached after a trivial accident. A sudden darkness eclipsed my vision as I sat gazing idly out of the office window one dull Wednesday afternoon.

There followed an ambulance, a half-frightening, half-comic consultation with a gathering throng of interested doctors, an emergency operation, a strange but not unpleasant period of fugue involving a fuzzy alliance of heavy anaesthesia, blindness and atropine drops. And then the peculiar decompression of a patient who emerges from a period in hospital to find that nothing has changed; the world has been going on as normal all the time that she has been sequestered from it. All that narrative, and not a syllable of it left written on the body.

A decade later there came the unexpected baby. 'You know that your stomach will hang down in folds like ruched blinds after you've had this baby?' threatened the (male) GP whom I visited in the early stages – apparently driven to make this dire prediction by fury at the fact that I proposed to go through with an unplanned pregnancy and bring up the resulting child alone.

(The urgent desire of the medical profession to impose order on the capricious, messy and mysterious terrain that is the female reproductive system is a fascinating subject, to which we will return. The tidying-up instinct is not confined to male doctors. Discussing contraception in my forties with a young woman GP, I rejected her suggestion of an implant. 'But it's a very safe method,' she protested. 'You'll be virtually sterilised.'

I tried to explain that that was exactly why I wasn't interested. That although it would be extremely inconvenient to become pregnant at this stage of my life, and although I was keen to take steps to avoid it, I nevertheless felt, on some primitive level, the need for a faint, residual trace of ambiguity; the vaguest of possibilities that some particularly intrepid sperm might navigate the contraceptive obstacle course. The expression of incomprehension and contempt on her face as I tried to explain this was very striking. We settled on the low-dose Pill.)

As the pregnancy progressed, I began to think that Dr Ruched

Blinds might have had a point. In the blithe haze of fertile detachment that muffled even the most urgent anxieties about what life might be like when this baby was born (where would we live? How? And on what?) I found myself curiously unworried about what my centre-front panel might look like once the baby was out from under it, although it did strike me that some of the changes that I had undergone might not be entirely reversible.

The everted navel, for example: was that really going to shrink modestly back into the tidy dimple it had once been? What about the sinister unknitting of the bony bonds of the pelvic girdle which, seeking an explanation for the stabbing pains in my hip joints, I had read about in a rare, unwise excursion into one of the pregnancy books that I shunned for their patronising tone and grisly illustrations? My loosened skeleton could be relied on to put itself back together, post-partum, as good as new, could it? Or might I find that I had begun to creak and rattle at the joints, like an old chair that someone too heavy has sat on?

When my son was born I was taken aback by the jellied mass of puckered flesh that was my deflated belly. When I sat down, it settled in my lap like a small, amorphous pet. It crept over the waistband of my jeans, pale and tender as a puffball. It was a striking change from the taut concavity that used to occupy the space between my hip bones. But in the shower one day a few weeks after the birth I looked down and the puffball had gone. The arc between my hip bones was now slightly convex, rather than concave, but smooth, unjellied, unpuckered.

'I've repaired myself as if by magic,' wrote Colette exultantly to a friend, after giving birth to her only child, a daughter, at 40. Magic was exactly what it seemed like – the restoration, after such a strenuous and deforming adventure, of the body to its accustomed shape as mysterious and improbable as the springing buds on dead-seeming twigs at winter's end. I considered making an appointment with the doom-mongering GP, just for the pleasure of whipping up my vest and showing him my unruched frontage, but found that I didn't care about him any more.

Apart from accident, illness or the stigmata of pregnancy, the other mark that time leaves on the body is the loss of beauty. For the very beautiful, the process begins horribly early. 'I've lost my bloom,' said a friend one day when we had barely turned 24. I was still hoping to grow into my looks, and said with asperity that it seemed a bit soon for the dying fall, at which the friend (whose extreme cleverness gave her beauty – pale translucent skin, grey eyes with black eyelashes, waving chestnut hair and a fine, straight nose – an almost moral force, like one of Shakespeare's more serious-minded and enigmatic heroines, so that beside her I often felt not merely plainer and dimmer, but less virtuous as well), patiently explained the difference between mere looks, which we all have when young, more or less, and bloom, the luminous quality that lends some girls and very young women a mythic, almost archaic air of unconscious self-possession, driving men and modelling scouts into frenzies of acquisitive desire.

Painful though it is to acknowledge that one will never know what it feels like to possess the authority that beauty lends, there are certain consolations: 'You are so fortunate not to be a beauty,' says the exquisite homosexual, Cedric, to his wholesome-looking confidante, Fanny, in Nancy Mitford's novel, *Love in a Cold Climate*. 'You'll never know the agony of losing your looks . . .'

And it is true that, with a robust constitution, a sensible diet and skincare regime, a fast metabolism, good stomach muscles and decent middling looks, it is possible to prolong the illusion of youth right up to the moment at which your body suddenly begins to deliver intimations of mortality – which, if you are cautious, may not be until the onset of the menopause, for which the average age in the UK is the early fifties.

I had not yet begun to experience symptoms of the menopause when I fell from my horse, and I was partly mistaken when I believed that I would never recover. Once again, the body performed its miracle of self-healing. After a week I stopped limping, after two I could get out of a chair without wincing, and the only sign that I'd harmed myself was the spectacular thundercloud bruise of purple, yellow and green that extended from my left hip halfway down my buttock.

All the same, it wasn't nothing. By coincidence or not, it was the first of a series of events – small shifts of emphasis, minor bodily afflictions, changes of circumstance – that precipitated me out of the blithe, heedless relationship that I had had with my body ever since adolescence towards something more anxious and foreboding; a period of change and – however fiercely I resisted the idea – decay.

It was the accumulation of physical failings that I noticed first of all. Small, almost insignificant – the sort of thing you'd hesitate to bother the doctor with: a grating stiffness in the elbow and shoulder, a blurring of the vision. Childishly, I refused to acknowledge them, thinking that if I pretended for long enough that they weren't there, in the end they would get bored and go away. When that didn't work, I went to the optician, telling myself that it was about time I had a check-up anyway.

But the appointment didn't go quite smoothly: something was bothering the optician. He fiddled patiently with different combinations of lenses, but none of his ingenious permutations could get us past the third line of letters on the chart, and even with my eventful ocular history that was worse than usual. 'It almost looks as though you might have a cataract,' he said, referring me to a consultant.

'You've got a cataract,' said the consultant. 'Small, but in a very inconvenient place.' She explained the treatment: entirely routine and straightforward, replacement lens, fixed focal length and then – sensing my dismayed resistance – added that I didn't need to decide immediately. I could wait for surgery until the inconvenience became intolerable. (In about thirty years' time, thought I, with relief – my 80-year-old aunt had just undergone a successful cataract operation.) In about two years' time, said the consultant.

Trivial as they were, these small malfunctions of the body bit deep into my sense of myself. 'Considering how common illness is,' wrote Virginia Woolf in her essay, 'On Being Ill', 'how tremendous the spiritual change that it brings, how astonishing, when the lights of health go down, the undiscovered countries that are then disclosed . . . when we think of this . . . it becomes strange indeed that illness has not taken its place with love and battle and jealousy among the prime themes of literature.'

As a peaky child, prone to migraines and fainting fits, I had relished my occasional excursions into the undiscovered countries of mild ill health with their attendant privileges: days off school spent reading in bed, punctuated by the arrival of special little meals on a tray and the opportunity to amuse myself with the glittering contents of my mother's jewel-box.

I had observed, also, the adroit use my grandmother Shilling made of her reputation for being 'delicate'. Well schooled in fairy stories, I knew that a fragile constitution was the infallible sign of noble birth. It didn't occur to me that her unspecified malaise might be a form of mute protest.

Years later, long after I had grown out of my childhood sickliness and into the kind of grimly splendid constitution essential for single mothers and the self-employed, I did once fall seriously ill. Disagreeable and wildly inconvenient though it was to find myself on a drip in a hospital bed, there was – once the drugs had begun to work – a kind of delicious fecklessness about this half-illicit flight from the duties of health into the realm of sickness that reminded me of those childhood illnesses.

But that dramatic lapse from health was nothing like these furtive degradations. In her book, *Fracture*, the sociologist Ann Oakley, describing a fall when she was in her mid-fifties that damaged irreparably the nerves of her right hand, notes the paradox that, 'while the body is the most abiding presence in our lives, the main feature of this presence is actually absence. Indeed, one definition of health is not to feel one's body... Ageing,' she adds, 'is a time in our lives when it's hard to pretend that we are in any sense separate from our bodies.'

Exasperated by my own growing estrangement from the body that had served me so unobtrusively until now, I was alarmed by the proliferation of small mechanical failures: after the grating and creaking of the joints and the dimming of vision there came a treacherous imperiousness of the bladder.

Relations between me and my bladder had always been fraught. Aged three, I sat in my white poplin frock with matching knickers and a pink grosgrain belt at Miss Thompsett's ballet class and, too shy to ask for the lavatory, made a warm, shaming puddle on the floor. When my son was born, I noted with misgiving that among the possible consequences of pregnancy was post-partum incontinence. I thought myself lucky to avoid it, and it was without surprise, although with acute dismay, that I found myself at 47, hopping urgently from foot to foot as I had four decades ago as a little girl waiting for the school bus in cold weather.

I mentioned the clamorous bladder to the practice nurse when I went for a routine check-up. 'It's your age,' she said, briefly. 'Any hot flushes?' I took to visualising my bladder as a dried-up horse-chestnut husk during the final agonising moments of the hour-long, traffic-choked, daily school run. It helped a bit. If my job had been one in which it was impossible to make an urgent dash to the loo the instant one became necessary; if, that is to say, I had worked as a traffic warden, waitress, bus driver, police-woman, sales assistant, surgeon, lawyer, teacher, banker, nurse or businesswoman – indeed, in almost any occupation other than that of home-based freelance writer – the quality of my working life would have become utterly wretched at this point.

An extraordinary degree of self-possession is required for a middle-aged woman to explain, several times a day to a younger colleague (even a sympathetic one), a criminal whom she is in the process of arresting, or a class of scornful schoolchildren that she has to go to the loo, now, this second, no, sorry, can't wait even for an instant. Even if one contrived to muster that degree of self-possession (and managed to keep it intact, day after day, week after week), the effect on one's authority and professional standing could hardly be other than ruinous.

Incontinence is something we are encouraged, as infants, to relinquish as soon as possible. The moment at which we gain mastery over our excretory functions marks the transition from impotent babyhood to autonomous personhood. To lose that mastery (and just when one might expect to be reaching the height of one's success and responsibility at work) is not merely infantilising, but un-personing. One ceases to be who one was, and becomes the 24-hour-a-day attendant of a querulous bladder.

On a practical level, I took to organising my life outside the house as a point-to-point between handy loos. Bond Street and Piccadilly could be negotiated without anxiety because of the plethora of conveniences along the route – the stately Victorian thrones of the London Library, the Royal Academy's design-conscious essay in inconvenience: blond wood, slate floors, always with a long queue of desperately chattering women snaking back into the entrance hall; Fenwick's chintzy cubicles with white-coated attendant and gilt-and-glass scent bottles – all within easy dashing distance, while High Street Kensington was a desert without oases, to be avoided at all costs. 'You'd better go now, while you've got the chance,' I used to say bossily to my toddler son. Now it was myself that I was chivvying.

Together with the comic horror of finding myself reincarnated as the lady with the fancy hat and the pinched expression, looking shifty at her daughter's wedding in the advertisements for incontinence pads at the back of the newspaper colour supplements, there came that other cheerless metamorphosis: the vanishing of the features which I'd been accustomed for the past twenty-eight years to see gazing back at me when I glanced in the mirror, and their replacement with those of a stranger – haggard, bun-faced (the expanse from cheekbone to jawline somehow contriving to appear both hollow and doughy in consistency, as though if you poked it, the impression of your finger would remain in the flesh), the skin not fitting glossily over the features, but crinkling a little, as though it was no longer attached to the underlying tissue but beginning to separate from it.

At university I had bought in a junk shop a pair of very old, very soft, long kid gloves in palest ivory-pink. I had always loved the way the kid moulded itself over the hand when I wore them, stretching and wrinkling as the fingers flexed. But it was less entrancing, now, to see something similar happening on the surface of my face. Like the little old woman in the nursery rhyme, I felt like exclaiming, 'Lawks a mercy on me/This is none of I!'

3

Because I'm Not Worth It

It was at this moment that the editor of the newspaper section for which I then wrote rang and suggested I have a facial. An American society dermatologist, a Dr Foster, who specialised in 'non-surgical rejuvenation', was setting up a practice in Mayfair.

Not only was this doctor apparently acknowledged by his peers in the field of skincare as the Derm's Derm; he had even been immortalised in fiction. My editor had heard that he was the model for the dermatologist who smoothed the ravaged faces of the Park Avenue princesses in a recent work of chick lit about the New York gratin. His über-facial was said to take years off one's phiz. So, did I want to go and see him?

I did. Facials had never been part of my regime. I thought they were a way for women with too much money and time to divest themselves of the superfluity. But that was before the stranger's face began peering out of the mirror at me. If this Dr Foster could give me back my old face, restore the connection between my inner and outer self, I'd be happy to suspend my disbelief in the rejuvenating powers of calendula, grapeseed oil, micro-crystals, blasts of oxygen or anything else that he cared to apply to my skin.

I had recently read a short story by A.S. Byatt called 'The Djinn in the Nightingale's Eye' in which the heroine, Dr Gillian Perholt, a scholar of narratology in her mid-fifties whose children are grown up and whose husband has left her for a woman of 26, suffers an attack of *le réveil mortel*. Speaking at a conference of narratologists in Turkey on 'Stories of Women's Lives', Gillian Perholt has a vision, or hallucination, of a terrible hag, flat-breasted, 'its withered skin . . . exposed about the emptiness, the windy hole that was its belly and womb'.

Later, in the bazaar in Istanbul, she finds a small dusty glass flask, dark blue, with a pattern of whirling white stripes – a pattern known as *çeşm-i bülbül*: nightingale's eye. Rinsing the flask in the sink of her hotel bathroom, she accidentally loosens the stopper and from the flask there emerges a 'fast-moving dark stain' that resolves itself into an immense, greenish djinn.

Since she has released him, the djinn tells Gillian, he is required to grant her three wishes. Her profession has taught her all about the spiteful nature of wishing; of the tendency of wishes, when granted, to turn nasty, leaving the wisher at best disappointed, at worst chastened, undone by the rapacity of his own wanting.

' "You must wish for your heart's desire," ' urges the djinn.' And so, cautiously, she does. ' "I wish," said Gillian, "for my body to be as it was when I last really *liked* it . . ." ' An instant later, retreating into the bathroom, she sees in the mirror the reflection of 'a solid and unexceptionable thirty-five-year-old woman'.

What the djinn has given her back is not the disturbing, dangerous beauty of her extreme youth, but a firmness both corporeal and spiritual. He has restored her to herself, banished the vision of the empty-bellied spectral hag. 'That was an *intelligent* wish,' thinks Gillian of her subtly altered appearance. 'I shall not regret it.'

I thought of Gillian Perholt's transformation while watching a television show called *10 Years Younger*. Both story and TV show are haunted by the subtext that rages beneath all projects of self-rejuvenation. On whose behalf is the hopeful searcher for lost youth pursuing her quest? For the self who inhabits the ageing face and body, or for the people on the outside, looking on?

In *10 Years Younger*, ordinary-looking middle-aged women (and a few men) who have won the privilege of participating submit to a pitiless scrutiny of their bodily flaws – missing and discoloured teeth, drooping breasts and bottoms, bad hair, cellulite, varicose veins, hammer toes, gnarled hands, pouched eyelids, drooping jowls, saggy necks, swags of surplus flesh – all the assorted afflictions of advancing age.

Then they are taken out, dressed like penitents in their un-flattering everyday garments – shapeless old fleeces and baggy trousers – to the modern equivalent of the marketplace: the shopping mall or high street, where passers-by are urged to guess their age. The presenter and her subject watch a video of the process, at which the subject often weeps, before being consoled by the thought of the various procedures that can reverse the process into triumph.

The challenge is for the presenter and her team of djinns – a cosmetic surgeon, a dentist, a hairdresser and make-up artist – to reduce the initial public estimate (invariably higher than the woman's actual age) to the appearance of an age at which, like Dr Perholt, the candidate for a makeover liked herself.

Trimmed, tidied, snipped, tightened, veneered, peeled, bleached, implanted, painted and re-dressed in clothes that are shorter, tighter, more vivid, more enticing than the dowdy camouflage in which they have been accustomed to shroud their imperfect bodies, the women are returned to the marketplace for the public vote, which invariably reduces by at least ten years the earlier public estimate of their age.

A premise, both of the story and the reality show, is the worthwhileness, the healing property for a woman of a certain age of even a temporary return to the appearance of a younger stage of life at which she felt comfortable in her skin. This is the programme's sole objective. The format leaves no time to explore the narratives of the past, and certainly none for speculation about the shape of the future. The effect, when these occasionally burst into the triumphant present, is disconcerting.

'Bet it's a long time since you've seen your wife looking like that,' chirps the presenter to a husband, rendered temporarily speechless by the sight of his wife's metamorphosis from saggy hag to tucked and uplifted cutie. 'I've *never* seen her looking like that,' blurts the befuddled husband. There follows a beat of silence, during which the swarming resonances of his response hang in the air, the significance of what he has said beginning to register with presenter and TV audience alike. Then the camera averts its gaze, the moment passes and we shift to a safer shot of the cosmetically enhanced lady's enthusiastic girlfriends exclaiming about the success of her new look.

The show's format is too rigid to accommodate ambiguity – a quality in any case inimical to television. Sometimes the made-over women look doubtful, hesitant, as though startled to find themselves so different and the world around them still the same as they left it. They often seem, before the roar of approval from family and friends engulfs them, diffident about the granting of their wish to look younger, as though uncertain of how to inhabit their accustomed surroundings in their new guise.

At the end of 'The Djinn in the Nightingale's Eye', Gillian Perholt is invited to another narratologists' conference. She chooses to speak on Wish-fulfilment and Narrative Fate, pointing out the unreliable properties of wishes in fairy tales, with which the characters granted them try to deflect their fates, only to discover that the intervention of magic merely hastens or complicates their existing destiny.

Modest wishes, Dr Perholt observes, tend to prove more successful than grandiose ones. The simple desire of the innocent fool or the downtrodden heroine without ambitions beyond food on the table and someone to keep them warm at night has a better chance of being granted without some spiteful extra twist than the peremptory demands of those who wish to alter time, or the laws of nature. Of these, examples can be found strewn all over the history of narrative: King Midas, whose greed turned all he touched – food, drink, his own warm, breathing little daughter – into cold gold; withered Tithonus, the mortal lover of a goddess, Eos, who secured immortality for him, but forgot to ask at the same time for immortal youth; Dorian Gray, whose history was scrawled across his ravaged portrait while his enchanted person retained the freshness of innocence.

Not that such hopeful monsters are confined to the realm of storybooks: ' "We can make humans into works of some kind of art or artifice," ' Dr Perholt reminds her audience. ' "The grim and gallant fixed stares of Joan Collins and Barbara Cartland are icons of our wish for this kind of eternity." '

This is easy for her to say, having been magically spared the choice between the grim and gallant fixed stare and the unmitigatedly haggish alternative of unimproved old woman-hood. Her distaste for the pitifully enamelled old women seems based on a conflation of good taste with virtue (a fairly common delusion among the aesthetically sensitive).

Those tightly stretched old ladies with their wigs, their lacquered maquillages, tarantula eyelashes and immobile features, their unnaturally wide-awake regard and wardrobes selected from the sprightly girlhood of a far-distant era are monuments to what happens when you engage in the wrong sort of wishing. Which leaves unresolved the question of what, in the realm of real life rather than stories, might be the right kind of wishing about your appearance once you arrive at middle age.

It was in the Perholtish hope of a return to the (after all quite recent) time when my face and I had been on good terms that I went trotting briskly (very briskly, since I'd got tangled up in the maze of red-brick mansion blocks behind Wigmore Street and was thoroughly late for my appointment) down the London pavements that early summer morning. I had no idea what Dr Foster was planning to do to me, but I was convinced that it would be something marvellous – magical, even.

A reputation for being the best dermatologist in New York – a city where (I had read) the young women were so highly groomed that they had the insides of their nostrils regularly waxed – could hardly be based on the perfunctory smearing on and off again of ineffectual scented unguents. I had always wondered what it would be like to be well groomed and now I was about to find out.

I crossed and recrossed Wigmore Street, getting hot and flustered, while the tarnished silver lamé vest top, which I had worn with jeans as a stab at negligent New York chic, began to emit a steely smell of overheated metal. At last I turned a corner and there was the salon, its windows filled, like a glamorous funeral home's, with arrangements of white lilies, its reception desk thronged with a flock of pretty little girls, like severe black-and-white-clad fairies, none of whom looked up as I approached, breathing hard and smelling of birdcages.

'I'm here to see Dr Foster?' said I, interrogatively. 'Downstairs,' said one of the fairies, still not looking up.

Downstairs were assembled a PR, the PR's assistant, a discreetly made-up person in a white medical smock who looked like an actress playing the part of a nurse in a soap opera, a photographer and his assistant (for all this was being photographed for the article that I was to write about my experience), a collection of tripods, lights and silver foil reflectors and a barista brewing cappuccinos behind a little coffee counter. There was a distinct air of anticipation. I was afraid it was me they were all waiting for and gasped my apologies, but no, not a problem, soothed the PR. Dr Foster was not yet in the building.

As she spoke, her eye became fixed on a point behind my shoulder. Descending the glass staircase (down the side of which there streamed a miniature waterfall) was a fine pair of shiny black shoes, attached to legs encased in pinstriped navy suiting. A double-breasted torso followed, a flash of pale blue shirt and glossy silk tie, then a mane of swept-back silvery hair. In a shimmering nimbus of charisma, Dr Foster had arrived.

The tide of assistants surged briefly, then subsided, leaving the Doctor and me becalmed on a squashy leather sofa. He had very bright blue eyes, startlingly black-fringed, a gaze like a medical scanner (I could feel him assessing the imperfections of my face, even as he shook my hand) and a miasma of charm as powerful as a general anaesthetic. Generally rather resistant to charm, I could feel myself succumbing as he spoke: ten, nine, eight, seven . . . and I was under.

The Doctor, it turned out, shared my fondness for horses. He used to hunt in Virginia, until prevented by injury. He loved also his dear old grandmother, whose wrinkles, he confided, he was forever offering to smooth out. But Grandma wasn't keen on this idea. 'I haven't got any wrinkles,' she always used to say. 'I go into the bathroom in the morning, I brush my teeth, I look in the mirror. I don't see any wrinkles. After that I put on my spectacles and I don't look in the mirror again for the rest of the day.' I liked the sound of Grandma, and wanted to hear more, but Dr Foster had turned to the subject of his own looks. 'See,' he said, 'I can raise my eyebrows.' And he wiggled them, reassuringly.

I was not reassured. In fact I was extremely unnerved by the idea that I might be in need of reassurance. I was being told that I would not emerge from this salon looking like the Bride of Wildenstein, but it had never occurred to me that I might. I had taken 'non-surgical rejuvenation' to mean face packs containing essential oils and mineral-rich mud; massage, possibly some more outré forms of treatment with oxygen, crystals or coloured lights, to a soundtrack of whale music or Tibetan temple bells. In short, I had expected magic. In this I had made a category error. Non-surgical rejuvenation meant . . .

'Just a little Botox here,' said Dr Foster. 'Some silicone in the cheekbones; perhaps some Restylane around the mouth . . .' I felt as one does in nightmares in which one is frozen, sentient but paralysed as some horrible fate advances.

Long before my skin began to slacken and wrinkle, I might have considered myself a candidate for cosmetic improvement. I had friends whose parents had offered to pay for a rhinoplasty as an alternative to a coming-of-age party, and if I had had that sort of parents, with that sort of money, they would undoubtedly have made that kind of offer to me. Large, unlovely noses run on both sides of my family and a hawkish example had come down to me from my paternal grandmother.

Then I was born without a left pectoral muscle, which left me, after puberty, with a flattened concavity on the upper part of my left breast, where the right was nicely rounded. A shortened left shoulder-blade meant that I looked asymmetrical from the back as well as the front. This was a kind of deformity with which spinal curvature was sometimes associated. As a child, I had been regularly taken to see a consultant at St Bartholomew's hospital in London; there was talk of physiotherapy, but never of surgery.

Neither my parents nor my doctors ever raised the idea of breast reconstruction and, although I was vigorously bullied about my flat chest at school, and minded the bullying very much, I was untroubled by my flawed appearance. I minded much more about the practical effect of the missing muscle, which meant that I couldn't do a handstand or a cartwheel as I longed to.

There was an afternoon at my village primary school when the headmistress suddenly decreed that the junior school girls should do a handstand apiece against the classroom wall. Standing in the sunny playground, in the middle of a chattering line of excited little girls, each of whom in turn stepped up to tip herself effortlessly forward and hang for an instant inverted in the air with her skirts suspended bell-like over her head before curving deftly back to earth and the headmistress's smiling approval, I was overcome with dread and a sense of lacking something that all the other children possessed. They were plump with the certainty of being able to perform this graceful physical trick. I was hollow with the certainty of not being able to.

Ours was a devoutly Christian school; we had been vigorously instructed in the efficacy of prayer. We prayed daily in assembly for the well-being of those less fortunate than ourselves. In these exceptional circumstances, I reasoned, I *was* one of those less fortunate than ourselves. Arriving at the front of the queue with a small tail of the less athletic children behind me, watched by the triumphant mêlée of those who had successfully accomplished the task, I hurled myself into space, trusting to Divine Providence.

I think I really believed that there would be a miracle. An angel would come and catch me as I pitched headfirst towards the earth, straightening and supporting my upflung legs with a strong, ethereal arm before returning me gently to the upright position. But no angel came. I landed in a heap with an ignominious crash and thump, scrambled to my feet and slunk to the back of the class in misery and shocking disillusion. Where were the Ministers of Grace when I needed them?

That momentary failure stung like an embedded thorn all the way into adulthood, while my irregular breasts never worried me. If I had been able to correct them by wishing, I don't think I would have bothered. I did sometimes wish that my nose were more regular. If a djinn had appeared and offered to convert it into a noble, symmetrical statement like the one on the face of Anjelica Huston, say, or the model Cecilia Chancellor, I would have accepted. But the idea of voluntarily submitting to having my nose broken and reshaped terrified me; not because of the pain (I never came close enough to considering surgery even to think about practicalities like pain, or what it would cost), but because of the fear that on some deep, mythic level I would emerge from such an operation no longer myself.

The make-up artist, Bobbi Brown, now in her fifties, described her consternation when she was about 20 and her mother and stepfather 'sat me down and said they had something serious to tell me. I was terrified. I thought they were about to say they were getting divorced.' But no, it wasn't that. 'We think you're really pretty,' they said, 'but you'd be beautiful if you had your nose fixed.' Brown remarked that she wasn't angry with her parents' suggestion, but 'it made me realise that my nose is part of my identity. It was the moment my views on cosmetic surgery were formed.'

That robust sense of self: the feeling of involvement with one's body as nature formed it, combined with a confidence that it is not necessary for a body to be perfect for the self that inhabits it to be lovable, has dwindled sharply since Brown and I were young women. Our untroubled accommodation with our imperfect looks now seems like a luxury.

Among the girls with whom I spent my provincial adolescence, the hierarchy of looks was strikingly parochial, and the range of comparison tiny. At the upper end of the scale it encompassed such creatures of fable as Jerry Hall and Marie Helvin (whose beauty we regarded as beyond aspiration – we might try to copy the looks we saw them modelling in *Cosmo* or *Vogue*, but we were no more likely to make serious comparisons between ourselves and them than we were to match ourselves against a unicorn or a giraffe). Then it swiftly dwindled into a strictly local league table, confined to the school, the year, even the class in which we found ourselves. There were a couple of acknowledged beauties in my year, one or two rebellious style queens, an unlucky few with spots or squints, and in between everyone else, neither outrageously lovely nor painfully plain, but more or less content to occupy the unspectacular middle ground.

Though intellectually narrow, the atmosphere at my school retained the faint imprint of the tradition of plain living and high thinking espoused by the great pioneers of female education. Our childhood was prolonged to a degree that would seem now bizarrely unworldly. Although we were sufficiently interested in sex to take a circuitous route home that took us past the boys' school (rolling up our skirts and removing our hideous uniform hats as soon as we were out of sight of the school gates), our competitiveness was confined mainly to our schoolwork.

What we lacked, growing up in the Seventies, was the sense that looks are of pre-eminent importance – that not until you had those sorted out could anything else important happen in your life. Around us the social shift was gathering momentum that would soon extend the condition of adolescence – coltish figure, acute body-consciousness, uncertain sense of identity and all – backwards into prepubescence as well as forward into middle age, and defer the acknowledgement of female 'adulthood' until almost the moment of the menopause.

But in those pre-internet days the idea had not yet taken hold that to be a woman implies automatic participation in a permanent, worldwide beauty pageant in which ordinary schoolgirls and menopausal women measure themselves against film stars and supermodels, and feel diminished if they find themselves plainer than these freaks of exceptional beauty.

In the decades since I was an adolescent, tolerance of difference – of race, gender, sexual inclination, physical and mental capacity – has increased vastly, underpinned by legislation; while at the same time the range of what is regarded as acceptable when it comes to female appearance has narrowed so as to exclude, sometimes very harshly indeed, the faulty, irregular, odd, quirky, counter, original, spare or strange.

The news-stands are filled with magazines and newspapers gleefully anatomising any minor flaw in the looks of women in the public eye. Photographs reveal in cruel close-up the wrinkly knees, batwing arms, gnarled hands, lardy bum or dimpled thighs of female celebrities, and chronicle with spiteful mockery their unsuccessful efforts to shore up their looks: the desperate diets and heroic surgery, grotesquely swollen lips, wind-tunnel facelifts and immobile, Botoxed serenity of expression.

If it is a gaffe to be plain, it is a pure affront to grow older. Who could be the repulsive object of this description: 'Her bosom is not what it was – these days no more pneumatic than a couple of bicycle tyres . . . With her butch upper arms, long hair and wing-three-quarters legs . . . she is the siren of lost ideals, fading youth, an Orpheus for the generation that still doesn't want to grow up'?

Not one of Roald Dahl's mephitic hags, but the middle-aged mother, Madonna, described by a (not especially young or lovely-looking, as far as one can tell from his picture byline) male journalist, her crime apparently to have the effrontery to sing and dance in public while past her first youth. And not just to sing and dance, but to present herself, in her fifties, as a woman still interested in sex, still confident of her power as a woman.

The week before my appointment with Dr Foster, I had lunch with a friend. We had met at work when we were in our late twenties and for a couple of decades, until I turned to freelance writing, our careers had run along parallel tracks. After that we grew a little apart, although we still kept in touch. Now, although I hadn't seen her for a while, I knew that she had been made redundant from one job and soon afterwards found another, better paid and more prestigious. It was a great success story.

She looked very beautiful when we met. Her clothes were exquisite – a pale silk suit, a putty-coloured bag of the sort that has a name. I had on a dress from H&M – a successful dress, I had thought when I bought it. But beside the silk suit it looked ill-fitting and unsuitably young. I felt awkward, graceless, at once less poised and much older than my friend, whose unmade-up face had the creamy firmness of a young woman's skin.

We talked about our lives. Her new job, she said, was exciting and very demanding. She hesitated for a moment, then, lowering her voice, she said, 'You mustn't tell anybody, but I've knocked ten years off my age.' 'You're telling them that you're 40? And they believe you? And you remember to be 40 all the time? With all the right music and everything?' said I, idiotically amazed. 'But why?'

She shrugged. 'The deputy's 33,' she said. 'The subs are in their twenties. The editor is the same age as me . . .' Another shrug. We carried on piecing together the jigsaws of our lives, finished our lunch, parted affectionately. She returned to her office and I to my desk at home, thinking rather ruefully about her beauty, her poise, how composed and successful she looked, with her pale suit and her opulent bag and her lovely creamy skin.

At the same time I felt a sort of vertigo, as though the solid ground had just tilted beneath my feet. Ten years of her life had vanished at a keystroke of the personnel department's computer. We'd known each other for twenty years. That was half our friendship obliterated: a decade of experience disavowed and now, it seemed, she had, by wishing it, made herself ten years younger than me. I felt both stupidly cheated, like the only person not in on a secret, and obscurely troubled. If I kept on getting older while my contemporaries grew younger and younger, whatever would become of me?

With all this racing in flustered, fragmentary fashion through my mind, I sat in squashy sofa-bound proximity to Dr Foster while he explained that the flesh of the face is like a grape, or a balloon, or some other plump, resilient object. At any rate, when young it is fresh and firmly attached to its bony armature, and when old it goes a bit saggy, which seemed unarguable, as far as it went.

And so his radical idea, the thing that had made him the Derm's Derm and the star of chick lit, was to rehang the flesh upon the structure of the face by augmenting the cheekbones with silicone, softening the nose-to-mouth lines just here, lifting the brow a little, plumping up the lip line . . . OK? Are you ready for this, Jane?

No! I want to say. No, indeed I am not. I'm with your grandma. I have no wrinkles – at least not until I put in my contact lenses in the morning. And, thanks to the kindly blurring effects of my cataract, if I shut one eye I can still imagine I look pretty much as I did twenty years ago. Or at least ten years ago.

At any rate, my face is my own and although I should very much like it to go back to what I quite recently remember it as looking like, I still believe this might be achieved with a good face cream and less domestic stress. I have no desire to see a synthetic simulacrum of that younger face in the mirror (not yet, at any rate. Though naturally I reserve the right to change my mind, particularly if those purple under-eye hollows begin to turn into actual pouches. In which case I will be on my way to the plastic surgeon's consulting room before you can say blepharoplasty.)

In fact I don't say any of this. A small internal civil war takes place, between my horror of plastic surgery and my sense of professional obligation. I agreed to do this story. It isn't my editor's fault that it involves syringes and Botox rather than, as we imagined, seaweed and Siberian throat music.

If I followed my instincts and launched myself out of this sofa at top speed, past the entourage of eerily kempt PR people, up the stairs with the tinkling waterfall, past the reception desk thronged with dismissive sprites, out into the anonymous red-brick expanse of Wigmore Street and the soothing hot-rubber smell of the Tube, I could be home in half an hour. Home where the grey Thames flows and the geese fly honking in V-formation across the pale evening sky, the cormorants roost on the ruined hulks of the old wharves and the sun shines on the shabby little streets of Victorian brick terraces, at the end of one of which is my own front door, surrounded by blown Gloire de Dijon roses.

Indoors the cat will be curled up on the chair by the door, smelling comfortingly of hot fur and purring when I press my faded face into his cushiony side. Soon my son will be home from school, full of news. He doesn't mind what I look like. (It is true that once, glancing at a photograph on the kitchen pinboard of me looking fond and fragile, balancing his huge, bald, soggy-nappied six-month-old self on my bony knee, he remarked, 'Gosh, Mother, you were quite pretty once'. But that is not to say that he'd prefer it if I suddenly appeared with the face of that fifteen-year-old photograph.)

If I went home now, in half an hour's time I could be emailing my editor, explaining that the non-surgical facelift wasn't what we thought. That it meant semi-permanent changes to my face, that I couldn't go through with it. She would understand. I'd work again. Only . . . her story would be wrecked, the photographers' fee wasted, the expensive derm's time booked for nothing. There would be an element of the dud racehorse refusing to leave the starting stall, which would hurt my *amour propre*. Then there was the curiosity of looking over the hedge that is the reason people become journalists in the first place. This, if I declined it, would be the first hedge I had ever refused to look over.

'OK,' I said, 'I'm ready.'

Having cajoled me into the starting-stall and slammed the gate upon me, Dr Foster stopped flirting and became brisk. His assistant, a pigeon-plump person in a white smock with a slightly alarming style of reassurance and the smooth, almost featureless face of a nicely speckled brown egg with a pair of glossy pink lips attached to it, installed me in a chair and the Doctor, snapping on a pair of rubber gloves, advanced with a large needle.

'Have you ever been to the dentist?' he asked. 'Every six months!' said I, furiously, taking the question as a slight on my (well tended, but distinctly British) teeth. 'Then you'll be quite familiar with *this*,' he said, sticking the needle into the crease by my nose and wiggling it about. 'Soon you'll feel quite frozen, just like at the dentist's.'

Quite frozen, yes. Just like at the dentist's, no. Even for big stuff – the shoring up of horrible old fillings, the fitting of a crown to a crumbled premolar – I was accustomed to rise from nice Mr O'Malley's dentist's chair still able to converse politely, drooling only a little, about the cricket (he was Australian) with only the area around the particular bit of jaw where he had been excavating immobilised.

This was something altogether more powerful; in a few minutes my whole face become nerveless and numb, as though someone had moulded a close-fitting rubber mask over my features. When I touched my cheek it felt dead, like the flesh of a chicken I was about to rub with butter before putting it into the oven. I shut my eyes. Over my head, Dr Foster and the photographer chatted matily as they went about their respective jobs.

'See the difference there?' said the Doctor. 'Ooh, yes!' said the photographer, unnervingly. Behind my closed eyelids there came flashes of red as he took his pictures of whatever was happening to my face. Prodding, prickling, a sinister flooding sensation around the cheekbone – all this, it suddenly struck me, was like a nineteenth-century engraving of a surgical operation, with the Doctor and me still wearing our respective day clothes, swarming with the accumulated bacteria of our journeys to the salon, and me with the remains of my make-up still smeared across my face, coating the point of every piercing needle with traces of Boots No. 7 translucent powder and London grime.

'There,' said the Doctor, eventually. 'That wasn't so bad, was it? Do you want to take a look?' In the dimly lit surgery mirror an eldritch figure appeared: wild-haired, the livid grey skin dotted with crimson pinpricks and glassy with sweat; the eyes the only things moving in a face of rigor mortis. 'It's great,' I mumbled, sliding the words through paralysed lips like coins into a slot. Then I fled, head down, grotesque and mortified, for the safety of home.

The outcome of the transformation turned out to be less dire than the process of undergoing it. Once the nerve block wore off and the pinpricks faded, what remained was my own face, almost unchanged as far as I could tell, but for a subtle difference around the eyes and forehead, and two significant alterations: a large blackberry-coloured bruise which appeared on my upper lip, and lingered like the Dark Mark for several weeks, and a fascinating paralysis of the muscles that allow you to furrow your brow vertically, so I could still raise my eyebrows, but could no longer draw them together.

The other legacy, which lasted for about as long as it took the bruise on my lip to fade, was unexpected: a sort of ruefulness that, after all the misgiving about the changing of my face, so little actually had changed. No one noticed any difference (except my son, who wondered about the origins of the bruise but didn't think, when I explained what I'd been up to, that I looked any younger), and by the time it came to go back to the salon for the 'after' pictures to be taken, I was wondering whether to accept Dr Foster's offer to top up his treatments; intrigued by the idea that my imperfect face might be perfectible; beginning, almost, to wonder whether – even now, so late in the story – my fortunes might be transformed by a change in my features.

The fantasy dwindled along with the mark on my mouth, and got its final quietus when I discovered that my all-but-imperceptible improvements would have cost an ordinary client around £3,000 – enough to carry out the much more urgently needed rejuvenation of my house; more than enough to buy a picture that I had fallen in love with in the window of a Bond Street gallery.

The seductive illusion of self-esteem urged by L'Oréal's advertising slogan hadn't worked. What was a plumped and uncreased face worth to me? Less than the cost of a new door frame and some yards of tongue-and-groove panelling. Less than a few square inches of canvas daubed with the stylised representation of a ghostly honesty plant in white oil on a black background. Because I'm not worth it. Or because, though I was nowhere near reconciled even to the very first signs of ageing, in my heart I knew I was entering a realm in which my accounting of my own value had better depend on something – solid bulwarks of love (or at least friendship); beautiful objects to look at; a useful purpose in life – beside the reflection of my face in the mirror.

4
Mapping the Future

Some of the time, for quite long stretches – months, even years – I had a fairly robust sense of who I was and the space I occupied. I felt firmly lodged within the envelope of my flesh, like a musical instrument bedded in the velours-lined recesses of its carrying case. On the upper deck of the bus on the way to work, walking to meet a friend, or sitting at my desk I could see myself as though from above: the centre parting bent over a book, the tapping fingers strumming the typewriter keys, the clicking heels striking the pavement, and it seemed to me that I fitted as neatly into my world as a piece into a jigsaw.

But at other times the sharp image would grow cloudy; my sense of who – and more troublingly, why – I was would become vague and drifting. Even during the solid patches, I was accustomed to reinvent myself each morning when I sat before the mirror to sketch on to the blank canvas of my naked face the mask that I turned to the outside world. But in the drifty periods I shouldn't have been surprised to look in the mirror and see no face reflected there at all.

The habit of making myself up – of having to imagine myself into being before I could go out and face the world – began in childhood, when I did it not with cosmetics, but with books. Each morning I would emerge from sleep to find myself (slightly to my surprise, for I was an avid and credulous reader of fairy stories, whose heroes were always undergoing dramatic shifts of shape or fortune) still here; not turned into a mouse, a seal or a swan, but still inhabiting the same body, still lying between the same sheets, in the same bed in the same room in which I had gone to sleep the night before, with the same noises of the household stirring as its life started up: the rattle of my father riddling the ash out of the boiler; the clink of my mother making tea.

And before life could get at me and begin the daily process of pressing me into a form to suit its own convenience, I would spend the secret moments between waking and getting out of bed deciding who to be: considering a selection of personae borrowed from my reading, just as a grown-up woman might lie in bed mentally reviewing the contents of her wardrobe.

Maria Merryweather from Elizabeth Goudge's *Little White Horse*, Pauline from Noel Streatfeild's *Ballet Shoes*, Bobbie from *The Railway Children*, all four of the March sisters from Louisa May Alcott's *Little Women* . . . I spent long periods of my childhood parasitically lodged within one imaginary character or another. It seemed both safer and more interesting than being myself. When adolescence came, rather than vanishing with the games of childhood, the habit of taking cover inside somebody else's fictional creation – cleverer, more attractive, more competent than myself at tackling the world – became entrenched.

Our school biology lessons addressed the topic of sexual reproduction in terms of the life cycle of the Japanese anemone, rising resolutely above the ripening of the female body in which we were all too obviously engaged. But the public library in my home town held a large collection of Colette's novels in Antonia White's excellent English translations, so for my sentimental education as a teenager I was able to rely on Colette's 15-year-old archetype of female adolescence, Claudine, for whose sweetly perverse fictional memoirs the writer drew on memories of her own village childhood.

In the confusion of puberty it seemed miraculous to have discovered a girl my own age (even if Claudine, having turned 15 in 1899, was technically ten years older than my elder grandmother) whose caprices and anxieties mirrored my own, but (unlike my own) made an orderly, amusing and beguiling pattern.

Her attachment to, and impatience with, her village education and provincial upbringing; her fascination with her own appearance; her erotic skirmishes with her schoolfriends – dress rehearsals for more serious skirmishes to come with male lovers; the passionate sensuality she bestowed without distinction on clothes, stationery, books, her cat, the woods around her village; her storms of temper; her nostalgia for her not-yet-vanished childhood; her abrupt retreat into that childhood when the advance into the Tom Tiddler's ground of adulthood became too alarming: all these disparate longings were familiar to me.

Experienced at first hand they felt messy, overwhelming, contradictory – sometimes too disturbing to be endured. They attracted the disapproval of authority, in the persons of my parents and teachers (I envied Claudine her haphazard education, conveniently dead mother and vague, scholarly malacologist father, whose warmest attachment was to slugs, the scientific observation of which was his life's work). To encounter in Colette's heroine a character whose sensibility hovered uncertainly between boldness and diffidence, and whose author evidently approved of the farouche nature of her creation, was an amazing liberation: it seemed to give me permission to exist.

Almost twenty years later, in the crisis of an accidental pregnancy, it was again to fiction that I turned for comfort and information. Little better informed than I had been in my teens about my hormonal cycle, I abandoned the monthly packets of contraceptive pills – primrose-yellow seeds lodged in blister-packs of peridot-green metallic foil that once seemed the essence of sexy spontaneity, but lately had begun to seem not glamorous but toxic.

The Pill and I had got along wonderfully well all this time. I swallowed it without ill effects; felt, when taking it, exactly the same as when I wasn't. Only, after a decade and a half, I suddenly began to feel a powerful nostalgia for my natural cycle. No doubt this intense wistfulness for an authentic experience of my own body had everything to do with the emotional artificiality that permeated the long and miserable attachment to which (despite my boyfriend's vigorous efforts to escape) I had been clinging since university.

So I stopped taking the Pill. I had a sketchy idea of the means by which those minuscule beads frustrated the lodging in the womb of the monthly phantom baby (a tiny homunculus, I imagined it: a shrill-voiced Thumbelina slithering down the chute of the Fallopian tube and out, furiously protesting, through the sluice-gate of the cervix on a tide of menstrual blood). But I imagined that all the years of synthetic hormones must have rendered me at least temporarily sterile – and in any case we were getting on so badly that it was rare for us to share a bed.

One night we had one of our occasional rapprochements, during which the thought suddenly came to me that I was pregnant. An instant later I dismissed the idea as ridiculous. But my first instinct was true. In the time it took to formulate the thought, I had conceived.

To begin with, I didn't say anything to my boyfriend. Once, long before, there had been a pregnancy scare. That time I had told him what I feared; we had worried together and when, at a New Year's party, there came the welcome cramp in the belly, as the other guests cheered out the old year and in the new with champagne and exultation and I expanded in delicious relief from the terrible unknowing of what might or might not be growing inside my womb, he said quietly, 'Pity.'

The moment of regret for something that might have shifted us from the aimless deliciousness of early love into something more permanent hung in the air. We didn't discuss it. Nor, until long afterwards, did I identify that as the forked instant at which our feelings flowed into one channel rather than another. This time I didn't tell my fears. I conjured a seed of hope that when told, he might remember his momentary regret at the missed conception and find something to celebrate in this second accident; but really I already knew what his reaction would be, and that whatever I did with the pregnancy, I would have to do on my own.

I really was on my own: almost exhilaratingly so. My grand-parents were dead. I was on distant terms with the rest of my family. My girl friends hadn't yet begun to have their babies. My closest male friend flew into a rage when I told him over a drink in a bar near St Paul's Cathedral; said, 'How dare you! Get rid of it! It ought to have been mine!' then turned away, leaving me desolate in the warm spring evening among the traffic, the rushing City commuters and the busy pigeons. I knew absolutely no one who could advise me.

My boyfriend's landlady, who had had her first child a year before and took a keen and not entirely malicious interest in the messy drama unfolding in instalments on her doorstep, lent me a couple of baby books. But when I took the first, by Sheila Kitzinger, to read in the train on the way to work, it fell open at a full-page picture of a splay-legged labouring woman.

For someone glad and confident about a new pregnancy, the image might have been inspiring: the hair-rimmed nether lips gaping to allow new life into the world a powerful reclaiming of the pornographic men's magazine image of the sanitised, unpro-ductive vulva spread wide for voyeuristic gratification. But for me, reluctantly pregnant with a baby celebrated by no one, it was too much. I clapped the book shut in dismay and never looked at it again.

It had not occurred to me (because I hadn't thought about being pregnant at all, until suddenly I was) that there might be different styles of pregnancy, as there are different styles of writing, clothes or interior decoration. But reading Colette's description of her late, 'masculine' pregnancy, I realised that there are, and that the absence of interested friends and relations meant that to some extent I could at least choose how to conduct mine.

The trouble was a shortage of role models. Apart from the gloomy precedent of *Tess of the D'Urbervilles*, I couldn't think of any. But then I remembered *The Millstone*. I had gorged myself on Margaret Drabble's fiction in my early twenties, continuing the pattern of reading entrenched during an English degree by consuming one book after another as though I were mastering her *oeuvre* with a view to writing an essay on it. I had an unlucky knack (for an examination candidate) of forgetting the plot of a novel as soon as I had finished the final sentence, but I remembered that *The Millstone* was about a young woman in something like my predicament, and took it down from the shelf.

Drabble's novel was set in the mid-Sixties, when accidental pregnancy attracted more surprise and dismay than in the early Nineties (though not as much more as you might think – the reaction of all but two of the people I told I was pregnant was some variation on, 'Oh dear. But surely you can get rid of it?').

After a half-hearted attempt at a self-induced abortion, Drabble's heroine, Rosamund, conducted her pregnancy with grave, scholarly composure. I wasn't composed at all. Still, if I didn't manage to mimic Rosamund's poise, or her patient endurance of the indignities visited by medical staff on expectant mothers (it was curious to note how little these had changed in the generation between 1965, when *The Millstone* was published, and 1991, when I was expecting my baby), I kept my head just enough to note the ways in which a woman wrong-footed by biology and her emotions could assert herself. I bought no layette, attended no pregnancy classes, prepared no nursery (there wasn't room for one, anyway, in my tiny basement flat), experienced none of the softening of the brain and physical debility that is supposed to affect pregnant women. On the contrary, between fits of misery, I felt very well and very clever. In other circumstances, it would have been an ideal pregnancy.

After a brief, tearing labour which, since it was the mirror image of the one in *The Millstone*, was pretty much as I had expected – dazzlingly painful and attended with brutal scepticism by the receiving midwives and fuddled dismay by the very young duty obstetrician – my son was born.

'It is neither wise nor good to start a child with too much thought,' wrote Colette, who would have been interested in the complicated and contradictory manoeuvres executed by women of my generation at first to avoid conceiving a baby, and later to try and get one to stick. 'I was struck by the recollection,' she added, 'that intelligent cats are usually bad mothers, sinning by inadvertence or by excess of zeal . . .' I was with the unintelligent cats. I found it deliciously easy to be a good mother to an infant. It was an enormous relief to give up the habits of egotism ingrained for three decades in favour of having someone to take care of.

'You look as though you've done this before,' accused a friend of the baby's father, finding me changing a nappy with uncharacteristically cheerful competence when he popped round soon after the birth to scout the lie of the land. I hadn't, but for once in my life I knew what to do by instinct, with no need of a book to tell me. It was only much later in my career as a mother, when the primitive, wordless relationship of early childhood was replaced by something more reasoned and sophisticated, that the malady of intelligent cats overtook me.

'Each period in the life of woman is uniform and monotonous,' wrote Simone de Beauvoir in *The Second Sex*, 'but the transitions from one stage to another are dangerously abrupt; they are manifested in crises – puberty, sexual initiation, the menopause – which are much more decisive than in the male.'

De Beauvoir takes an exceptionally bleak view of the experience of menopause. Her lengthy depiction of the prolonged menopausal 'moral drama' of the underemployed bourgeois housewife: the erotomania, incestuous urges, pathological creativity (interminable crochet, amateur watercolours, book groups and other horrors) and oppressive meddling in assorted good works (charities, school boards and local councils tremble, says de Beauvoir, at the approach of the energetic middle-aged female), reads quaintly to a twenty-first-century woman trying to schedule time for mourning the end of her fertility between a full-time career, running a house and bringing up children, whose own moral drama of adolescence may well be clashing inconveniently with hers of menopause.

An underlying monotony in the pattern of one's existence is harder to perceive when life appears to unfold in a state of continuous crisis – as it does when one is preoccupied with paid work, or children, or a combination of the two. Intense busyness can mimic a sense of forward momentum with eerie accuracy. Minutes pass, hours, days, weeks, months and years, in a flurry of spent energy. Jostled and buffeted by deadlines, salary reviews, sales conferences, SATs, GCSEs, Christmas, the school holidays, the sales, the start of the new school year (and Christmas again, already!), one labours doggedly to achieve the official landmarks of a fulfilled existence as a woman – a love, a home, a job, a child.

At the beginning of the great expanse of one's years of sexual maturity, the broad, flat, three-decade plateau of fertile womanhood, one feels, like Jinny in Virginia Woolf's *The Waves*, that 'Days and days are to come . . . we have scarcely broken into our hoard.' Time passes, the seasons turn, the river flows idly; distracted by duty and business we fail to remark a quickening of the current until in an instant something startles us: a change of circumstance, a divorce, an illness, an accident or unexpected loss. Then we look up and see that the landscape has altered. While we were busy, the tide has swept us downstream. Places where we hoped to step ashore and linger, to pursue a friendship or a love affair, follow an ambition, raise a child, now lie behind us, just out of reach.

Ahead the current hurries towards rapids and beyond them a chasm clouded in spray, by which the lie of the land in the distance is obscured. The hoard of time is half spent – and on what? The minutes and hours, days and weeks not run together into the 'whole and indivisible mass that you call life' (*The Waves* again), but frittered away in boredom and triviality, in housework, office work, idle chat, bad love affairs, silly quarrels, phone calls, shopping trips, school runs, PTA meetings, and hours and hours of terrible television.

As half a life's work, as a bulwark against the crisis of meno-pause and a foundation for the rest of our lives – a time as long again, perhaps, as the time that we have already lived – the fruit of the fertile years can seem dangerously insubstantial. At 50, I feel that I am still working out what I want to be when I grow up. I am not ready to be told that it is too late, that I've had my turn and must get off the ride now and let someone else have a go.

Here, more than ever, is where the consolations of narrative are needed. To turn something into a story is to give it shape, solidity, dignity, a presence in the world. To gather up some scraps of nothing and mould them into an artefact is to lend them a value. Like old-fashioned patent remedies, storytelling is both soothing and stimulating, sovereign against all known maladies, from dread of the unknown to the state of sick disgust with the tedium of everyday life variously known as accidie, ennui, *cafard* or (particularly when presented to busy doctors by middle-aged female patients) depression.

Gripped for the third time in my life by the whirling sense of being swept into a liminal state from which I would emerge once again fundamentally changed – myself, but not myself – I felt once again the need for a fictional prototype to give me a lead; someone to make the process seem coherent, shapely, resonant, rather than confused and disorderly.

The trouble is that – according to Germaine Greer – there are no middle-aged fictional heroines. Greer argues that, 'In fiction, whether written by men or by women, middle-aged women are virtually invisible. All our heroines are young.' As evidence of the dismissive treatment of middle-aged women by novelists she produces Jane Austen's dithering Miss Bates, the object of the heroine's brutal scorn in *Emma*, and Mrs Gaskell's tremulous Miss Matty, whom even her Cranford neighbours think older than her real age of 52. Both are, in fact, women whose pusillanimous manner hides a character of real courage in the face of age, loneliness and financial disaster. All the same, Greer has a point: as models for the task of opposing the indignities heaped on middle-aged women by twenty-first-century society, they're not really up to the job. I felt in need of someone fiercer, more sceptical and mocking, more self-assured, as a household goddess for my middle age.

Shimmering on the margins of my mind were the images of several middle-aged women, figures from texts that I had read long ago when my preoccupations were different. One was the Virgin Mary's barren middle-aged cousin, Elisabeth, who conceives a son when 'well stricken in years' and speaks in a transport of joy at feeling her child leap in her womb the beautiful biblical verses that are the preamble to the Magnificat.

Her appearance in St Luke's Gospel is fleeting, but in the space of a few sentences she establishes herself as something more than a mere submissive receptacle of God's will: a woman vividly engaged with life and resilient enough to accept whatever surprises come her way. (I also liked this story for its thunderous reproof of the prudish hand-wringing with which modern stories of middle-aged motherhood are often reported. No one in St Luke's account thinks for a moment that Elisabeth's son – who grows up to be the prophet, St John the Baptist – is anything other than a miraculous blessing.)

If you cast back far enough in literature, the squirming coy distaste that currently infests the subject of middle-aged sexuality vanishes in a blaze of bawdy pragmatism. Chaucer's Wife of Bath is an early, magnificent specimen of a type of middle-aged woman (Paulina, the fearless champion of Leontes's wronged wife Hermione in Shakespeare's *Winter's Tale*, is a later example) who occupies something rather like the privileged position of a court fool: a person standing at an angle to society, licensed by virtue of a certain institutionalised powerlessness to observe and utter uncomfortable truths about the state of the world around them. A shrew, is one word for the type, but the Wife and her successors are not shrews merely. Their experience of life, the extent of their self-knowledge, is too richly complicated to be contained by the insult.

At 40, the Wife of Bath has been married five times, most recently to a 20-year-old scholar, Jankin, whose lovely legs caught her eye at her fourth husband's funeral. (The coupling of middle-aged women with much younger men was a far less outré phenomenon in past centuries than its contemptuous modern label of 'Cougar' implies.)

The Wife brings a stringent clarity to the volatile cocktail of sex, power and money that is domestic life. She has a strong sense of the kind of ménage that will suit her, and she has bent all five husbands to her will, by browbeating, sexual manipulation or, on occasion, violence. There is a sharp intelligence about her understanding of her own appetites – for sex, money, admiration, amusement and good clothes (Chaucer describes these in detail: red stockings, fine linen, fashionable shoes of buttery-soft leather) – that extends even to her sense of regret about growing old.

Lord, she says, how it makes her laugh, now, to think of the high old time she had when she was young: 'But age, allas! that al wol envenyme,/Hath me biraft my beautee and my pith;/Lat go, fare-wel, the devel go therwith!/The flour is goon, ther is na-more to telle,/The bren, as I best can, now moste I selle;/But yet to be right mery wol I fonde . . .'

I was captivated by that 'Lat go, fare-wel, the devel go therwith!' – the stylishness and courage of it: the antithesis of the ludicrous process of shoring up my ageing face that I'd undergone in the Wigmore Street beauty salon. And I was intrigued by the idea of selling the bran now the flour had gone. My success in selling the flour when I was younger had not been very conspicuous. But who knew – perhaps, with the newfound courage and self-knowledge of middle age, the bran might yet find a taker. Of all the things bothering me about the future, it was the lack of love that gnawed me most sharply.

From the inchoate mass of anxiety that was my feeling about growing older, some ideas began to form. The Wife of Bath's distinctive autumnal pragmatism, her determination to squeeze from life whatever last drops of sweetness it might still hold, seemed more attractive, more possible as a formula with which to affront the future than any of the alternatives I'd yet encountered. I liked her voracious hunger for pleasure of all kinds, her keen instinct for self-preservation and her unapologetic determination to mould life into a shape that suited her.

Everything I read about middle age in my own era stressed that it was a time for women to begin feeling extremely apologetic about themselves. The proper occupation of middle-aged women, the newspapers and magazines and television programmes and menopause self-help books made punishingly clear, was to take whatever steps – cosmetic, sartorial, surgical, pharmaceutical – might be necessary to conceal for as long as possible the shocking reality of lost youth. The only alternative was a sort of licensed institutional battiness.

All my life I had been apologetic – the infallible mark of a child who thinks itself unloved. But now I began to wonder if the changes of middle age might include gains as well as losses. Perhaps, even so late, I could learn how not to be apologetic. Age would narrow the range of things I might wish for, but I began to consider whether there might still be time in which to please myself.

If the Wife of Bath is a sketch, a perfect miniature of a woman living her middle age with ingenuity and relish, Colette's great belle époque courtesan, Léa, heroine of *Chéri* and its sequel, *The Last of Chéri*, is the finished portrait. Stephen Frears's movie adaptation captured none of the nuance and hard-won grace of a woman who has learned to face life without illusions – or rather, who has learned which illusions are worth preserving and which must be jettisoned in the casting overboard of half a lifetime's ballast that is one of the disciplines of middle age.

Léa's regret for the passing of her own physical allure has about it something of the steely objectivity of a racehorse trainer who realises that his great champion has passed its peak and now faces a future that has shrunk to just two alternatives: a well managed decline, or a badly managed one.

Schooled by decades of having exchanged the illusion of love for the solid stuff of financial independence, Léa still places the real thing at the head of her hierarchy of what makes a life worth living: the sensual housewife's list of good food, excellent clothes and jewels, a well run household, friendship (of the sharp-edged, beady-eyed female variety) and a seasoning of gossip and intrigue. The luxury she denies herself is that most commonly resorted to by women of a certain age who haven't made a living from love: nostalgia.

When the novel begins Léa is 49 and Chéri, her lover of six years, is 24. When he leaves – a little sooner than she had antic-ipated – to make a suitable marriage to a girl his own age, Léa takes it well, makes little fuss, falls back on her well-regulated habits as armour against the terrible intimations of mortality brought on by the end of this, her last love affair.

Of course the perturbation of her climacteric isn't as easily resolved as that. There follows a bitter struggle in which she experiments with as many different personae as an adolescent trying out adulthood for size. She plans cosy soirées of knitting and poker with her friend and rival (and fellow former courtesan), Chéri's terrible old mother, Charlotte. 'Do you knit?' enquires

Charlotte, startled. 'Not yet,' replies Léa. 'But it will soon come . . .'

When Chéri returns it seems, for the space of a few blissful hours, as though all the confusion is resolved. But at dawn the idyll falters. Jaded, Chéri watches through his eyelashes the figure of his lover, 'not yet powdered, a meagre twist of hair at the back of her head, double chin and raddled neck . . . exposing herself rashly to the unseen observer'.

Watching him from the window as he leaves, Léa sees him pause in the courtyard and imagines for a moment that he is coming back. Catching sight of herself in the long mirror, she wonders who the old woman is, gesticulating crazily, and in the same instant sees her lover look up at the spring sky and take a long breath, like a man released from prison.

'I invented Léa as a premonition,' wrote Colette. Her biographer, Judith Thurman, remarks tartly that Colette wrote her endings so that she did not have to live them herself. But although the metamorphosis of Léa from idolised blonde beauty to rich middle-aged *demi-mondaine* to (in *The Last of Chéri*) grossly obese and unsexed old woman, appals the reader as it appals Chéri – and for the same reason: that it brings us face to face with our own mortality – the premonition is not without ambiguity.

Stephen Frears joked that he filmed only the first of the *Chéri* novels because he could hardly expect his star, Michelle Pfeiffer, who was then 50, to play fat and old. It is hard, in fact, to imagine a modern Léa abandoning the struggle to keep her looks. The money that her beauty earned in the first half of her life would be spent in the second on preserving her beauty by every stratagem of the surgeon's art. Liposuction, a strict regime, perhaps a gastric band, would banish the slab-like carapace of fat; Botox and chemical peels would preserve her dewy skin from weathering into the 'varnished hide' that so repels Chéri when he meets his former love at 60.

In fact, if a modern Chéri were to return to his mistress eleven years after their first parting, the chances are that he would find her scarcely changed. There would be no metamorphosis, no catastrophic confrontation, no tragedy. Just an interminable synthetic idyll, with the dying fall that makes the last assignation between Léa and Chéri so poignant vanquished by HRT and Restylane.

Would this be a better ending than Colette's premonition? Although I was disturbed by the changes I felt in myself, and reluctant to admit that the process of post-menopausal masculinisation had already begun, I found a sense of recognition – almost of exhilaration – in the defiance of Léa and the Wife of Bath.

In more conventional narratives of middle-aged love – the libretto of *Der Rosenkavalier*, say, or the screenplay of *The Graduate* – the loss or renunciation by a middle-aged woman of her much younger lover is presented as a form of expiation or punishment for her 'sin' in seducing him. But the Wife and Léa defy convention with a passionate individualism: a determination to shape for themselves the narratives of their middle years, rather than dwindling into the roles that convention prescribes for them.

Their intelligent willingness to taste the strangely compromised flavours of middle age – the bitterness of menopausal experience: the scandalous emptiness of children not borne, lovers not seduced, beauty vanished, the power to please withered, the inevitability of death; and mixed with it the sweetness of seizing the opportunities that survive; the pleasure of an orderly, settled life, self-knowledge and formed tastes, as well as what remains of the wilder joys of love and sexual exploration – hints at a state of mind more complex and durable than mere happiness – or at any rate, of more use as a shield against the diminishments of old age. Happiness is a gift; a matter of luck and circumstance. You can't practise it, or acquire it by force of will. Composure, on the other hand, you can.

'Immunity...' wrote Virginia Woolf, aged 50. 'To be immune, means to exist apart from rubs, shocks, suffering . . . to have enough to live on without courting flattery, success . . . to be mistress of my hours . . . Immunity is an exalted calm desirable state, & one I could reach much oftener than I do.'

Woolf was already working on *To the Lighthouse* when she began writing *Mrs Dalloway*. In the central characters of her overlapping novels she captured the contradictory emotions of middle age: the blurring of the present with memories of the past and foreboding for the future; the perception that strikes Mrs Ramsay as she serves her daube that there is 'a coherence in things, a stability; something [that] is immune from change'; the feeling that one is the person that one has always been, but at the same time changing irrevocably into someone quite different.

Mrs Dalloway, Woolf writes, 'felt very young; at the same time unspeakably aged. She sliced like a knife through everything; at the same time was outside, looking on. She had a perpetual sense . . . of being out, out, far out to sea and alone; she always had the feeling that it was very, very dangerous to live even one day.'

The internal reveries of Woolf's heroines are built on a sturdy armature of their position in society, to which they are attached by ligatures of love and friendship. They are matriarchs: mothers, wives, hostesses; objects of desire and affection, fecund, benevolent. In a way, they can afford the luxury of speculative fragility. Their apprehension of the perilous amorphousness of the middle years spoke eloquently to me, but I lacked their resonant, almost grandiose, sense of entitlement. My own experience of mid-life felt thinner, more contingent than theirs.

In 1958 Angus Wilson published *The Middle Age of Mrs Eliot*, in which he imagined the fate of a middle-aged woman stripped of the traditional trappings of female dignity. His heroine, Meg Eliot, is a woman of substance: courted, admired, the darling of charitable committees, and a benevolent friend to her flock of lame ducks – single women of a certain age with less fortunate lives than her own. But when her husband dies suddenly, she undergoes a baleful metamorphosis. The change is not simply a matter of loss and grief; not even a question of identity, although she has no children or job to support her newly bereft sense of self. The real shock is her social demotion from a person of consequence to someone who effectively doesn't exist.

Wilson compares Meg Eliot's dilemma with that of her brother, David, who is homosexual. Homosexual himself at a time when it was still illegal, the novelist was well acquainted with the feeling of belonging to a despised and invisible group. Historically, the position of middle-aged women, particularly those not attached to a man – widows or spinsters – had been ambiguous, com-promised, uncertain. But not invisible. However unenviable their state, the Miss Bateses and Miss Mattys, the maiden aunts and dowagers and shrews and grandes dames and adventuresses of a certain age were still a formidable presence in their families and communities.

Until the mid-twentieth century they are an indispensable part of literature. Fiction swarms with them. Plots revolve around them. Younger characters tell them their secrets, court them for the legacies they might bestow, pity them, dread turning into them – and sometimes even marry them. But then comes Angus Wilson's premonition of middle age as a form of exile; a solitary deviation whose only solace is a lonely self-knowledge, hard won after heroic emotional struggle. And after that, in 1966, comes Dr Robert Wilson's *Feminine Forever*, the bestseller that would convert middle age from a stage of life rich in ambiguity and nuance into a curable medical condition.

The project of finding a remedy for the symptoms of the menopause and restoring 'femininity' to ageing women had fas-cinated physicians for centuries. Many before Dr Wilson had experimented with hormonal therapy on their menopausal patients. His particular distinction in the field was arguably not so much medical as literary: by synthesising the factual language of science with the flowery emotional hyperbole of romantic fiction, he produced an account of middle age as a transformation narrative from youthful femininity into 'castrate' and – thanks to the magic of oestrogen therapy – back again that would prove extraordinarily seductive to women throughout the decades to come.

It is puzzling that fiction, traditionally the realm in which women felt most free to describe themselves, should fall almost silent on the subject of the middle years, and doubly strange that it should do so at a point in literary history at which women's writing about their own lives became richer and bolder than ever before.

If it had worked as its advocates envisaged, HRT should have resulted in a great flowering of the literature of middle age. With all the traditional benefits of the middle years – freedom from child-rearing, a formed character, the competence and confidence that only decades of experience can bestow – combined with liberation from the physical effects of the menopause, middle-aged women ought to have become unstoppable. You might have expected that from their resurgence would spring a body of work at least the equivalent of the passionate twentieth-century love affair with their own experience of middle-aged male writers.

The sense of the middle years as a period of life whose task is to grapple from the hostile void of time some evidence of reality, some permanence, some tangible proof of having existed, became a rich source of inspiration to male novelists of the twentieth and early twenty-first centuries: from John Updike to Martin Amis, they roamed the labyrinth of the ageing male psyche, recording the wonders they found there.

But the great swell of younger women's fiction that emerged from the social and sexual liberation of the 1960s was not accompanied by an equivalent portrait of a rejuvenated and invigorated generation of middle-aged women. It is as though Angus Wilson's vision of the middle-aged woman as an unperson was a premonition of an age of anxiety – or denial – that began with the 'liberation' of women from their sexual destiny.

HRT turned out to be a fairy's gift, with the spiteful tendency of such gifts to bring trouble to their recipients. Along with the reports of increased risk of certain cancers, heart attack and stroke, hormone therapy spread a canker over the narratives of middle age. Human instinct is to shun disease, and the effects of diagnosing half the female population with a mortal malaise were predictable. Vanished, the flowering of the autumn rose, the half-amused, half-melancholy subtleties of late love, the selling of the bran now that the flour is gone. Vanished the dignity of the matriarch, the notion of a composure hard-fought, wrenched from suffering and experience, and quite distinct from the invulnerable complacency of extreme youth and beauty. All deleted by the myth that since middle age is a malady for which palliative care is available, its stories are without interest.

Helen Paloge, an American academic and author of *The Silent Echo*, a critical study of the contemporary narratives of women's middle age, puts it like this:

> Contemporary women novelists have not only ignored the opportunity of addressing the 'identity change' that hits women between the eyes at some point in middle age, but by doing so, they have helped perpetuate the regressive myth about female identity . . . that such identity is formed and finished at one stroke in young adulthood. In their novels, middle age is either a bogus problem that can be remedied by a change of diet, lover, location, or husband; a bogus time that can, nevertheless, be turned back with enough repetition of concepts such as 'Today's 50 is 40'; or a bogus idea altogether . . .

The trouble with modern fictional accounts of midlife is that they tend to stop at the fence that makes the Wife of Bath and Léa, Mrs Dalloway and Mrs Ramsay such rich and resonant characters.

Instead of acknowledging the spectral figure of mortality that she sees grimacing behind her own lined and softening reflection, attempting to make his acquaintance, even flirt with him a little, the post-HRT heroine tends to resort either to hopeless resignation or a sprightly denial that anything has essentially changed.

Angus Wilson's wounded heroine prefigures a group of later middle-aged fictional females who find themselves wrong-footed by life – Anita Brookner's fastidious perpetual spinsters; Rebecca Davitch, the protagonist of Anne Tyler's *Back When We Were Grown-ups*, who feels, at 53, 'a superfluous woman'; Edie Boyd, the subject of Joanna Trollope's *Second Honeymoon*, who is driven to the point of madness by empty nest syndrome.

The world-view of these women is disturbingly browbeaten: powerlessness is their leitmotif. They are hapless, beleaguered, effaced, querulous, uncertain: unable to establish a secure footing between the clamorous demands of the young and the properly old. Their prevailing tone is one of inchoate but dreadful misgiving, spiced with a lively resentment towards who- or whatever (men? children? the family? society? fate? biology?) is to blame for the dreadful reversal in fortune that attacks women of a certain age. That or the mute narcissistic passivity of intelligent women who decline to involve themselves in the cruel battle for the predominance of the most attractive and share the belief of Jane Austen's less spirited heroines – Jane Bennet, Elinor Dashwood, Fanny Price, Anne Elliot (a belief not much vindicated outside the world of the female imagination) – that a serene and beautiful nature will prove more effective when it comes to securing a kindly fate than the flaunting attractions of good looks and sex appeal.

Nothing in the experience of these defeated or deluded fictional forty- and fiftysomething heroines interested me. Not their dignified retreats from the vulgar hurly-burly of an engaged life, not their circular journeys back to the place from which they started, nor their wistful acceptance of middle age as a diminished, paler, more sedate version of their more vivid and exciting younger lives. I thought there must be something more to it than that.

The spirit of Léa de Lonval survives in the rackety, difficult, sexy and resilient heroines of Mary Wesley's fiction. The stubborn, questioning high seriousness, the interest in how to lead a good life, of the heroines of Margaret Drabble's early novels persists in her later depictions of the middle-aged condition. And in short stories by A.S. Byatt and Amy Bloom the desires and passions of middle age are beautifully anatomised.

But in the end none of these became my guide to middle age. Eventually I resorted to a different kind of personal narrative, more venerable even than fiction. I began writing letters. My friend Prudence Entwhistle and I had known each other since our twenties. She, like me, had never married but was living her menopause against a backdrop of adolescent male drama – lots of adolescent male drama in her case, because she worked as a matron at a boys' boarding school.

We had always been close but suddenly, during odd gaps in the day's work, we began to exchange emails about the things that were bothering us: the changing texture of our skin; the atom-isation of experience in middle age so that, like Woolf's Mrs Ramsay, we were perpetually Thinking about Life, but never managing to finish the thought; the superb selfishness of teenage boys; the urgent need for a completely different wardrobe at 50, even though our old clothes all still fitted perfectly well; the importance of a proper Plan for the second half of our lives so that they shouldn't be a muddle like the first half; the desirability of Composure, Order and *douceur de vie*; the attractions of becoming Formidable; the best ways of dealing with loss; the possibility – likelihood, even – that our days of falling in love were over.

It was a strange process, this daily recording of our experience. We were like ancient mariners sailing into uncharted waters, mapping the shoals and reefs as we went; mistaking whales' backs for solid land; fearful of the monsters and prodigies that swarmed and thrashed in the heaving swell beneath us; the change of weather gathering on the far horizon. We were much too busy for our exchanges to echo the delicious speculative languor of adolescence; but still, something about them did remind me of the endless, aimless chatting of my teenage years. Making up a life, trying it on for size, putting it aside, trying another one. Talking the future into existence.

5

Feminine For Ever?

In the absence of stories about middle age, we must make do with what purport to be the facts. With certainty one can say that at some point between the ages of fortysomething and fifty-something, previously fertile women will become infertile. Everything else is provisional. Unlike successful pregnancies which, in their neatly contained drama of three trimesters, essentially resemble one another, the narratives of menopause are diffuse and hard to categorise. Each middle-aged woman is menopausal in her own way.

As with puberty there is a clearly identifiable point, after passing which one will have moved into a different state of being. In medical terms, that point is marked as the year's anniversary of your last period, a definition that sounds reassuringly precise until you realise that you'll only know in retrospect (and then only if your menstrual record-keeping is remarkably well organised) which flow was the last. The effect of this game of biological cat-and-mouse is a disconcerting mirroring of the uncertainties of late childhood.

For thirty-odd years, I gave the efficient mechanism that was my reproductive system scarcely a thought. Two or three times in those decades I wondered if I were pregnant and waited impatiently for the fall of the unfertilised egg that would tell me it was not so. Apart from those alarms, the prodigal succession of potential children formed, ripened and was shed without my paying it much more attention than I give to the monthly waxing and waning of the moon in the night sky.

In my mid-forties, having rejected my GP's offer of temporary sterilisation by implant, I began to take the low-dose Pill – at which the flow of blood that had marked each month with infallible regularity for so many years suddenly became erratic: first dilatory, then too frequent.

I stopped taking the Pill, but the cycle remained erratic. I wondered if I might be pregnant. The prospect was bizarre. I thought of the terrible, inconsolable crying; the long night watches; the unwieldy impedimenta of infancy that shoulders its way into every vacant space – the pushchair looming in the hallway, waiting to catch your ankles like a troll under a bridge; the nursery cot with its prison bars and packets of nappies stacked around it like straw bales in a barn, the trash of gaudy toys, each with its call sign of squeak, plink, tinkle or maddening snatch of electronic ditty.

I thought of the fact that we live in a house with four cramped rooms, only two of which are bedrooms and as I did so I had a flash, lurid as a photographed murder scene, of the inexorable way a baby would take over every inch of that small space.

I thought about telling my son, who had lived his whole life in the full beam of my undivided attention, that he would now have to share it with a baby brother or sister. I thought about the shit-smeared psychodrama of potty training, about the remorseless egotism of small children, the exquisite tedium of their conversation, like the shrill, repetitive calls of tropical birds, and of myself sixteen years hence, still thrashing in the snare of GCSE coursework while my contemporaries who had slipped the leash of parenthood sped away from me, into the airy freedom of the rest of their lives.

I thought of having to summon the energy to start again from the beginning, just as I'd begun to luxuriate a little in the thought that it was almost over. I thought of what it would be like to raise another child, still on my own, but sixteen years older than I was the last time. And I hoped with a thrill of longing like falling in love that I might be pregnant.

Perhaps I dared hope because I knew it was quite safe; there would be no pram in the hall because it wasn't pregnancy that had staunched my flow of blood, but the last of the long line of dream babies that had passed at the rate of one a month for hundreds of months, but now was dwindling; the tail end of the column of phantom children that used to extend over the far horizon now visible; one or two last stragglers vanishing from sight and then no more.

And as I had when I was a girl waiting to become a woman, I lost the complacency with which I had grown accustomed to inhabit my body and became once again watchful and uncertain, began looking out for signs that I'd passed the frontier from one state to another.

As a teenager I could feel myself living in my body as though it were a garment that didn't quite fit; as though I'd dressed up for a game in one of my mother's outfits and was now trapped where everyone could see me, wearing a dress that was too big for me, too grown up, whose womanly cut of bust darts and hip yoke hung mockingly ample on my bony, curveless frame. In my bedroom I examined the imperceptible swelling of my breast buds; the few pale hairs growing at fork and armpits, and wondered how long I must wait in this unformed, fledgling state, too big for the nest, too small to fly, and in everyone's way as a consequence.

Now the feeling of suffocation came again: as familiar as though it hadn't been absent for thirty years, this uneasy sensation of waiting for a change to take place that will leave you vulnerable and exposed, but about which you know nothing – not when it will come, nor how – other than that its coming is inexorable.

Perhaps it is the feeling a snake has when it is about to cast its skin.

When the blood ceased to appear I felt strange: stopped-up, dry and hollow, like an unwatered plant. I looked at the packets of tampons in the bathroom cupboard, for light to medium flow, and thought, well I won't be needing you any more, for I am a woman whose flow has dried up. I didn't care for the sound of the phase. It reminded me of Judith Starkadder in *Cold Comfort Farm*, announcing darkly that she was a Used Gourd. Once again, I felt I was inhabiting a body that wasn't mine.

Still, I thought, in time no doubt I'd get used to this peculiar stopped-up feeling and after a while it would become a part of my normality, in the same way that gross myopia struck me as an affront when my sight first began to fail around the age of nine; but I'd since forgotten what it might be like to open my eyes on waking and see anything other than a formless astigmatic blur. If that was it, I couldn't really see what all the fuss was about the menopause.

In fact, according to the plethora of menopause handbooks, the end of bleeding was only the beginning. Indeed, it was generally agreed to be altogether the best bit of the menopause – the tidying-up of the 'mess' and 'nuisance' of the menses acting as a sort of consolation prize for all the other inconveniences. I felt, sulkily, that I'd always rather liked the lunar ebb and flow of femaleness, relished the *Dame aux camélias* drama of blood and grand emotion for a week in every month. I thought life seemed a bit dull and shapeless without it.

If the narratives of middle age in modern fiction are somewhat thin and apologetic, there is rich compensation to be found in the handbooks of menopause, which tackle their subject with a certain grim relish for the indignities their readers are about to experience. They tend to have pink on the cover and titles in which mild facetiousness competes for the upper hand with a certain euphemistic optimism: *A Change for the Better; Is It Me, Or Is It*

Hot In Here?; The Woman's Guide to Second Adulthood, and so on.

Manuals tackling other problematic aspects of female life – pregnancy, say; the raising of toddlers or teenagers; losing weight; finding and keeping a lover; decorating a house; deciding what to wear – do not, on the whole, begin with a litany of reassurance about how what you're about to experience won't be anything like as terrible as you think it might be. But this is a common feature of guides to coping with middle age and the menopause.

Dr Hilary Jones, the GP, newspaper columnist, telly doctor and ice dancing star, concludes the introduction to his *A Change for the Better* ('How to survive – and thrive – during the menopause') thus:

> In this new millennium the menopause need no longer be regarded by women as a time they most come to dread. It need no longer be associated as it once was with negative attitudes, intractable physical symptoms and mind-altering psychological turmoil.
>
> Nor should it any longer be the subject of such widespread but misguided medical mythology. HRT does *not* make you gain weight. You do not suddenly cease to be sexually attractive or responsive, you do not become socially redundant in the eyes of your family and society as a whole, and it is not the final chapter in a woman's intellectual life by any means. Far from it.

Rather in the way that it didn't occur to me, while pregnant, that I might suffer from pre-eclampsia, placenta praevia, breech presentation, toxoplasmosis or an incompetent cervix and, by shunning handbooks, antenatal classes or any other source of anecdotal information on my condition, failed to apprehend the frightful dangers to which by a single careless act I might expose my unborn child, striding my way through a pregnancy in which my contact with unpasteurised cheese, germ-laden cats and the stress of extreme unhappiness was equalled only by my excellent physical health and preternaturally low blood pressure, it hadn't struck me that the end of my fertility might be attended by any of the hobgoblins of which Dr Hilary was kindly urging me not to be frightened.

The apprehension of my own mortality after the fall from my horse, the sudden vivid certainty that I would grow old and die – and that this wasn't a process that would begin at some unspecified time in the distant future, but was happening right now – might at a stretch be described as 'mind-altering psychological turmoil'.

It had altered my mind in the sense that it wasn't a transient thought, but had taken up lodging there and now sat in the recesses of my consciousness, emitting a low psychic hum, like the sound of a distant hive of bees, or a cat purring in an airing cupboard. I was aware of it most of the time, but mainly it was disconcerting, rather than terrible, though every so often a spectral whisper would pop into the foreground of my consciousness as I was performing some mundane task – making a cake, changing the sheets, cleaning my boots.

'Remember you must die,' it would hiss. And, 'Yes,' I would obediently think, with a little twist of dread at the prospect, 'one day I will die. My spirit will leave my body, which will be burned, or buried in the ground, where the flesh will rot from my bones and I shall cease to exist, except in the memories of the people who loved me; and when they in turn are dead, I shall be obliterated entirely. Before that I shall grow old, probably decrepit, perhaps mad.' And then I would carry on creaming butter and sugar, tucking in my hospital corners or trying to raise a shine on the scuffed toe of my boot.

Not much was left of the childhood Christianity in which I had been vigorously schooled, but just enough for me to feel a certain superstitious ambivalence about the aftermath of death, about which I managed to entertain two quite contradictory convictions. On the one hand I felt certain that my own consciousness would not survive the death of my body. On the other, when I thought about the people I loved who were dead, it was always in the context of a biblical passage whose words and cadences I knew by heart long before I understood what they might mean. 'Seeing we also are compassed about with so great a cloud of witnesses. . . .' it began, 'let us run with patience the race that is set before us.'

When I thought of the cloud of witnesses I imagined my grandparents, who seemed, in this posthumous version of them as spectral witnesses of what I was up to down on earth, much as they did when I was a child: old, but cheerful and vigorous, inhabiting a landscape of fields and gardens – an idealised version of the places where they had once lived. They didn't speak or offer advice, but they were definitely there, benevolent spectators of my mistakes and struggles, in a form more vivid (I thought) than that of mere imagination.

Garrison Keillor's novel, *Pontoon*, opens with a scene in which death, in the form of a silent angel, appears 'like a deer' in the bedroom of a lively nonagenarian, Evelyn, who is propped up in bed, reading, and says, 'Not yet. I have to finish this book.' The angel laughs ('He'd heard that line . . . before. He was always interrupting people who were engrossed in their work or getting ready for a night at the opera or about to set off on a trip . . .'). He takes Evelyn's hand and 'they flew up into the sequinned sky . . . through a meringue cloud into the mind of God and the embrace of her sainted ancestors all gathered at her grandfather Crandall's farmhouse on a summer morn, the patient horses standing in the shade of a red oak tree, white chickens pecking for bugs under the lilacs, Grandma whistling in the milk house . . . The weathered sheds and barn, the hayfields of heaven.'

When I first read this, it was with a shock of recognition: I realised that it was like this that I had imagined my own death: the old woman in bed (the image borrowed from the sight of my grandmother resting, small as a withered child, under the pink silk eiderdown of her own deathbed; still present but also profoundly absent: utterly absorbed by the intense silent drama of the transition from life to death); the swooping flight away from earth and into the spacious firmament on high, the solid familiarity of things on earth dwindling smaller and smaller, until suddenly all the ties that bound me to them were loosened and, bursting through the meniscus that separates life from death, I found myself a young woman again, at home (as it were), in a Kentish apple orchard on a warm day in early May, where the kind approving figures of my dear grandparents were to be seen coming to meet me among the blossomy branches.

The hopeless incompatibility of this vision with my conviction that death really was extinction didn't bother me unduly. If I were pressed to reconcile the two, I would say that the vision of meeting my sainted ancestors among the apple trees was my stratagem for avoiding Dr Hilary's mind-altering psychological turmoil.

The experience of middle age is one of many different losses. All sorts of things go missing around this time: youth, looks, ambition, eyesight, teeth, husbands, lovers, parents (and with them one's accustomed role as a child), children (and with them one's accustomed role as a parent); or the hope that one might one day bear a child. As outriders to all this loss come a handful of grim gains: in particular, the *timor mortis* that comes with waking on the morning of your fiftieth birthday to the realisation that (increasing numbers of centenarians in the population notwithstanding) your store of life is running out: you have lived for more years than remain to you.

To wrestle from this intractable catalogue of large and small diminishments a life that remains rich with hope and interest, while at the same time not denying that you're on the downward curve of the arc that leads from the stark simplicity of birth to the answering simplicity of death, is the proper business of middle age. As with puberty, mental turmoil is an essential part of the process of moving from one set of certainties to another. I felt rather suspicious of Dr Hilary's assurance that these days, the menopause could be accomplished without it.

I was all in favour of anything that would mitigate the 'intractable physical symptoms' that apparently awaited me. But what pill, what preparation of red clover, black cohosh, yam, HRT or selective serotonin reuptake inhibitor could conjure away the anguish of the middle years? And if such a magic draught existed, what would be the consequences of taking it? For surely there must be consequences. It was hard to imagine that you could chemically obliterate an entire passage of female experience without setting up some answering physical, psychological and social ripple somewhere further down the line.

That had been the promise on which the contraceptive Pill was marketed: the obliteration of the dread and horror of unwanted pregnancy and the toxic cloud of anxiety that hovered over all sexual activity. As a teenager, the delicious licence offered by the Pill, the *laissez passer* that it bestowed into an entrancing world of consequence-free sexual exploration, seemed marvellous to me.

Only later, after a decade and a half's suppression of fertility, did it belatedly become clear to me that I had claimed my sexual freedom at a heavy price. Along with my natural cycle, I had suppressed a longing for marriage, children, the deeply boring and comforting sensation of occupying a double bed with the same familiar old body as years and decades passed. The freedoms that seemed wild and precious at 17 struck me as thin and comfortless at 30. I was weary of the interminable prolongation of my adolescence. I wanted to be a grown-up woman.

Approaching 50 I found myself painfully conscious of the damage I had done to the prime of my life, the years between 30 and 45, by clinging to the habits of my 20-year-old self, refusing to listen to the insistent internal voice that spoke the truth when it said that I found my insouciance a burden, that my unfettered life gave me vertigo, that I longed to be tied down and held captive by responsibilities.

The opportunities of which that voice had spoken so urgently were vanished and would not come again. No internal voice now urged me to embrace the experience of middle age. Still, if it had been reckless to squander the chances of early adulthood by continuing to behave like a teenager, I thought there might be equally pressing disadvantages in refusing to give up the tricks of one's sexual peak once it was past.

I was haunted by a series of pictures I'd seen in a newspaper of the slender, pretty 52-year-old wife of an adulterous television presenter. 'Finding out your husband of 15 years is a philanderer is not usually to be recommended,' said the accompanying text. 'Then again, there are some benefits. The 52-year-old housewife and mother of four says she is emerging from her heartache as a woman in her best shape ever. "I'm feeling great – 50 is the new 40, without a doubt . . ."'

Beneath the headline, 'Look What You're Missing!', the betrayed wife posed in fishnet tights, a crimson basque and tight black pants, teetering on pole dancer's black patent-leather shoes with mountainous platform soles. Her eyes were thickly lined in black, her face a painted geisha mask of stylised allure. Dressed in this burlesque costume she was evidently putting on some sort of performance. But what was it a performance of? And who was its intended audience?

Her faithless husband was clearly meant to understand that the wife he'd betrayed was a figure of powerful sexual allure. Or perhaps the subtext was not that of wishing to lure him back with a public display of erotic energy, but that of revenge. By exposing herself to millions of newspaper-reading strangers, dressed in the formal uniform of sexual performance (a garb that specifically denies privacy or intimacy – the qualities that his faithlessness might be thought to have damaged), his wife perhaps felt that she was, in effect, repaying the humiliation he had inflicted on her by making him a virtual cuckold.

Perhaps, too, an element of altruism was involved in the performance. The newspaper was one popular with women and much given to a sort of voyeuristic empathy with women's preoccupations. Many of its readers might have felt the same shock of betrayal as the television presenter's wife, and been consoled by reading about her experience.

It wasn't the difficult mixture of revenge and defiance that haunted me, or even the way that the newspaper, while appearing to champion the injured wife, was also subtly exhibiting her as an object of ridicule (not coincidentally, it was the same paper in which appeared the scathing description of the middle-aged Madonna). Nor was I troubled by the expanse of 52-year-old flesh. On the contrary, I felt quite strongly that the more familiar the sight of the middle-aged female body, the better. The ambiguous cocktail of tenderness, sauciness, admiration, embarrassment and a trace of comic disgust that accumulated around the naked calendar modelled by middle-aged members of the Rylstone branch of the Women's Institute (and the subsequent film, *Calendar Girls*) struck me as a useful starting point for a discussion of the ways in which the female body might continue to be an object and instrument of desire, even when softened and marked with signs of wear and past its brief moment of adolescent perfection.

The thing that disturbed me about these pictures was the stripping away of any such complexity. These were not pictures celebrating a 52-year-old body in excellent condition, which had nevertheless borne four children and become a physical palimpsest of half a century of living, but of a menopausal woman demonstrating that she could pass, well lit and with plenty of make-up, for someone who wasn't a menopausal woman.

Which seemed not just uninteresting, in the way that reproduction anything – whether paintings, furniture, jewels or youth – is more kitsch and boring, less resonant than the authentic article of which it is an imitation; but also to miss the whole notion of middle age as an interesting stage of life in its own right: troublesome, painful and difficult, as such transitional periods inevitably are, but with the beauty, depth and poignancy that clings to endings, late works, Indian summers . . .

However you romanticise it, the transition from youth and fertility to age and barrenness is bound to be unwelcome, so it is understandable that the menopause manuals should concern themselves mainly with tactics for deferring or mitigating the effects of the change.

Buried among the lists of symptoms, questionnaires ('How Stressful is Your Lifestyle?'), diagrams of the ovary and graphs of oestrogen levels pre- and post-menopause in Dr Hilary's book there lies the following statement: 'Epidemiologists are aware that one of the reasons for the menopause having such a bad press is that only the views of women undergoing severe problems are ever represented . . . In fact, overall most women have a fairly uneventful menopause, with the majority experiencing a few short-lived adverse effects, and some blissfully sailing through menopausal waters with not a care in the world.' He adds that in his own experience as a GP, 'many women suffering from so-called menopausal symptoms are in fact encountering problems due to other unrelated medical conditions or environmental factors'.

This partly explains the mystery of why the phenomenon of menopause as a physical malady should be so strangely absent from pre-HRT female fiction and memoirs, but proposes an alternative notion: that the great incapacitating drama of menopause – the dismal catalogue of affliction listed in the BMA's handbook, *Understanding the Menopause & HRT* – from anxiety, depression, dry vagina, fatigue and irritability, to palpitations of the heart, poor concentration, urinary problems and loss of interest in sex – might be, not a cultural construct exactly, nor precisely an artefact of the medical profession or the pharmaceutical industry, but an event defined as much by personal style and expectation as by science.

Dr Hilary's modest endorsement of the 'uneventful' menopause notwithstanding, the advice of menopause handbooks is overwhelmingly preoccupied with hormone replacement. The BMA handbook on *Understanding the Menopause & HRT* advises, 'Try simple measures and lifestyle changes first' (for menopausal symptoms), and describes as 'a myth' the belief that 'oestrogen could be used as a panacea for all the effects of ageing', but devotes just 20 pages (of 177) to these 'simple measures' (including the crucial factors of exercise and diet), and then states unequivocally that 'HRT is the most effective treatment for menopausal symptoms'.

The notion of the menopause as an illness both reflects and compounds the low status of middle-aged women. But although Dr Robert Wilson characterised the menopause as a 'serious, painful and often crippling disease', his view of the climacteric would have gone the way of all sorts of other eccentric medical theories of the Sixties, if it were not for the fact that significant numbers of women remain willing to share his view of themselves as 'diseased'.

At a college reunion I fell into conversation with a female doctor a little younger than myself and was surprised by the vehemence, almost the relish with which, when I said that I wasn't taking HRT, she began to describe the shrivelling of flesh and crumbling of bone that would soon overtake me if I continued to reject the drug. I began to wonder, as I had during the conversation with the GP who warned that my post-partum belly would sag in pleated folds, or the young woman GP pressing me to accept chemical sterilisation, whether there was some extra agenda to our conversation, besides the unnecessary medication of a healthy middle-aged body.

It is easy to imagine what a delicious promise of liberation hormone replacement therapy must have seemed to women entering middle age in the Sixties, with the catchy jingle of 'Hope I die before I get old' ringing in their ears. The forty- and fiftysomethings offered the hope of perpetual youth must have felt they were helping to build a future in which their daughters' experience of middle age would be scarcely different in quality from their carefree twenties and thirties.

It is disconcerting, now, to consider the gap between that ideal and the twenty-first-century reality, in which middle-aged women face a bleak choice between the strenuous, expensive, time-consuming, and possibly risky pursuit of synthetic youth, or a state of invisibility so powerful that it can cause female television presenters to vanish from the screen as though they had never existed, while their male colleagues accumulate gravitas with every passing year and are even permitted, as an extra privilege of age, a certain playfulness; the licence to explore soft subjects – late fatherhood, say, or their hobbies – which they would have scorned when younger as women's-page stuff.

The medicalisation of childbirth eventually engendered a counter-movement whose enthusiasts argued the case for the inherent good health of the female body and its reproductive functions, and sought to restore to the narratives of pregnancy and childbirth the mystical element of which they felt the clinical approach had stripped them.

There are writers, including Germaine Greer and Ann Oakley, who argue passionately in favour of a holistic approach to the physical and psychological phenomenon of the climacteric, and there is a thriving industry in 'natural' remedies for menopausal symptoms. But the project of reclaiming the menopause from its dire clinical description as a female epidemic has not yet gathered the fashionable momentum that eventually made natural child-birth a mainstream, rather than an alternative, choice. If anything, the current of fashion still runs the other way.

'We'll have to decide,' wrote Jenni Murray in the introduction to her menopause guide, *Is It Me, Or Is It Hot In Here?*, 'whether we want to go along with science that seeks to keep us young and nubile, either through pills and potions or the surgeon's knife, whether we want to grow old disgracefully with a hairdresser with a great line in hair dye as our constant companion, or whether we'll be graceful and grey in the distinguished manner so far only open to the male of the species.'

Why Murray believed it the prerogative of men to be 'graceful and grey in the distinguished manner', she did not say, but it is a common conviction. In an episode of the television makeover programme, *Trinny and Susannah Undress the Nation*, devoted to older women, the presenter Susannah Constantine, who was then 45, underwent a transformation with make-up and prostheses into an imaginary version of her 70-year-self.

Having spent many hours having twenty-five years added to her age (the viewers were not told how much time she habitually spent applying make-up in order to make herself look twenty-five years or so younger than her real age, though the comparison might have been interesting), Constantine opened her eyes in front of a full-length mirror and burst into tears at the sight of herself dressed in dowdy, ill-fitting clothes, her shirt buttons and skirt waistband straining over pendulous prosthetic breasts and swollen belly, thin, grey hair straggling about her shoulders, her face pouched and deeply wrinkled.

'There is no way I'm going to look like this when I'm 70,' she wept to her co-presenter. 'I will not dress like this and I will not allow my face to become like this.'

It was a transformation as lurid and fanciful as Colette's incarceration of Léa de Lonval in sexless slabs of fat. But it was never explained why (or at what point in the coming quarter-century) Constantine thought she might undergo the dismal transformation from someone who cared what she looked like, to someone who didn't.

One reason for engaging in such grotesque reverie is as a way of testing what the future might hold; of imagining a dismal destiny as a kind of charm against its coming true. Just as many adolescents engage in Gothic daydreams about living fast and dying young, the middle-aged flirt tremulously with the spectral versions of themselves when withered by the frost of old age.

In *Break of Day*, her autobiographical novel of middle age, Colette conjured a disturbing vision of an old age in which flesh was already halfway to rejoining the earth from which, dust to dust, it sprang: 'The only old people I can tolerate are bent over towards the earth, cracked and fissured like chalky soil, their hands gnarled as old branches, their hair wild as birds' nests,' she states, and she describes a Provençal woman of 72 who fits this farouche description.

On her way back from working among the vines and vegetables on her smallholding, the old peasant pauses to caress a flower-bud with a finger like a dry twig, crooning, 'Isn't it pretty?' With her arms full of green peppers and onions, an egg cradled in her wrinkled palm, she looks the very embodiment of productive old age. But if the life force still flickers within her, so too does a deadly urge to destroy: she crushes shrews on the path, squashes dragonflies against the windowpane, snuffs the life out of newborn kittens as casually as if she were shelling peas.

When it came to her own ageing, Colette took energetic steps to avoid resembling the mineralised peasant whose version of old age was the only one that her fictional alter ego claimed to find tolerable. At the age of 48 she underwent what her biographer describes as the 'brutal and rather crude operation that a face-lift was in the early 1920s'. A decade later, she set up an institute of beauty, opening shops in Paris, St-Tropez and Nantes selling beauty products and cosmetics of her own devising.

'I find the women beautiful as they emerge from beneath my writer's fingers,' she wrote. But in practice her writer's fingers were less assured with the make-up brush than the pen – at least when the face they were working on was that of a young woman. The formidable American Sapphist, Natalie Barney, observed that Colette plastered her own daughter with make-up until the girl resembled a streetwalker, and Martha Gellhorn left a devastating account of being made over by Colette. Gellhorn's lover at the time was Colette's stepson, Bertrand de Jouvenal, whom the novelist had seduced when she was 47 and he a 16-year-old virgin.

Colette persuaded Gellhorn to pencil her blonde eyebrows with black crayon 'so that the lines almost met in the middle . . . And it was three days before some kind, candid friend said to me, "My dear, what dreadful thing have you done to your face?" She [Colette] was jealous of me . . .'

Certainly if one were to harbour in middle age a jealous wish to spoil the looks of younger, prettier women, the beautiful faces of one's daughter and the girlfriend of one's stepson and former lover might be high on the list of candidates. The envious despair of ageing women whose fading looks are eclipsed by those of younger, more beautiful rivals is richly recorded in myth and story.

But now the revulsion seems to flow in the opposite direction, from the beautiful young towards the less beautiful old. Often it assumes the form of a quasi-filial contempt: the impatience and faint disgust that young women feel for the mothers whose sexual competitors they have become. But the sexual rivalry masks something else as well: an unacknowledged sense of dread at the fate that lies in store.

'As I am, so shall you be' run the inscriptions on old tomb-stones, above the carved image of a grinning skeleton, jovially reminding the passer-by of the common fate of man (and woman). Now that death is tidied away, its dreadful shape removed from common view, our first and only direct encounter with last things – apart from the odd goldfish or childhood hamster – is quite likely to be the moment of our own death.

We lack a personalised image of mortality – and into that void steps the figure of an ageing woman, for whom a real sense of loathing crops up in the most surprising places: not just in the horrified dismay of Susannah Constantine at the sight of her grotesque imaginary older self, but in the advice of newspapers and magazines on grooming for the older woman.

'Acceptance is, in part, a solution. Keep buggering on,' was the terse advice offered to middle-aged women by a journalist in a newspaper's 'Age Defiance' beauty series. For 45- to 55-year-olds, the advice was, 'Should you have the stomach and the wallet for it, now is a prime time to embrace plastic surgery.' But if courage or funds are lacking, 'console yourself with the thought that age comes to us all, and that fresh-faced lovely who just caught the waiter's eye before you will, in ten years' time, find herself in precisely the same boat'.

As for the over-65s: 'The good body now needs more medical help than maintenance . . . If you succumbed to breast implants in your younger years, now might be a good time to have them taken out, as a young woman's bosoms on an older frame is not a good look. Besides, you are above all that now.'

By 'all that', the writer apparently meant sensuality, the desire to please and be pleased, to take (and bestow) pleasure with one's appearance. She seemed to discount altogether the possibility of an older woman's enduring power to fascinate. By her reckoning, 'all that' was a commodity so perishable that it had already begun to take flight by a woman's mid-twenties (according to the article, the years from 26 to 36 are 'when the rot sets in').

What is strange about this account of women's maturity is not just its grim tone: the need to shore up against decay beginning even before the prime of life has been reached; by the forties, a straight choice between plastic surgery or taking spiteful consolation from the thought that younger women will soon be as ugly as oneself; by 65, entirely desexualised – a woman only in the sense that one is not a man. There is also the writer's evident sense that she is saying nothing unusual, simply articulating a universally acknowledged truth: that women begin to become physically repulsive soon after the first bloom of their youth has vanished, and what remains thereafter is a more or less heroic programme of resistance to the catastrophe of age, until the mid-sixties when all options are exhausted – at which point you have your breast implants removed and give up.

Germaine Greer devised a macaronic neologism for this sometimes veiled, sometimes quite explicit, loathing of ageing women: anophobia, she calls it, 'from the Latin anus, meaning old woman'. And she notes how 'the tradition of ridiculing older women seems neither to surprise nor to infuriate them . . . Fifty-year-old women laugh along with everyone else when male comedians guy whiskery-chinned shrieking old bags in ridiculous hats'.

This is prescient: she was writing more than a decade before *Little Britain* kept the nation in a roar of amusement at the antics of its terrible old women – the chatty old dear who pisses uncontrollably in public places; the tweedy ladies who project torrents of yellow vomit everywhere on learning that the vol-au-vent or slice of Victoria sponge they have just tasted was prepared by someone gay or from an ethnic minority.

The comedy is double-edged: hilarious as it is to see posh old women humiliated, their impregnable self-assurance ravaged by the base bodily functions that publicly overwhelm them, there is also an undertone of fear. These old women have no shame at all: beneath their cable-knit twinsets and pearls they are completely anarchic, like huge incontinent toddlers, with a toddler's over-weening egotism and lack of inhibition. There is no knowing what they might do or say. They are terrifying as well as despicable, unsightly and disgusting – a living affront to the world of the young.

On a personal level, Greer claims this waywardness, this outsider's perspective on the world, as the means by which an ageing woman can reclaim an inward power and control over her own destiny once her powers of sexual attraction have waned: 'Once we are past menopause we are all oddballs,' she writes. This thought, or a version of it, evolved into the hugely popular *Grumpy Old Women* franchise of television series, books and innumerable other spin-offs, to which Greer is a notable contributor.

The premise of the series seems, at first glance, to be a sort of Old Girl power: an affirmation of women's comradeship, an insouciance about physical decay and the contempt of the young, a cheeky egging-on of one another about such manifestations of 'grumpiness' as complaining about poor service, or the dauntless confrontation of bad behaviour by youth in public places. Threading the comedy, though, is a disturbing strand of self-loathing.

In the *Grumpy Old Women* version of it, the poignant cessation of the struggle to stay young becomes a riotous celebration of grotesquerie. The pleasures of farting and nose-picking are vaunted as more than adequate substitutes for vanished sexual pleasure; the uncontrollable sprouting and sagging of increasing age pitilessly anatomised; men, old people, young people, sales assistants, bosses – in fact other people in general – energetically excoriated. From beyond the self-mockery there rises a pungent reek of melancholy, of discontent, of regret and envy of 'people like Helen Mirren who looks maddeningly good for her age'.

For all its bravado, there is not an air of underlying serenity or security in its own position about the Grumpy persona. You have the powerful impression that the women who laugh along with the Grumpies are more than likely to be channel-flicking between that and *10 Years Younger*, thinking that if only they had the nerve and the money they, too, would go for the veneers, the lipo, the face lift, hair extensions and the room full of admiring friends exclaiming about their miraculous rejuvenation.

Nowhere, either in the reflective Greer examination of the physicality of the middle years or in the commercialised Grumpy version of it, does there appear the notion that grace, allure, attraction (of which conventional beauty is an element, but not a necessary condition) might not be a perishable commodity of which one was granted a finite ration at birth, but a quality more in the nature of a talent of which one could make what one chose at different times in one's life.

The 'maddening' good looks of Helen Mirren are maddening only because their owner insolently ignores the tyrannical idea of allure as the exclusive property of youth, which from middle age must either be faked or austerely relinquished. It is a peculiarity of the Hollywood concept of beauty, in which the UK is also saturated, to dismiss the notion, more common in the matriarchal cultures of Europe, of the power (and desire) to attract as a continuum: a quality retained throughout adult life, depending not on the firmness of one's flesh, but the firmness of one's sense of self. Not a fixed sense of the self one was when young, but a shifting sense of the self one becomes with experience.

The actress Penelope Keith, asked by an interviewer whether she had been approached to appear in *Grumpy Old Women*, said that she had – 'But I'm an actress, not a turn.' Which is a neat précis of the crisis of middle age, in which you wake one morning to find that you have been demoted from the star of your own life to a turn: your choice of roles limited to a handful of caricatures – old dear, battling crone, faux gamine. What woman, reading this in her late thirties or early forties, could think of herself as settling with any satisfaction into any of those personae in ten years' time?

'The trouble is,' says my friend Prudence, as we discuss our awkward age, 'that you've been giving a performance all your life, but when you become middle-aged, suddenly you don't know who the performance is for any longer. When you're a child it's your parents and your teachers. Then it's your mates at school and college; then, when you're starting an independent life, it's lovers and work colleagues. Then suddenly you're middle-aged, and who is the performance for now? It has to be for yourself.' And it's true. One's personal drama doesn't stop just because the house isn't as packed as it once was.

Simone de Beauvoir, writing at the age of 54 in her memoir, *Force of Circumstance*, described with memorable bitterness the sensation of life closing in, the dwindling of horizons that came with the passing of youth. Often, she wrote, she dreamed that she was dreaming. In her dream-within-a-dream, she would imagine that she was 54. Then, in her dream, she would wake with relief to find that it wasn't true, that she was only 30, before realising, while still asleep, the crushing truth that her joy at finding herself not old was illusory.

Everything, she wrote, was infected by the 'pox of time', even her sense of connection with the world. 'Never again shall I collapse . . . into the smell of hay. Never again shall I slide down through the solitary morning snows. Never again a man . . . In spite of everything, it's strange not to be a body any more . . .' Even the richness of memory has deserted her – the books she read, the places she visited, the music she heard: 'They made no honey, those things... [no] nourishment.'

Ten years later, another volume of memoir, and the landscape has altered again. The convulsion of change is over: 'As I see it, there is not much difference between being 63 and 53, whereas when I was 53 I felt at a staggering distance from 43.' The scandal of ageing, the sense of being excluded by the world – spurned by the very snowflakes and hayfields – has receded. The affronted feeling of being betrayed by her own memories is assuaged. Now, 'What strikes me is the way the little girl of three lived on, grown calmer, in the child of ten, that child in the young woman of twenty, and so forward . . . Through all my changes I still see myself.'

Hovering on the threshold of the changes that older women describe with such misgiving, I find myself gripped both with a silly conviction that it won't happen to me (even though it already is). But also by the longing for some directions to this difficult terrain. The ones I have consulted so far seem somehow faulty. Trying to find a way by them feels like trying to navigate a city centre with a guidebook published in a previous century. The major landmarks are just distinguishable, but all the thoroughfares have shifted; the places of interest have changed; I cannot recognise my journey as the one charted by the people who travelled before me, even quite recently.

In the end, I get out the photographs of myself from a baby onwards and spread them out on the table. There aren't many of them: just a handful from my childhood, teens and twenties; and although a mass of pictures begins once my son is born, it's almost always me behind the camera, so I am mostly absent from those.

But between the absences there are just enough fixed points to map a life: a newborn baby with pop eyes, clenched fists and an inexplicable shock of wild black hair; a bandy-legged toddler peering suspiciously at a daffodil; a beaming five-year-old in the first class of infant school and then a series of passport photographs: sombre at 11 in crooked, swooping-framed glasses at least fifty years too old for me; grimly disaffected six years later as I prepared to leave home in a hurry; mousy and formless at 25; all in black with dark lipstick a year later, like a newspaper photograph of a nineteenth-century French lady poisoner.

After that a gap of almost ten years, and then a mixed clutch of a dozen tender pictures with my son taken over a decade and the same number of pictures taken in various guises for work: a pretty picture byline taken when I was so much in love that the glow of it quite effaced the fearful hangover from which I was suffering; pictures of me cooking, shopping for groceries, on horseback at a meet of hounds, before-and-after Botox shots of me looking pale and furious (even beneath the drag-queen's slap of the 'after' picture).

Two of the photographs – the first two, of the smiling five-year-old and grave, bespectacled 11-year-old – make me sad; it seems to me that I can see between the two pictures the shutting down of whole areas of personality which wouldn't come to life again for decades – not until I had a child of my own. Like de Beauvoir I can see the child of five in all her later metamorphoses: the sullen teenager, the formless twentysomething whose life had taken a wrong turning, the new mother, the middle-aged woman. But although I can't help wondering what might have become of that child if her circumstances had been only a little different, I haven't quite de Beauvoir's sense of having been cheated.

What failures and disappointments befell the girl I was – at any rate the 17-year-old I was – were mostly my own work. And after all, if you'd asked the five-year-old what she wanted when she grew up, three of the most urgent items on her list of ambitions (to write, to have a baby and a horse of my own) have been realised.

Fate saw to it that I discovered fairly early the unreliability of some of the bigger deceptions that life dangles in front of women – the ones to do with thinking that everything will be all right, that you'll be taken care of, that love solves everything. But it strikes me that the biggest lie of all has been saved up until now, and it's the one I could still fall for, because one is so vulnerable, so soft and shell-less at this moment of change that it requires every bit of self-control not to believe that some alchemy, some cocktail of hormones, surgery, diet, cosmetics and positive thinking can stop time and keep me poised for ever just at the moment before I grow old.

6
The Body's Body

It is well known that one of the baleful symptoms of female middle age – along with hot flushes, sudden weight gain, incapacitating vagueness, wrinkles, invisibility, powerlessness and an interest in gardening – is not having a thing to wear. Sure enough, as I arrived at 50, without warning my clothes seemed to turn against me.

I might have sensed the problem earlier if I hadn't resigned from my last office job at 40 and begun to work from home, which I mostly did in a utilitarian uniform of jeans and cardigans. Working at home, and the extra homeboundness of single parenthood, meant that I hardly ever had to assume a public face. It was not until almost a decade later, when I began to attend a weekly ideas meeting at a newspaper office, that I realised something had gone wrong.

I was a voracious reader of fashion magazines, so I'd kept my eye in – or so I thought. I had cupboards crammed with the sartorial love affairs of the past decades – a journal of my adult life in chiffon, leather and wool. And although time had softened and slackened the flesh on my bones, a metabolism-boosting temperament of high anxiety meant that the zips and buttons of my old garments still fastened willingly enough. So at first, when I started to dress for the office, I did it with the unaccustomed pleasure of getting ready for an occasion.

I'd leave the house convinced that I looked tremendous: elegant, original, with a fascinating vintage twist. But during the journey from Greenwich to London a curious transformation would take place. Looking at the other people on the bus and train, my confidence in what I was wearing would begin to seep away, and by the time I reached the office, full of busy, efficient young women, all looking indefinably *right* in their clothes, it would be clear to me that what I had on was, equally indefinably, *wrong*. Not risibly unfashionable or disastrous mutton dressed as lamb, just very dowdy and a bit eccentric. I could see myself through the eyes of the confident young women in their neat, tight officewear and teetering high heels: an opinionated old bird in flat boots, trailing peculiar bits of vintage finery.

In the television schedules, programmes on the restoration of shabby, run-down old houses were outnumbered only by programmes on the restoration of shabby, run-down middle-aged women. The main difference between the two was that the presenters of the house restoration programmes seemed to regard their projects with a certain tenderness, even before their renovation, while the people in charge of the human makeovers seemed specially picked for their ferocious manner towards their charges.

They rampaged through their wardrobes like updated versions of the dreadful Scissor-man in the nursery rhyme, brandishing huge pairs of dressmaker's shears with which they cut their victims' favourite old clothes to shreds; they made them strip to their underwear in front of 360-degree mirrors, then grasped their sagging breasts and hoisted them into the air, to show the improvement that proper corsetry might make.

They chivvied their victims out of their shapeless monochrome garments and stuffed them into control pants and fitted ensembles in cheerful bright colours. Their universal ideal of perfection seemed to be a flared skirt or bootcut trousers worn with mid-high heels and a tightly fitted short jacket, low-cut to show to best advantage the newly uplifted cleavage, saucily embellished with a dangling paste jewel. 'Soooo sexy,' was their constant refrain, as though the primary purpose of women's clothes was to express the sex appeal of the body inside them.

I watched these programmes at first with derision and later with pity. I was taken aback by the humility of the women who submitted themselves to the makeovers. I longed for them to snatch back their treasured old garments from the snipping shears, or for one of them to rebel and tell the presenters (like the popular school bullies whom everyone fears and wants to be friends with, I thought they were, with their queasy mixture of insults and caresses) exactly what she thought of their hateful formula of control pants, uplift bras, high heels and garish colours. Above all, I wanted to someone to say that clothes are about more than sex.

All my life I had loved the expressive mutability of fashion. I was intrigued by garments as artefacts, by the mysterious energy of them, and by the technical business of making them. The desire I felt when choosing a dress or a pair of shoes was the same that I experienced when I bought a chair or a picture, or picked up a stone, a shell, a feather or a dead leaf when I was out walking. I relished the negotiation of choosing some object or another which would, once it was mine, assume the responsibility of acting as my interpreter.

I had always relied on my clothes to make up stories about me – as fantastical and mendacious as possible. I trusted them to take on the world in a way that I felt my plain undecorated person could not. What I did not require of my clothes was that they should act as my pimps or panders. No doubt some erotic transaction was involved when, in my twenties, I dressed up as Vita Sackville-West in land girl's breeches and boots, as Patti Smith in my boyfriend's old school suit, as Nancy Cunard in leopardskin and bangles like weapons. But I felt that it was a private one between me and my clothes. The purpose of the fancy dress was narrative, rather than advertisement.

Occasionally I did contrive to look sexy, despite myself. 'You can join my regiment any time you like, hen,' said a burly sergeant of the Black Watch, following me up the stairs of an Edinburgh bar which I was ascending in a Black Watch tartan miniskirt, fastened with little mother-of-pearl buttons, that I had bought with the pay packet from my first proper job.

A few years later there was a combination of white jeans, heavy silver belt and navy voile shirt that induced a young man to ask me out to tea when he fell over me in Blackwell's music shop one summer afternoon in Oxford. But when this sort of thing happened it was generally by accident. I had no clear idea of what constituted a 'sexy' outfit and in any case I was inclined to think that when my true love came along, he would see past the gypsy queen finery to the naked person within, and love that.

There must once have been a time when I didn't notice what I or anyone else was wearing, but I don't recall it. I even imagine that I remember wearing my christening dress – white rayon satin with the eerie, dead-white sheen of uncooked meringue, smocked in pink and blue with imitation pockets, pearl-buttoned, lace-edged – but this must be a memory confected from seeing pictures of my baby self wearing it. At any rate, from an early age I relied on clothes to do the hard work of self-expression. There was something miraculous, I thought, in the way you could slide into a dress like a spirit creeping into an inanimate body; become someone else at the buzz of a zip and the snap of a press-stud.

At intervals during my childhood, packages would arrive containing outgrown clothes that had belonged to an older cousin. Her taste, which ran to the fancy, exactly coincided with my book-fostered vision of myself as an orphan princess. Out of the brown-paper parcels sprang a hand-me-down puff-sleeved party dress of blue nylon net spangled with white flock snowflakes;

another of crimson velvet with mother-of-pearl buttons and a collar of handmade ecru lace, and a full-skirted day dress of white cotton pique with bands of rose and dove grey, and pointed, rose-piped sleeves like vestigial wings.

Like the heroines of my storybooks, I was entranced by fabric and cut – perhaps because, like them, clothes were the only visual aesthetic experience I knew, besides nature. I relished with the child Laura Ingalls the dresses that her Ma and aunts Ruby and Docia put on to attend the sugaring-off dance in the Big Woods of nineteenth-century Wisconsin. Ma's dark green delaine with a pattern of strawberries and knots of green ribbon; Aunt Docia's dark blue, sprigged with red flowers and green leaves, with buttons like juicy blackberries that Laura longed to lick; Aunt Ruby's wine-coloured calico with a feather print in a lighter wine colour and gold buttons carved with a little castle and a tree.

I suffered with Pauline Fossil and Meg March the vicarious humiliation of threadbare velvet audition dresses and limp tarlatan party frocks, and noted for future reference the ingenuity of Sandra in *The Swish of the Curtain*, who buys ten yards of cheap lining material to make into a huge-skirted ball gown. It looks dreadful in daylight, but under artificial light is transformed into an ethereal cloud of silvery pale-blue.

In my everyday life I began to develop a critical eye for the clothes of grown-ups. Mrs Turner, the headmistress of my primary school, who was tall and slender with dark curls and bright dark eyes, glittered with a quality that I had not yet learned to call chic. In the winter she sometimes wore a narrow, clinging jersey dress of black and tawny horizontal bands that made her look sharp and dangerous, like an elegant wasp. For summer she had a dress with a tight bodice, a square neck and a vast skirt in white cotton satin printed with large blue roses that I thought simply beautiful.

In a different way I could see that my Shilling grandmother, with her furs and ever-changing hats and good jewels, also had a distinctive sense of style. Alone among the other adult women in my world – the teachers, dinner ladies, friends' mothers and Sunday-morning church ladies – Mrs Turner and Grandma Shilling had clothes that said something about their own essential Mrs Turnerishness and Grandma Shillingness. The blue-rose dress could hardly have been less like the striped wasp dress in style, but each had an insolent wit, a quality of dash, that was the essence of Mrs Turner.

My grandmother's furs, some with beady glass eyes and mummified claws still attached to their dangling limbs, gave off a faint feral smell beneath the grandma scent of powder and dead-rose potpourri, as though they might nip back to the wildwood, given half a chance. The biting spark of a diamond, the musky animal tang, revealed something about my grandmother, something wilful and instinctive, a glint of whiskers and sharp teeth beneath the old-lady uniform of hat, gloves and handbag, that contrasted strangely with the stately rhythm of her life, of spring cruises to Madeira and Sunday afternoon runs down to the front at Hastings beside my grandfather at the wheel of the great, grey, rolling Rover.

I was growing up in the 1970s. In London and the big provincial cities, branches of Miss Selfridge and Wallis were filled with cheap Ossie Clark and Bill Gibb knock-offs. A revolution was beginning in which mothers and daughters shopped at the same places, swapped outfits with each other, wore clothes that were interchangeable and not defined by age. But that revolution hadn't yet come to Sittingbourne.

My mother, like my friends' mothers (younger, all of them, than I am now), wore mother clothes: constricting undergarments – a girdle with elastic sides, metal and rubber suspenders and an unforgiving satin centre-front panel; everyday skirts and toning twinsets from St Michael and occasion wear for Ladies' Nights from a dressmaker – Madame Stuart of Canterbury – whose workshop, crammed with bolts of shocking pink crêpe and rolls of silver and metallic purple braid, tangerine shot-silk shading to bronze when you held it to the light, garnet brocade and jewelled sea-green taffeta with floating chiffon panels, seemed like a cave of hoarded treasure.

There was no common ground between the world of grown-up clothes and my clothes, which came, until well after I had started at grammar school, from the children's department of Hulburds of Sittingbourne. But by my mid-teens, Sittingbourne High Street had sprouted a boutique and a branch of Dolcis and I, obsessed by now with Nancy Cunard's kohl-smeared eyes and skinny arms laden with heavy ivory bracelets, had begun to explore the power of clothes to outrage and affront.

It was a pair of granny shoes that opened hostilities at home. Even now, with a Seventies revival going on and the identical twins of these shoes to be found in every high street shoe shop, I marvel at the trouble they caused.

My mother was a generous and rather daring shopper when it came to my clothes. Aged 14 I owned – and regularly wore to church on Sunday mornings – a forest green jersey dress with a front seam slit almost to the crotch, and a wet-look navy PVC coat with a heavy silver buckle that clanked on the pews when I knelt down. But for some reason my parents absolutely drew the line when it came to high heels and make-up. They were forbidden.

For my sixteenth birthday my friend Angela Spark bought me, from Woolworths, two Miners powder eye shadows, one white, one a glaucous blue-green, and a lipstick of virginal pale pink. It was all but imperceptible when on, but my mother perceived it just the same. There wasn't a proper row, just a stiff dose of more-in-sorrow-than-in-anger and a grieved suspicion that I had encouraged Angela to give me make-up in order to outflank the parental ukase against buying the stuff with my pocket money.

For the same birthday, someone gave me some money. I had seen these shoes in the window of Dolcis a few weeks before and there had passed between me and them the strange silent transaction – the moment of exhilarated recognition, like love – that takes place between women captivated by clothes and the objects of their desire. I knew without doubt that something very bad would happen if I gave in to the temptation to own them. And I knew with equal certainty that I was going to buy them at the very first opportunity, even if it meant keeping them in their box for ever.

So I took my birthday money and I went into the shop: the very antithesis, it was, with its crackling nylon carpet and slouching, insolent assistants, of Armitages, the nice, reliable shoe shop where all my footwear had until this moment been purchased. Armitages was warm and dim, with an atmosphere of studied calm, like a cross between a doctor's surgery and a church. There were the reverent rituals of fitting – the assistant genuflecting as she raised my foot in its wrinkly pale-brown sock into the wooden foot-measuring contraption.

Then the murmured consultation with my mother (or, on one startlingly irregular occasion, my father), the disappearance into the secret sanctuary of the storeroom and the re-emergence with four or five almost identical pairs of flat, shiny, conker-brown Clarks or Start-rite lace-ups (in winter) or buckled T-bar sandals with a dully decorative fanlight cut-out on the broad toe (in summer).

By this time I would have begun to protest; even, as I entered my teens, to snivel with rage and humiliation: muttering, snarling, arguing that my friends, even the ones with really strict parents, were allowed a little heel, a tiny decoration, a scrap of fashionable frivolity, and pointing furiously at alternatives in black patent leather with gold bits.

In vain. Every time we came away with a cardboard box containing a terrible pair of flat, brown, leathern foot-platters. Which, after an astonishingly short time (given the stupendous Start-rite reputation for solid reliability), would be crushed by my hatred into down-trodden, slip-slop caricatures of their original neat practicality.

No wonder that opening the door of Dolcis felt like a transgression – its very name a byword for the wicked deceiving sweetness of cheap fashion. Inside, the light was harsh and fluorescent, the smell not the good earthy reassurance of brown leather, but a badass toxic reek of PVC and nylon. There was no nonsense about fitting, either. 'What size are you?' asked the bored assistant. I told her. She fetched a box with the shoes inside it and left me to it. No expert palpating of the toe to check whether there was room for my feet to spread out, no probing finger slipped between the flesh of my heel and the back of the shoe to make sure that it fitted snugly but not too tight. Out of habit, I did it anyway, trying to persuade myself that if the toes didn't pinch and the heels didn't slop, the parents would have nothing to complain about.

The shoes fitted fine. They were lace-ups. Their toes were round, not pointy. They were, in fact (except that they had a three-inch heel and were made of shiny black plastic), not unlike the dreary horrors that I had been wearing for the past sixteen years. Perhaps my parents wouldn't notice the difference.

They did, of course, and there was a fearful row, which rumbled on for days. It centred on the offensive 'unsuitability' of the trashy plastic and vertiginous heel, but seeped outwards to encompass my nasty duplicity in sneaking off to buy in secret the forbidden articles, and my culpable extravagance in spending the birthday money that my kind relations had given me (expecting that I would use it to make some worthy and improving purchase: preferably a book, though a modest piece of jewellery would also have been acceptable) on a pair of shoes whose principal function was not that of coming between my feet and the pavement, but the insolent defiance of all respectable standards, not just of footwear, but of morals.

Clothes, said Erasmus, are the body's body. And that was what the row was really about. Not the cheap unbreathable plastic, a breeding ground for the interstitial fungal infections so dreaded by my father that he covered the bottom of the bath each evening with a scurf of medicinal foot powder. Not the inevitable distorting effect of the high heel on my spinal column, pelvic girdle and the fragile metatarsals of which Armitages had taken such exemplary care for sixteen years. Not even the mildly fetishistic effect of perching a plain schoolgirl's lace-up on top of a three-inch heel, but the obtrusive insistence of my body's body: the lamentable metamorphosis from child to adult so outrageously signalled by the contraband pale-pink lipstick, the greeny-blue eye shadow, the cheap high heels.

The odd thing was that when it was all over I seemed, unprecedentedly in my skirmishes with my parents, to have won. The violent battle for possession of the shoes (for which I had been bracing myself ever since I left the shop, with a sense of dreadful foreboding mixed with inexplicable excitement) never took place. They weren't confiscated, not thrown in the dustbin or cast on to the bonfire. After a while I was even allowed to wear them to school. And after that the sumptuary laws relaxed to such a startling extent that a year later I sat the university entrance examinations in the sketchiest, most contemptuous approximation of school uniform that I could devise, wrists jangling with bangles, eyelids ringed with black kohl, hair straggling down my back, reeking of Havoc. 'Woah,' jeered my son when he saw a photograph of me from this era: 'You were an *emo*.'

In the nineteenth-century novels for whose anaesthetisingly plotty narratives I developed a passion in my mid-teens, an interest in dress often appears as a signifier for moral imbecility, if not actual vice. Emma Bovary is the archetype of the tragic heroine whose fatal flaw of character is chronicled in details of haberdashery, millinery and rouge, but she is a close cousin to Trollope's adventuress Bella Trefoil, Edith Wharton's Lily Bart, even Dickens's Little Em'ly, whose future ruin is dismally prefigured in a childish love of adornment: the blue bead necklace that is the first thing the child David notices about her; the innate vulgarity of her innocent wish, 'If I was ever to be a lady' to dress her weatherbeaten fisherman uncle in 'a sky-blue coat with diamond buttons, nankeen trousers, a red velvet waistcoat, a cocked hat, a large gold watch [and] a silver pipe . . .'

A reading of the heavier-handed nineteenth-century novelists may lead one to suspect the motives behind the authors' symbolic use of clothing imagery. The conflation of plain clothes with virtue and elegance with vice can appear to spring less from an admiration of womanly modesty than from a dislike of females indulging in any form of self-expression at all – even if mute and exclusively confined to bonnets and shawls.

But two of the most articulate and strong-minded of these heroines approach the question of self-adornment from fascinatingly opposed perspectives. In Henry James's *Portrait of a Lady* there occurs a telling conversation between the heroine, Isabel Archer, a young woman infused with passionate idealism in everything she undertakes and her nemesis, the subtle, deeply attractive, profoundly wicked and entirely worldly 40-year-old Madame Merle. Early in their friendship the young woman and the older fall to discussing the nature of the self.

' "What shall we call our 'self'?" ' asks Madame Merle.

> 'Where does it begin? where does it end? It overflows into everything that belongs to us – and then it flows back again. I know a large part of myself is in the clothes I choose to wear. I've a great respect for *things*! One's self – for other people – is one's expression of one's self; and one's house, one's furniture, one's garments, the books one reads, the company one keeps – these things are all expressive.'

' "I don't agree with you," ' Isabel responds:

'I think just the other way. I don't know whether I succeed in expressing myself, but I know that nothing else expresses me. Nothing that belongs to me is any measure of me; everything's on the contrary a limit, a barrier, and a perfectly arbitrary one. Certainly the clothes which, as you say, I choose to wear, don't express me; and heaven forbid they should!'

'You dress very well,' Madame Merle lightly interposed.

'Possibly; but I don't care to be judged by that. My clothes may express the dressmaker, but they don't express me. To begin with it's not my own choice that I wear them; they're imposed upon me by society.'

'Should you prefer to go without them?' Madame Merle enquired in a tone which virtually terminated the discussion.

Isabel's fear of the power of objects to reify the person they adorn proves well founded. She, like Dorothea Brooke, the heroine of George Eliot's *Middlemarch*, believes that to bedeck the person is to place a barrier between themselves and the pure, stripped, unmediated engagement with the world of ideas and ideals that they believe lies somewhere just beyond the restraining conventions of the material world in which they live. It does not occur to either woman that the semiotics of clothes will get them anyway: that a plainness of dress is as eloquent and studied a performance as the most elegant *tenue*.

There is a school of twentieth-century feminist thought that shares Isabel and Dorothea's austere distaste for self-adornment. In *The Last Gift of Time*, her memoir of life beyond 60, the American scholar, Carolyn Heilbrun, included a chapter 'On Not Wearing Dresses' in which she described exultantly how in late middle age she liberated herself from the conventional feminine clothing that feminists of her generation referred to as 'drag', and adopted instead a comfortable 'androgynous' uniform of trousers and tunic.

'Androgyny defeats semiotics,' she wrote, arguing that by dressing in a neutral version of male clothing, a woman can achieve the tricky dual object of making a political statement – a refusal to be defined in terms of her 'femininity' – while remaining, semiotically, invisible, so that nothing in her appearance obscures the essence of her 'self'. And she quotes Susan Brownmiller: 'The nature of feminine dressing is superficial in essence. To care about feminine fashion, and do it well, is to be obsessively involved in inconsequential details on a serious basis. There is no relief . . .'

I thought that 'Androgyny defeats semiotics' was a good slogan, but like most slogans, more of a wish than a truth. And Brownmiller's ideas about fashion seemed an unexpectedly reductive view of a rich and complicated area of human experience – as though someone tone deaf or colour blind should dismiss music or art as 'superficial in essence', and assert that to be captivated by them is to be 'obsessively involved in inconsequential detail'.

Middlemarch is a novel haunted by the power of clothes to represent feeling, and in the end it is a change of clothes that signals Dorothea's shift from idealistic self-delusion to redemptive self-knowledge. She has been very unhappily married, then widowed while still young and is now convinced that she is as badly mistaken in a deeply felt second love as she was in the futile sacrifice of herself in her first marriage.

After a sleepless night of moral crisis, she looks out of her window and sees the world going on outside: a man with a bundle on his back, a woman carrying her baby, a far-off shepherd with his dog, just visible in the pearly light of the new day. In an instant she understands that 'she was a part of that involuntary, palpitating life', and there comes to her mind, 'like a haunting, the tradition that fresh garments belonged to all initiation'.

As for a christening, a wedding or a burial, she knows that she must dress in new clothes to begin this new phase of her life in which she has resolved to live as best she can without love. And Dorothea, the brave, the unconventional, the careless of her own beauty and appearance, 'grasps after even that slight outward help towards calm resolve. For the resolve was not easy.'

There is a moving mixture of humility and self-possession in the act. By giving up her disregard for outward appearance and calling on a dress to help her at a moment of emotional crisis (something of which she would have been incapable at the beginning of the novel), Dorothea is symbolically clothing herself in the self-knowledge towards which she has been struggling throughout Eliot's narrative. The new dress with three folds at the bottom of the skirt and the new bonnet with plain quilling aren't after all arbitrary barriers to self-expression, but eloquent inter-preters of feelings that would otherwise be inexpressible.

Somewhere between the believers in self-adornment as a betrayal of the female spirit, and the television purveyors of control pants and cleavage-revealing jackets in garish synthetics, I felt that there must be a way of pursuing my love affair with clothes into middle age. More than that: a way of marking my transition from one state of womanhood to the next in clothes, just as the high heels had signalled the crossing of the bar from childhood to adulthood.

'When you are getting older,' says Carine Roitfeld, editor of French *Vogue*, 'you have to find some new tricks.' But how? Despite frequent news stories that fashion houses were turning to middle-aged models – Jerry Hall, Helena Christensen, Madonna – in order to attract older, richer customers, very young models continued to predominate in the editorial and advertisements of women's magazines, and fashion advice for the over-forties invariably concentrated on prohibition: no exposed knees, no bare arms, no leather; long hair is an outrage on women past the age of 40.

The list went on and on. No tight jeans (in case of giving passers-by a nasty turn by looking like a lissom teenager from behind, and a skinny crone when they get a glimpse of your front elevation). No bare midriff. No 'directional' shoes: they are 'undignified'. Nor should you 'cling to the styles of yesteryear' (this meant no kitten heels). What the hapless fortysomething is supposed to walk about in was not clear. But it's a fair bet that bare feet are out of the question, as well.

When the advice was positive, rather than simply a list of forbidden fashion fruit, the results were often odd, or disturbing, or insultingly dull. In 2008 Marks & Spencer launched Portfolio, a range of clothing for 'the older woman' that combined hectic impracticality (a sleeveless, zip-front jumpsuit) with bizarre dowdiness (elastic-waisted jersey trousers) and a fearful coyness (a trench coat, sawn off at hip level, in sickly raspberry pink). The effect was astonishing: a horror parody of every grim cliché of middle-aged dressing.

Two years later Debenhams also had a crack at the market of what they described as 'forgotten women', launching 'the Style List', a campaign intended to show women in their forties, fifties and sixties 'how to achieve fashionability and enjoy trends traditionally worn by consumers half their age'. The campaign seemed better considered than Marks & Spencer's. It used models the same age as its target consumers, who actually looked their years. And the clothes were nicer. They weren't really my thing: very urban and sophisticated, whereas my get-ups always seemed to have a vague whiff of the stableyard about them, even when I was doing my best to look soignée. But at least they avoided the dreaded cliché (the only resort, it sometimes seemed, of fashion editors faced with the task of advising the over-forties on their wardrobes) of 'timeless classics': cashmere cardis, crisp white shirts, the essential black trouser, the perennial trench, good shoes, good bags, a string of pearls, a bright silk scarf or funky bangle to add a jolt of colour.

I was too narrow across the shoulders to carry off tailoring, too pale to wear a crisp white shirt – and in any case the prospect of spending the next four decades of my life in expensive mono-chrome made me want to weep with boredom. Why would I suddenly want to start dressing like a corporate lawyer when my whole life had been dedicated to clothes that put on a performance? All I wanted to do was to carry on looking like me. Whoever that was these days.

The disjunction between the person I felt myself to be inside, and the person my clothes announced me to be was intensely disconcerting – a sort of sartorial aphasia, as disturbing as finding oneself suddenly unable to communicate in a language one had once spoken fluently. Like the old woman in the nursery rhyme who woke from a snooze by the roadside on her way home from market to find her petticoats cut up to her knees, I didn't know who I was any more.

The rhyme describes the old woman in a state of cruel distress at what she feels is her loss of identity: 'She began to shake,/And she began to cry,/Lawk a mercy on me,/This is none of I!' She comforts herself with the thought that, 'if this be I,/As I do hope it be', her dog at home will know her. 'If it be I,/He'll wag his little tail,/And if it be not I/He'll loudly bark and wail!' But as she arrives home, 'Up starts the little dog,/And he began to bark'. The rhyme ends with the dog barking as though at a stranger, and the little old woman in her curtailed petticoats standing outside her house in the darkness, weeping bitterly and wondering who she is, if not herself.

Without my carapace of clothes to rely on, I began to feel as I had when as a child, I used to frighten myself by repeating 'Who am I? Who am I?' until overtaken by a vertigo of lost identity. I could feel that change was upon me, as it had been when I had precipitated the first great row of adolescence by buying the offensive pair of shoes. Only that time, clothes had been my allies; the armour of my new-fledged sexuality: it was me and my high heels, *contra mundum*. Now I was on my own. I retreated into my uniform of jeans and a jumper, and grieved.

One day I bought a fashion magazine: 'The Don't Miss List – *Vogue*'s need-to-know guide to autumn', said the coverline. I hoped it might point me in the right direction. Inside were pictures of Kate Moss wearing trousers sewn from a Union flag; a grey chiffon top with a fringe of silver and sulphur yellow beads. In a derelict room with shattered floorboards and walls of ruined azure she stood between a chipped metal chair and an electric kettle, wearing a ballgown of pleated platinum satin; a short dress of white ostrich feathers and another of white organza roses with a studded black leather motorcycle jacket; a ruffled rag of rose and peach-coloured chiffon beneath a frogged military jacket.

In a bodice of guipure lace flowers and a Union flag jacket she gazed without expression at the camera. Her bare feet were thrust into unzipped black boots with heavy wooden platforms, and she held a tulle crinoline above her waist so that her little black mesh pants were exposed. 'Knickers, Kate's own', said the caption.

A paragraph of text explained the purpose behind the apparently random juxtapositions of silk fringing and metal chain; embroidered tulle with goat-hair and horsehair, studded leather and old metal badges. 'Who wants to look like a fashion robot when the joy is adding the you, the me?' it enquired: 'From amulet-dripping necklaces to haute-bohemian rope belts, and from lace handbags to metallic stilettos, choose your self-expression.'

I was easily persuaded to comply with this sort of rhetorical exhortation. Choosing my self-expression was exactly what I longed to do. Shimmering at the edge of my consciousness was a notion of the sort of clothes I wanted. I owned a book of photographs of Balenciaga's designs from the 1950s and '60s. That lovely sculptural rigour was it exactly. Not sexy or girlish but strange, organic shapes like birds' wings, trees, or rock forms carved by wind and waves, in fabrics nubbly, sleek, slashed, hairy or granulated with beads and sequins.

I didn't care for the late-period sable jogging pants, but coveted a great, stiff, moundlike cloak of green tufted wool, like wearing a small grassy hillock as an outer garment. These were clothes for women with lived lives; intelligent, complicated clothes in which one might resemble a mythical beast – a selkie, say, half seal, half woman – or an animated feature of landscape. In clothes like those, one would look interesting at any age.

Such garments were still to be had – made by Galliano, McQueen, Lanvin or Hussein Chalayan and glimpsed from time to time in red-carpet photographs, generally with Tilda Swinton inside them. They weren't the stuff of high-street knockoffs, however: too clever and wrought to be reduced to something that could be run up in a Far Eastern sweatshop. These were clothes that you could only own if you had a very great deal of money, and I hadn't any, so that was a problem. I couldn't afford even the tamed, domestic versions of these daring, feral garments – the less alarming but still thoughtful mid-price creations of Donna Karan, Nicole Farhi, Sonia Rykiel or Agnès B.

I thought of humble, middle-aged Miss Matty in *Cranford*, standing among the newly arrived Spring Fashions in Johnson's, the Cranford shop that sold everything from cheese to millinery, fingering the rainbow shawls and lustrous silks of crimson, sage green, silvery grey and lilac with yellow spots and wishing like a girl that she might have a gown for every season. I thought of Clarissa Dalloway, stitching and stitching at the tear in her green silk evening dress, planning her party, deep in reverie, her mind turning at anchor between the girl she was and the woman she had become.

I thought of the women in Helen Simpson's story '*Wurstigkeit*' – not quite middle-aged, these two, but in their mid-thirties; considerable mature women in the prime of life, at the top of their game: formidable city lawyers, romping like children in the extraordinary dressing-up box of a nameless shop in a vile alley off a street in Spitalfields, trying on impossible, theatrical garments

– a pink-fawn pelisse, pleated like mushroom gills; a long dress of pear-yellow with mulberry-stained panels, another in blue and white like a willow-patterned teacup. Apotheosis clothes, says one of them to herself. That was what I wanted.

Avid for something new, for fresh clothes to mark my initiation into this new phase of life, I took to haunting the Blackheath thrift shops. Rich pickings were to be had there for little money: I bought a green velvet coat with a greenish fake fur collar, tipped with black, like the fur of slow-moving sloths on which grows a creeping, symbiotic lichen. It had, I thought, a sort of savage grandeur: the sort of garment Maid Marian might have worn to keep warm while queening it under the greenwood tree. But a friend gave it a quizzical look when I wore it to lunch.

I bought a pencil skirt of tawny orange corduroy, but it was too large and hung loose from my hip bones, which wouldn't have mattered when I was younger, but looked like a mistake now. Back it went to the charity shop, from which I brought home in succession a short lampshade-pleated skirt of felted grey wool and a jacket of fine black needlecord with a millefiori print of tiny green and fawn flowers, lined with cotton striped in black, pink and white, like a nineteenth-century muslin. I wore the skirt and jacket to an interview with a magazine editor, to whom I mentioned that I once wrote a style column for a newspaper. 'A style column?' she said, looking startled. 'Really?'

I bought a tight-fitting mouse-coloured heavy cotton jacket with leg-of-mutton sleeves, finely striped in grey with a jacquard pattern of a climbing vine in dull gold. It was laced at the back like a corset, buttoned from waist to neck, and from wrist to elbow. I wore it with a long, fox-coloured velvet skirt, but caught sight of my reflection unexpectedly and realised I looked like the most old-maidish of Chekhov's Three Sisters.

Then I found a narrow, plain, knee-length coat of plum-coloured suede. 'That's a nice coat,' said a friend. Giddy with success, I bought a pair of round-toed shoes in mushroom-coloured calf with very high stiletto heels in matching plum-coloured patent leather. 'They make you look a bit short in the pastern,' said the friend, grasping my elbow as I teetered across the road. In my late teens I used to stride the mile and a half between the town centre and my university college in towering heels, but the knack must have vanished at the same time as my knack for the alchemy involved in putting together a look, juxtaposing a disparate clutch of garments to create a coherent autobiographical mini-drama.

Declutter! urged my friend Prudence, in whose handsome Victorian closet there hung a tiny, perfectly co-ordinated selection of linen, cashmere and flowered crêpe de Chine, all of exquisite quality. I could see that this was the ideal of a middle-aged wardrobe – sophisticated, comfortable, well edited.

Women with much finer clothes collections than mine had relinquished them, handing over the best things to museums, then dispersing the rest among friends and charity shops. In *Vogue*, Joan Juliet Buck described doing exactly that, holding back a single, beloved jacket to stand for the multiplicity of memories, the magical surge of hope and excitement and change represented by each coat and dress at the moment of its acquisition.

I knew that at some stage that grand relinquishing gesture would become necessary, but I couldn't yet make it. It hadn't ripened in my mind. Instead I searched the magazines for pictures of women of my own age who had contrived to avoid the tentative, wounded look that I saw reflected in the mirror, who had succeeded in recalibrating the equilibrium between their outward appearance and their inner sense of self.

Helen Mirren, Tilda Swinton, Jane Birkin and Yves St Laurent's muse, Loulou de la Falaise, all shared a quality that was distinctive, although hard to describe. It was not precisely that they were well dressed (although I did like their clothes very much, particularly the fluid, fantastical quality they all shared: as far from muted classics or hoisting and confining undergarments as could be imagined). It was more that the ease and humour with which they wore their clothes seemed to reflect their personal histories: the spark of their early beauty still visible, tempered now with the tinge of melancholy that experience brings, and a sort of insouciance about being, despite everything, still themselves.

Having worked this out I began to feel calmer about not yet managing to do it myself. I recalled the awkward age between 14 and 17 when I had veered uncertainly between the quasi-adult sophistication of rolling the waist of my school skirt until it barely skimmed my buttocks, then taking fright and squeezing back into the child's clothes that were suddenly too small for me. That ungainly phase had resolved itself eventually – and so, in time, I supposed, would this.

7

The Awkward Age

I wasn't the only one in our house experiencing a metamorphosis. When the change began I was 47 and my son was almost 14. He was still half a head shorter than me: the supercharged growth spurt of his mid-teens not yet begun. The teeth flanking his two big upper incisors were the short, frilly-edged baby teeth whose eruption through his infant gums had seemed like such a lurch into grown-upness at six months old. His arms and legs still had the marshmallow softness of childhood, the muscles not hardened into the lean gangliness of adolescence. His face was a childish composition of tender curves: cheeks, brow, nose, chin – rose-freckled and dusted with a silvery down like a moth's wing or a green almond. His hair was bleached by the sun into gilt streaks. He smelt of hay and newly baked sponge cake.

He hadn't always been beautiful: the photographs record a bald, jaundiced newborn, so ugly that I was dismayed at my first sight of him in the delivery room and felt obscurely ashamed, as though I had failed at some tricky domestic task: my soufflé fallen flat; my jam failed to set.

At two years old he flowered from a wizened changeling into a handsome, laughing, long-limbed putto with dark gold curls and a grey-blue gaze. But in the pictures of him beginning nursery school eighteen months later he seems to have withered again: he is pale, peaky, self-conscious, ill-at-ease, the gilt curls shorn into a mousy crop, his expression tentative and withdrawn, his skinny arms folded across his body like a fledging's bony wings.

Arriving to pick him up I would look into the playground, spot him hovering at a distance from the yelling Brownian motion of the other children, his gaze averted, as though by avoiding eye contact he could make himself invisible, and feel a wrenching mixture of pity and irritation. Pity for the way that the experience of school seemed actually to twist him out of shape; irritation that it should be my son who was the poor doer, the cadpig, the outsider.

Why couldn't my child be one of the solid, jovial yellers? I felt, rather than thought, unwilling to let the horrible wish for a different child take shape in my mind. But still, why couldn't I be coming to pick up one of these robust, pink-cheeked children roaring and romping like puppies under the approving gaze of the class teacher with her iron-grey pudding-bowl hairdo, rather than the peaky, problematic wraith in the corner?

Looking back at the pictures of myself as a child, writhing nervously in front of the lens, legs and arms twisted together like bindweed, unable to meet the camera's gaze, it strikes me that the source of my daily playground jolt of irritation, the thing for which I found it hard to forgive my son, was that he resembled me as a child.

Long before I gave birth to him, from early childhood onwards, I had been weaving an elaborate fantasy of the sort of children I would have in the future, the sort of mother I would be. I wanted to be the mother of sons – of that I was certain. Lots of sons – six, perhaps – and no daughters. Or perhaps just one, late girl after I'd reared my brood of fantasy boys.

I had grown up in a household of flustered female meekness. 'Efface yourself!' my father used to demand. Victorian children were allowed to be seen, if not heard. But he apparently wished his daughter to vanish altogether. I tried to do as I was told – at least, I suppose that's what I'm doing in the photographs with the contorted posture and scrunched-up arms and legs – trying to make myself as small and invisible as possible; trying to efface myself.

My negligible worth as a daughter convinced me that I didn't want anything to do with girls when it was my turn to be a parent. Like Louisa May Alcott's Jo March in her adult incarnation, when I grew up I wanted a kind-but-firm husband with scholarly leanings, and a shabby-but-comfortable house filled with cheerful, manly, rough-and-tumble little boys, forever getting into wholesome mischief. How I thought I might achieve this fantasy, given the striking absence of cheerful rough-and-tumble in our family, which was more inclined to grim silences, compressed lips, speaking glances and raised voices behind closed doors, I have no idea. But it was an intensely persuasive vision.

Even now that it is relinquished I find myself still dreaming sometimes that it really happened; and that my present reality was an uneasy trance from which I have now woken: I see the shape of the house as though I'd lived there all my life – old bricks, a tiled roof, ancient yew and apple trees; a paddock edged with sloe and hazel rising away from the house towards woods and orchards and at the far horizon the glitter of the sea.

From the woods and the paddock I hear the distant shouts of children faintly rising (I'm always in the kitchen in this dream, cooking something. A tendency to wild over-catering, as though feeding the vast family I never had, has been a constant feature of my grown-up life). I sense, rather than see the shapes of croak-voiced adolescents slumped on the living-room floor and sofas, absorbed in some electronic game; feel the shadowy heft of a smaller child at my hip (they never have faces, these dream children, only the vague lineaments – the long limbs and tangle of dirty blond hair – of my real son).

The experience of being pregnant silenced conclusively the bravado of theoretical preferences. I didn't even think about what sort of baby I might be having, so stupefied was I by the fact that I was having one at all (and so startled by the astonishing, Scutari filth and brutality of the obstetric care at the south London teaching hospital where I was a patient).

I turned up for my 20-week scan untroubled, for the first time since childhood, by the urgent longing for a son (but surprised and rather impressed by my own uncharacteristic blitheness). Boy, girl, whatever, said I to myself as I climbed on to the sonographer's couch. As long as it's got arms and legs and fingers and toes. And a head.

'Would you like to know baby's sex, as such?' asked the sonar operator. As such, I thought I would, even while glorying in my virtuous indifference to the information. 'This,' said the sonographer, flirting a white arrow somewhere around the mid-section of the pulsating mass on the monitor that represented my developing child, 'is the willy area.'

The willy area? A boy, then? I was to be the mother of a son? I had studied *Coriolanus* for A level, and in an instant felt myself morphing into the terrible Roman matriarch, Volumnia, whose great glory is that she is her son's mother. Expecting a boy, eh? Well, *get me*!

My fantasy of myself as the mother of a son was so vivid that I didn't suffer a moment's anxiety about how I was going to do it. I knew nothing about the raising of boys; and not much about males in general. My only successful relationship with a man had been with my grandfather, who died when I was 18. It wasn't much of a base from which to undertake, single-handed, the nurture of an infant son.

And yet I was superbly sure I could do it. My child-rearing theory was simple: I would do the opposite of everything in my upbringing, and the result would be the cheerful, open, uncomplicated child of my imagining. Genetics, in the limited form in which I studied the subject at school, had concentrated on the inherited characteristics of pea shoots. I had read more than enough biography and fiction to understand that people, like peas, pass on traits down the generations, but still I failed to make the connection between peas and me.

No one forced me to be a single mother. I could have refused the role, but I chose not to. Strange, then, that I found it so hard to reconcile myself to my situation. My surreally conventional suburban background had suited me very poorly; yet when it came to inventing myself as a parent, I found I missed it. I couldn't think myself into the role of the cool young babymother, out to parties every night with the infant slumbering sweetly in a wicker basket among the abandoned coats; nor that of the well organised career woman, expertly juggling work and baby. I wanted very much to be a married lady with a ring on her finger, a white wedding dress in the closet, honeymoon photographs on the sideboard and lamb chops in the fridge for supper.

I went to work every day, came home, retrieved the baby from my next-door neighbours, who looked after him as kindly as though they were family – which in effect they were – and went home to cook lamb chops for one. By degrees I began to inhabit an atmosphere almost as permeated with powerlessness and rage as the one in which I had grown up.

Then Linda arrived. Most people can look back over a life and see in it a pattern of encounters – a couple, a handful – by which the course of their existence was shifted from one trajectory to another. Linda arrived at a moment of dire catastrophe when my son was 20 months old. I had, that morning, gone mad from a combination of chronic lack of sleep, a difficult house move and an intractable sense of loss, and was due to keep an appointment with a psychiatrist at the Maudsley Hospital, round the corner from my flat.

If my prospective nanny thought the set-up unusual – the gloomy basement flat, the absence of a father, the haggard and dishevelled mother, the strangely silent child, the hovering pair of concerned friends (there to make sure I didn't do myself a mischief on the way to the Maudsley) – she didn't say so, but agreed to take the job, with a start date a few weeks hence, by which time I was planning to have recovered my sanity and accomplished the move from my flat in Peckham to a cottage in Greenwich.

Linda was an unusually composed 19-year-old with a milkmaid's pink-and-white complexion and an air of implacable calm. Unlike Mary Poppins, who was always cross, and whose presence drove inanimate objects to jiggle in nervous frenzy – drawers slamming themselves open and shut; toys and books leaping to attention – she had a curious ability to impose stillness on her surroundings. She came, like Peggotty, from Great Yarmouth.

She took a dim view of the fact that Alexander, at almost two, scarcely spoke and of his quirk of referring to himself, on the rare occasions when he did utter, in the second person: 'You need a drink. You want to go home now . . .' In a matter of weeks, apparently without effort on her part or resistance on my son's, she had him potty trained, drinking from a cup rather than a mug with a spout, using a knife and fork and conversing volubly in conventional syntax. The hectic gloom in which we had been existing was replaced by a peaceful ordinariness so unaccustomed as to seem utterly exotic.

From the first day she made me question myself as a mother. I came home from work once to find her offering the baby a choice of yoghurts for his tea: would he like apricot or raspberry? It had never occurred to me that he might have a preference. Yet by offering him this insignificant choice, she gave him a degree of power over his own world that I had been withholding.

Linda's arrival tore great holes in our sealed world, through which the outside came rushing in bracing blasts of unaccustomed sensation. She took Alexander out – not just to the park on the doorstep, but up to London to see the pelicans in St James's Park, and to toddler groups, where she met other nannies and made friends. Sometimes I'd arrive home to find my living room filled with unknown young women drinking tea and the carpet swarming with their little charges.

As he grew older, she began to form his tastes as well, steering him away from the *Thomas the Tank Engine* books which were his first obsession. She took him to Legoland and Chessington World of Adventures, to petting farms and children's activity centres, to the swimming baths and the London Aquarium. They went to the circus together, to the Blackheath funfair and to McDonald's.

I minded very much about missing so much of the day-to-day, the solid warp and weft of the fabric of my son's life. Part of me felt sad and ashamed at having to acknowledge that if I had been able to take charge myself, I wouldn't have known how to do it half as well as Linda, with her natural authority and apparently effortless energy, inventiveness and sense of fun. Another part felt pure gratitude that Alexander was having the sort of childhood in which ordinary fun, free of improving content, was a feature; yet another part felt vast relief that I didn't, myself, have to go to Legoland or Chessington, ever, and could stick to what I was good at: reading bedtime stories and baking complicated birthday cakes in the shape of trains and football pitches.

But in my own role as a mother, it was hard not to feel cheated by circumstance. The six months of my maternity leave, though lonely and frightening in some ways, had also been filled with sweetness. I felt transformed as a person – the baby had smashed the defiant shell of egotism inside which I had been sheltering since childhood, and as the spring came and the leaf-buds burst I felt my small, hard, black, cramped soul expanding in sympathy as I learned what unconditional love felt like.

When my son was seven, I gave up my staff job at a newspaper and turned freelance. I was working for a woman who celebrated the masculine rituals of newspaper production: fearsome rows, impossible last-minute changes of plan, eleventh-hour ripping-up of pages to concentrate the minds of her underlings. On my first day in the job I had to telephone the widow of a well-known man who had just hanged himself and request an interview. The widow declined with a gentleness that I did not deserve.

I should have realised then that I wasn't cut out for this line of work, but the thought of money made me hesitate. My next task was to commission a series of articles on sex from 'great writers'. I did so, with predictable resistance on the part of the great writers. But when I produced the hard-won results, my editor flicked through them and said indignantly, 'I can't publish this! It's *filth*!'

I tried to feign insouciance in public and raged in private. But the rift between the Mannerist contortions of the executive hier-archy and the pressing simplicity of my son's longing for me to be at home (and my longing to stay with him) became so extreme that in the end I couldn't stretch myself across the gap any longer. With characteristic bad timing I resigned just as my editor was fired and her place taken by her deputy, a calm and diplomatic mother of two small children who contrived to reconcile the maternal and the professional with a grace I couldn't manage.

I launched into the flighty precariousness of freelance life and began to write from home. I wondered if this might be the moment when the wind changed and Linda left to exercise her calming influence on some other troubled family, but she didn't seem in any great hurry to be off. She settled in a flat with her boyfriend and had children of her own: a dark-eyed baby daughter, followed a couple of years later by another.

The professional relationship had long since grown into friendship; with the arrival of the little girls it began to blur into something more like an extended family. After a dozen years of shared history it seemed impossible that she should leave – except for the inconvenient fact that my son had grown out of his need for a nanny, though not out of his relationship with the young woman who had done half the work of bringing him up, and with her daughters, who were like his little sisters. But then there came an unexpectedly graceful solution to the problem of how and when to part. A house in Great Yarmouth became available. Linda had the chance to bring up her daughters near their grandparents, by the sea. It was the end of the chapter.

Her parting present to us was an album of photographs chronicling the decade of our life together: in the earliest pictures Alexander was still a baby. Here he was cutting a Henry the Green Engine cake at his fourth birthday party; looking apprehensive on a ride at Legoland; wearing a monster mask at a Star Wars exhibition; pushing Linda's elder daughter in her buggy, serious and responsible in his first pair of glasses. And here he was in the last picture, long-limbed and gangly, the planes of his face looking suddenly very defined and adult, camping it up to make the baby laugh, with a pink tutu pulled over his ripped jeans and surfer's T-shirt.

Laid out like this as a chronological narrative, the passage from baby to toddler, toddler to schoolchild, child to boy, boy to almost-adolescent, had a look of seamless coherence, a glossy, almost stylish inevitability which was not at all how it had felt to me as it was happening.

I had apprehended the changes in him more with my body than my mind, charting the transitions in terms of how far I had to bend down to speak to him face to face; the position of his hand when I was holding it; the ease with which I could hoist him on to my hip; the advance of the top of his head, with its pale parting, from knee level to waist height – then breast height, shoulder height. Now his eyes were almost level with mine and our joint perspectives were altered for ever. Quite soon he would overtake me and for the rest of our lives, our vantage points would be reversed: me looking up at him; him looking down on me.

Knowing that this would be the last summer of his childhood, I asked an artist friend to take photographs of him. Every stage of his childhood had always seemed so vivid, so burned into my consciousness that I could not imagine forgetting it, ever. Only the evidence of the photographs revealed what a slipshod cataloguer memory was: places, clothes, toys, outings, entire holidays were deleted from the record. Only the pictures remained to show that they had ever existed. Poised at the ending of the first part of the story, the moment at which the balance of power between us would begin to shift, I wanted a talisman; something to remind me what it had felt like to be the mother of a child.

The pictures are snapshots, taken in the park where Alexander had played in the sandpit as a baby and made his first unaccompanied excursions to play football. She caught him sprawling on the grass, for once not stiff or mugging for the camera but smiling, pensive, chin propped on his hand, at ease with the park, the summer's day, the old friend taking pictures. He looks younger than his age: his features, the pearly sheen of his skin, the plump hands and slender wrists are all those of a child. Only his long limbs and his expression, in which a faint trace of irony or melancholy, a knowingness is visible, suggest the transition into adulthood has begun.

He was almost as hesitant about his own shift towards the next stage of life as I was about mine. He'd been impatient for a while with the nursery atmosphere and restrictions of Linda's regime; surlily rejecting her insistence on good manners; her efforts to steer him towards assuming some of the responsibilities of the anteroom to adulthood. But while he resented the nursery, he was reluctant to leave behind the privileges of childhood.

We were both worried about what life would be like when Linda left. For twelve years we had been alone together only at weekends and holidays. If something went wrong, if we had a row or got bored, we were never more than a few days away from her mediating presence. What's more, the regular passage from Linda's care and Linda's house to mine made us seem exotic to each other: at the end of the school day I would feel a clutch of excitement at the sound of her car drawing up outside the house, the slam of the door, the footsteps up the path, the prospect of the day's news to come.

Weekends and the planning of how to spend our two days of freedom – where should we go, what should we do? – felt like a succession of small holidays. But I doubted my ability to sustain the variety, the imaginative energy, even as far as the end of the summer holidays, never mind indefinitely – or at least for the next four or five years, until the moment when he would (presumably) leave home.

I thought my nervousness about the future would make us uneasy with each other. That we would say our farewell and turn away with the hollow sense of people left behind, returning to our empty house after waving Linda and the girls off on their adventure. Linda and I, as we parted, couldn't speak. Our throats were full of dry sobs that we couldn't swallow. I had expected that Alexander would be desolate; that I'd have to control my own feelings in order to take care of him, but as we turned for home it was I who wept and he who seemed to take charge.

The combination of perimenopause and adolescence should have been volatile, but perhaps the long expanse of July and August was the right moment for the tidal shift of boundaries between child and parent. There was an unexpected companionable lightness to those summer months. It felt carefree, like sharing a house with a friend. The vapid sense of boredom I feared never came. I thought it would be impossible to work with another person in the house, wandering in and out for a chat, filling the house with noise, dirty plates, discarded socks and dense clouds of teenage languor. But we fell into a routine. The weather was fine, the days long. I got up early and worked. We ate lunch together and went out in the afternoons.

In August we went to Crete, where we stayed for a week in a stone house on a hillside with olive groves sloping away towards the lights of the valley. In the early evening swallows skimmed the pool, swooping to sip a few drops, circling and swooping to sip again. As it grew dark we lay flat on the stone terrace and watched the stars come out and the bats hunting overhead. I would have been happy to stay among the olive groves, the singing heat, the birds curving over the pool, the stars and the bats, but Alexander wanted to explore, so on the third day we drove to a Venetian port, 30 kilometres away.

The drive in the crammed streets of the little town was strident by comparison with the archaic peace of the house on the hillside: the one-way system convoluted; the traffic signs few and unexpectedly placed, issuing instructions in Greek that I couldn't transliterate fast enough to obey. We circled the suburbs fretfully before finding at last the route to the port. There we left the car and struck in from the city walls to the centre. A maze of narrow alleys between old stone houses opened into a starburst junction of wide thoroughfares roaring with cars, at the centre of which stood a cruciform covered market.

Stepping away from the hot shimmer of the traffic into the cool shade of the stone market building, with stalls in every direction piled with onions, tomatoes, aubergines, bundles of green herbs, hard quoits of bread sprinkled with seeds, buttermilk pucks of sheep's cheese, chunks of honeycomb bleeding gold, glinting scales of little silvery fish and the writhing purple arms and large reproachful eyes of octopus, the dreamy idleness of the past few days by the pool gave way to an avid longing to try all these new things. The violet artichokes, the waxy slabs of olive oil soap, the creamy blocks of halva jewelled with pistachios and powdery mounds of rose and lemon Turkish delight – I wanted them all.

More exactly, it wasn't the things themselves that I wanted, not the tourist's experience of asking for things in dumb show, fumbling for a handful of unfamiliar coins and carrying home my little trophy of local colour. I wanted to know what it felt like to be one of the plump housewives with their straw baskets, bantering with the stallholders as they assembled the ingredients for the day's meals.

Alexander, who didn't altogether share my passion for the groceries of other nations, was growing restive. On the way to the market, in the cutpurse maze of little streets, we had passed plenty of restaurants: appetising, some of them, with white walls, bright blue or dull green paintwork and dim tiled interiors exhaling cool air into the hot street.

We'd noted a couple of them to go back to, but now I had another idea. Among the market stalls were several cafes – narrow diners consisting of a single line of tables flanking a counter with a display of hot dishes – mysterious stews with sharp-angled fins and knobbly joints rising like wrecks from a choppy sea of ochre liquid; sandy heaps of fried dabs, orange loops of stewed squid. It was past noon and the diners were filling up with shoppers and stallholders.

'We could eat here, in one of these cafes,' I said. 'Those restaurants we saw are for tourists. This is where the market people eat.'

'But we *are* tourists,' said Alexander, looking unhappily at a writhing tentacle beckoning from a seething cauldron of crimson broth, 'and I fancied a pizza.'

'This is Crete, not Italy,' I said. 'And what's the point of visiting a place if you don't eat the food? I'm sure you could find something nice to eat in one of these cafes. You quite like squid, don't you?'

'Not this sort of squid,' said Alexander, firmly.

There rose in me suddenly a rage as urgent and vivid as love. I opened my mouth and incoherent shouting came out: 'I brought you on this holiday,' I screamed. 'I did all the work. I found the house and paid for it. I did all the packing and the driving and you didn't lift a finger to help. I've done all the shopping and cooked all the meals and we have to eat indoors because you're frightened of bloody wasps and now I can't even eat in the restaurant I want to because you won't put anything in your mouth that isn't pizza. I never get to do anything I want, because you won't let me. It's *not fair*.'

I paused for breath. Alexander was staring at the ground. A vivid, childish sense of injustice had given me a mad energy. But as I drew breath to carry on shouting, the energy leaked away and I subsided into bitter martydom. 'Fine,' I said. 'You win. Pizza it is. In the tourist restaurant. Why not?' And I set off at furious speed, marching back the way we had come, my son trailing dismally behind.

As I stamped my rage into the old paving stones a memory flashed into my mind, of a summer holiday in France with my parents when I was my son's age. It was lunchtime and something had gone wrong. We had meant to buy a picnic but it was half-day closing and the shops were shut. Instead of heading for the nearest bistro, my father had turned off the car ignition in the middle of nowhere and refused to move. We all sat there, raging, powerless and silent, staring out of the windows at the empty road, the pointless expanse of countryside, the wild flowers and hopping birds and chirping insects all getting on with their lives while we were stuck there in angry limbo. I couldn't remember the end of the story, only my sense of impotent fury and contempt that this grown man, this *parent,* was behaving like a stupid child because he hadn't got his way over a picnic.

Ah. And here I was, a generation later, enacting the same drama with my own child. Who was presumably judging me from twenty yards behind on the glaring Cretan pavement with identical loathing and contempt. This must be the moment, the subject of much wry hilarity among the Grumpy Old Women, when you realise in middle age that you have turned into your parents. Only it didn't feel hilarious to me. It felt as though our family life was a fragile construction that I'd been building since he was born – an intricate nest that I'd woven around the pair of us. And now I'd smashed it and however I tried to repair it, it would never be quite the same again. This moment would never not have happened.

Now that the exultation of rage had left me, I thought what a very middle-aged sort of tantrum it had been. If I'd been younger or older there would have been no discussion about where we should eat. In my twenties I would have swept us into the market cafe as soon as the idea had formed in my mind, never mind whether anyone else fancied the look of the squid. And if I'd been older, I might have mastered my unruly ego sufficiently to know that the peace of the day mattered more than the authenticity of the lunch. Either approach would have dispensed with the ugly scene, the blighting of the adventure over a plateful of food. But I was neither one thing nor the other and the gap between what I had been and what I might become was filled with fury and remorse.

We ate pizza in the tourist restaurant, conversing carefully like polite strangers, then spent the afternoon shopping for presents. In the early evening we returned to the harbour. The light was slanting now; the cafe tables at the water's edge filling up, the glamour of the evening beginning. It felt like the wrong moment to be going home. Along the harbour wall were ranged old-fashioned horse-drawn carriages with leathery black hoods like enormous prams, offering scenic rides through the town.

'We could take a carriage ride,' said Alexander. 'Go on. Let's. It would be fun.'

'But it's for tourists,' I said, for the second time that day.

'But we are tourists,' he said, also for the second time.

The horses stood patiently, their heavy harness decorated with a frou-frou of bright tassels and trinkets. Some wore straw hats with holes punched for the ears, roguishly wreathed with flowers. I wasn't sure what I felt about the use of equines in these circumstances; performed a hurried mental trade-off – animal welfare versus regaining of ground lost at lunchtime, with a brief side reflection on what an idiot I'd look, perched up there in a carriage trolling through the town like a carnival queen – before saying All right. Why not? As long as the horses are sound.

We walked up and down the carriage lines like show judges,

then picked one drawn by a flea-bitten grey with pink tassels. The driver, presumably used to middle-aged Englishwomen, waited patiently while I looked at his horse's legs. Alexander gazed into the distance, willing himself elsewhere. At last we got into the carriage and lurched off across the cobbles. I felt preposterous; conspicuous as the Queen in the state landau. I was going to make a joke about it. But then I looked sideways at my son sitting next to me on the old cracked leather seat, enjoying the trot through the crowded street in the busy warm evening, cars in front, cars behind, people on either side, with superb simplicity, not outside himself looking in, not analysing the moment, not taking a perspective, other than that of being in this carriage with me on a warm evening in an old foreign town. And for once I thought I wouldn't say anything, after all.

8
Belonging

In both the places where we had lived our neighbours on either side were bemused by our lack of family. In the Peckham flat and the cottage in Greenwich we were objects of intense sympathetic curiosity. Both sets of neighbours came from a clannish white working-class background, in which bonds of close family were both an obligation and the boundary by which their personal universe was defined. It was the background from which my own grandparents came. I recognised its intonations; was familiar with some of its vocabulary and customs, but like a visitor, not a native. In a couple of generations, my family had perfected a fluent impersonation of the cooler mores of the middle classes.

I met my first neighbour, Judy, over the garden wall. We lived in a curving, uphill south London terrace of raw-boned, yellow-brick Edwardian houses with cream stuccoed façades and long, narrow gardens at the back. Judy was a diligent gardener: tall, thin, a nervous chain-smoker with a reserve of tender energy that brought dahlias, gladioli, standard roses and busy Lizzie springing from the cold London clay.

She and her husband, Michael, who worked punishing hours as chauffeur to the chief executive of a department store, had bought the house when they were first married and lived there with their children, Richard, a taciturn teenager, and Michelle, a pretty schoolgirl on the turn of adolescence. I had bought the basement flat next door: two dark, low-ceilinged rooms with Pooterish vestiges of nineteenth-century character and a strip of rear garden.

Judy's side of the old brick wall that separated us had the fine, kempt look of a garden that has been planned, groomed and tended for years. The grass was smooth, the flowerbeds a riot of perfectly deadheaded seasonal colour. Even the bindweed shrank from the approach of Judy's vigilant hoe. On my side there was evidence of a plot that had once been loved but had fallen into neglect: a great lilac bush outside the kitchen door, a strip of coarse, uneven turf punctuated with thorny old roses.

One fine spring evening just after I had moved in I was on my hands and knees, planting sweet peas. Judy, out watering her French marigolds, looked over the wall, saw me crouching there and we fell at once into an affectionate gardeners' intimacy. She had a frank curiosity about my circumstances, and an openness about her own that seemed perfectly extraordinary to me. I had been raised on a strict code of discretion and secrecy. Don't ask other people's business. Don't tell your own.

In the fine summer weather we met most evenings with our hoes and watering cans, and very soon I knew what struck me as an almost reckless amount about her life. Even if I had been able to overcome my long-ingrained habits of emotional parsimony, I had a pitiful quantity of information to offer in return: one love affair, not going well; regular job; relations with family distant. In four years as Judy's next-door neighbour, the most exciting thing I did was acquire a couple of cats (they, too, were instantly absorbed into the extended family, their eccentricities cherished and indulged).

At last I contrived to produce a real *coup de théâtre* with the news that I was pregnant. And not just pregnant but unmarried and dumped by the father: a proper Victorian melodrama in the making. While almost everyone in my circle (including me) greeted the news as though it was at best a mishap, at worst a tragedy, Judy seemed as elated as though the baby were a welcome arrival. She hugged me, rubbed my 20-week bump and went straight out to buy needles and wool.

Over the garden wall came a stream of intricate, lacy cardigans, mittens, hats and pram blankets, while in the road at the front of the house my battered old car, which hadn't been washed in all the time I'd owned it, began unaccountably to shine. Waking early one Sunday morning I found Michael and Richard giving it the same painstaking waxing that they administered to the chief executive's great gleaming pristine Volvo.

When we moved to Greenwich two years later, it was into the force field of another family with an exceptionally strong gravitational pull. Violet was 81 when we arrived, but looked 60. She, too, had a front garden full of vivid flowers, but they were made of plastic, renewed twice yearly. Not for her dreamy evening chats while deadheading the roses and swapping advice about aphid control. Her evenings were spent at the Bingo, to which she set off around teatime, dressed in vivid costumes of peach, turquoise or cyclamen with co-ordinated shoes and bag, heavily bejewelled earlobes clinking and knuckles clotted with gold rings, her lipstick matching her manicured nails ('filbert nails', she said, stretching them out for me to admire).

The inside of her house resembled the interior of a gypsy caravan: the ceiling swagged with fairy lights and tinsel garlands, a cuckoo clock piping the quarter-hours, family photographs on the walls, lace drapery at the windows and on the tables, a throng of life-sized china dolls in frilly costumes directing a fixed stare at visitors from their positions on either side of the fireplace and beside the easy chairs. Violet's mother, she confided, was a Romany who had never worn a pair of shoes in her life.

Judy, for all her warm neighbourliness, was diffident, nervous, highly strung. Violet was indomitable. She had buried her husband (a fine-looking man with dark eyes and a pencil moustache whose portrait hung on the wall) and one of her daughters, but her spirit was high. She had a much younger boyfriend in his late sixties ('my toy boy') a meek, silent man, always dressed in a dark suit and a white shirt, who sheltered from the unrelenting barrage of conversation behind a copy of the *Racing Post*. And while she took a polite interest in my son, what she really wanted to know about was my sex life.

In vain I tried to explain that I hadn't got one; that I was too busy being a mother; that my reverses in love had put me right off the idea of men.

'Course you want a boyfriend, pretty young girl like you,' said Violet. 'Who was that I saw knocking on your door the other evening?'

'That was just a friend, Violet.'

'Huh!' said Violet, disbelievingly.

A couple of years after moving in I did take up for a while with someone who was away most of the time, a doctor serving as a reservist with the UN. He came to visit one weekend and locked us out of the house. We had to knock on Violet's door and ask if we could climb over her wall. I was mortified. Violet was enchanted. 'Lovely-looking feller,' she said, after he'd returned to his duties. 'You want to hang on to that one, my girl.'

She was so lively and sociable, her glamorously dressed departures to her Bingo evenings and raucous late-night returns such a reproach to my bread-and-butter life of office and nursery, that I didn't notice at first the web of family ties of which she was the centre. I knew she had a married daughter ('my Sylvia') who lived close by, and that she was frequently visited by her dynasty of grandchildren, great-grandchildren and great-great-grandchildren. But it wasn't until 13 years after I had met her, when she took to her bed in her mid-nineties and announced her intention to die, that I really saw the family close around her.

In the full vigour of a riotous old age, she still took a keen interest in the important frivolities of life. But one day she simply turned her face to the wall and said that she'd had enough. I had gone round just before Christmas to deliver her present (always so easy to buy presents for Violet, her appetite for pretty things not a bit sated by age – none of that nonsense about 'Don't bother getting anything for me, I've got everything I need'). But this time was different. Violet was sitting up in bed – very unusual for her not to be up and dressed in her best on Christmas Eve – discussing coffins with her daughter. 'Show Jane the catalogue,' she said. The funeral was all paid for in advance. It remained only to choose the details: oak or mahogany? Horses or limousine?

'Don't be ridiculous, Violet,' I said. 'You're not going to die. You're going to live for ever.' I was appalled, almost angry, that this healthy, elegant, sociable, amusing old woman should be planning her own funeral. It felt like a personal affront, as though we, her family and friends, weren't interesting enough to keep her attached to the world.

And something else frightened me – the idea that in old age the world might become, not unendurable because of pain or extreme decrepitude, but simply insipid: that tedium might prove stronger than love or gossip, the prospect of a new dress, a new baby grandchild, a new day. That you might wake one morning and find life too dull to continue living seemed entirely shocking. 'It's the cold weather,' I said. 'You'll feel better when the spring comes.'

Spring came, but Violet declined to get up. For the first time in all the years since we had been neighbours, she failed to make the trip to the pound shop to replace the plastic flowers in her front garden. She lay in her bed (dressed, I noticed, in a series of showy lace nightgowns, which made me hope that she hadn't entirely given up on life) and wept. There was nothing really wrong with her; not physically, at any rate. She got up to wash, ate regular meals, rallied at the prospect of amusement, sparkled for visitors, kept the mixed hospital ward in a roar of ribald hilarity when she was briefly admitted for anaemia, but continued to insist, without drama, that she'd had enough.

'Honestly,' said her daughter, locking up for the night, 'it's like closing up a tomb. She just lies there with the curtains drawn and cries. Doesn't even want to watch the telly any more.'

Another Christmas came and another summer – damp and miserable, this one – not worth getting out of bed for, even if you weren't tired of life. Violet continued to lie in bed, a little weaker from lack of exercise ('Look at me arm,' she said, producing a round, pearly, unwrinkled limb from under the bedcovers. 'It's wasting away!') but with her sharp wits and her remarkable constitution unimpaired. Death, the longed-for visitor, refused to call.

The way in which Violet's family gathered to support its matriarch struck me as exotic. In particular, I was fascinated by the matter-of-fact way they incorporated indignity, mishap and death itself seamlessly into the fabric of their lives. One day, as I bent to sit on the frilly counterpane at the end of Violet's bed, I noticed that a white plastic potty had appeared on the lace-draped bedside table, next to a vase of flowers, a glass containing Violet's teeth and a stuffed rabbit. Violet noticed me noticing. 'I can't walk no more,' she said, offhand, and went back to describing the night a couple of weeks before when her boyfriend (who had a history of manic depression) had got up in the small hours, dumped her in the bath in her nightie, then driven at top speed around the living room on her mobility scooter while the china dollies looked on with blank glass eyes.

It sounded a dreadful experience, and I said so. But I could see that my expressions of dismay weren't at all the required reaction: I was treating Violet as the victim of this alarming incident, but actually she seemed quite invigorated by the shindy. Upended in the bath, she'd given him a right verbal what-for, then Sylvia had come round and seen him off for good. It was a family triumph, of a kind; another detail in the rich mythology of Violet's indomitable resilience. I was glad, sometimes, that it was as an old woman that I'd met her; I thought she'd probably been a terror when she was younger.

Throughout everything, her own sense and her family's sense of her dignity as matriarch of her clan remained robust. When we went round on her ninety-fifth birthday the visit was received with a mixture of pleasure that we had come with our tribute of pink roses, and a powerful intimation that it was an expected homage to someone who had become a living monument of her own family history.

The contrast between Violet's old age and the widowhood of my maternal grandmother, thirty years before, was very marked. After my grandfather's death she lived alone in their hideous bungalow in a Kentish hamlet. She had never learned to drive so she relied on the village post office, which sold groceries, and the daily bus to Canterbury. The post office was run by a rackety ex-RAF man in a brown cardigan. He seemed discontented with life and sold sliced bread that was green with mould. So Grandma's options narrowed to the bus, which took an hour to get to Canterbury, stopping at every tiny village along the route of sick-making twisty back lanes.

She wrote frequent letters to me at university and during the vacations I went with my parents to visit her. My grandmother was knitting me, slowly because her hands were tremulous with Parkinson's disease, a scarf. During one of these visits she put down the knitting and said, very distinctly, 'I'm lonely.' There was a beat of silence. Then the conversation resumed where it had left off.

She got a kitten, which helped, and she contrived to stay at home until her final illness. She died in hospital. They rang to say that we should come, but we were too late. I kept the unfinished scarf with its dropped stitches and kitten-tangled skein of wool for a long time.

Diana Athill writes of death that, 'When I worry, it is about living with the body's failures, because experience has shown me that when that ordeal is less hard than it might have been, it is usually because of the presence of a daughter. And I have no daughter.'

I find it easier, in middle age, to imagine myself an old woman in thirty or forty years' time than I did as a teenager to look forward across the same expanse of time towards middle age. Even in childhood I found it possible to imagine a version of myself as an old woman, since my paternal grandmother, whose avid taste for clothes and jewels I inherited, was almost as small as me, with child-sized hands and feet and an enviable wardrobe of diminutive brocade and chiffon cocktail dresses and fur coats. The condition of being old seemed then, if anything, rather fascinating and even now that I am so much closer to it, I catch occasionally a distant echo of that childhood sense that being properly old might be quite an interesting experience.

It is when I think about the last stages, the preamble to extinction, that the swerving dread returns. No long-suffering daughter will be lifting me on to the plastic potty kept on the lace-swagged bedside table when my time comes. If my legs fail before my mind (or, almost more alarming, the other way around) I shall have to depend on the dubious kindness of strangers.

But apart from the quality of care and the warmth of human proximity, the real difference between Violet's protracted widow-hood and my grandmother's is one of identity. Extreme age is dismantling Violet bit by bit, shrinking her world inexorably, inch by inch, yard by yard. But while her mind is clear and her family around her, her sense of who she is remains intact. She is Violet Lee, matriarch, widow of one, mother of two, grandmother, great-grandmother and great-great-grandmother of dozens. And here they all are, popping in at all hours to remind her who she is.

My grandmother, on the other hand, alone in her house for hours and days, suffered the malaise of solitude: the sense of self fluctuating like an imperfect radio signal, depending on who you've spoken to that day – if anyone. Sometimes, if days pass without conversation beyond the monologue of the radio, you find your jaw and tongue almost paralysed at your next human encounter – the responses slow, the banter clumsy, the words thick in your mouth. The letters she wrote to me at university are droll and nimble-witted – full of the essence of herself, comic, loving, alive with news of the kitten and her sparse sprinkling of neighbours, avid for a response from me, out there at liberty in the world beyond her village to which the death of her husband had removed her *laissez passer*.

Sometimes in the holidays I caught the train to see her, then walked the couple of miles from the station through featureless green tunnels of coppiced chestnut, turning down through hop gardens and orchards to the hedge of nut trees and blackberries at the back of her house. But when we met it seemed to me that the real grandma, the grandma of my memory and of her letters, was trapped somewhere inside the hardened shell of a person whom solitude had calcified into a rattling bundle of survival stratagems and eccentric economies – the meagre sprinkling of coals on the living-room fire; the stale packet of crisps put to brisk up in the oven, which shrank in the heat to the size of a doll's-house snack.

Honestly, Grandma! said I, unable from my undergraduate eminence to understand why the old woman should be so upset at the comic dwindling of half a packet of cheese 'n' onion. She had been a good cook, when I was younger. The taste of salt bacon rashers frying in the house in Cumberland where she and my grandfather lived when I was a child, the dark, sweet burn of her rhubarb-and-ginger jam on toast, the crisp sugary top of her sultana cake were still vivid in my mouth. I wanted her to be the same. I didn't want to know about the circumstances that had led her to be dismayed by her failure to warm through a half-eaten packet of crisps.

I had left my parents' house a few weeks before my A levels. I stayed with my Latin teacher while I sat the exams, spent the summer as an au pair in France and the remainder of the vacation with my grandparents. But my grandfather died suddenly, just before he was to have driven me to Oxford to begin my university course, and I made my own way there on the train.

'Are you homesick, Miss Shilling?' asked the Principal of my college, bald and awe-inspiring across the expanse of her book-crowded desk. 'No!' said I, incredulous in her winged armchair, feeling myself at ease for the first time in my life in this place of books and ideas, where no one knew me; exulting in my detachment from my family. I had prided myself on the flourish of teenage rebellion – the outlandish clothes and unsuitable boyfriends that had affronted their anxious respectability so gravely. But now I was expanding in the unaccustomed ease of not being at odds with my surroundings.

I envied my grandfather the blank page of his beginnings: the singularity of his foundling origins as an infant picked up by a policeman from the pavement of a side street behind St Pancras station. He was his own invention, I thought. His successes and failures were his alone: he had no one to blame him for the latter or appropriate the former. There seemed something heroic about the lightness of his passage through life, free from the encumbering drag anchor of family history and expectation. I don't know whether he ever felt, himself, this sense of lightness, because I didn't think to ask him about it before his death.

In retirement he began to write his memoirs. I have the manuscript, a fragment of 70 typed pages which reaches only as far as his teens when he discovered, on joining the Navy from a foster home in Essex, that he had no family, no ties, no history at all. Of his teenaged self he wrote that he had 'always hoped that one day I would be reunited with my real father and mother, and perhaps with brothers and sisters'. In middle age he tried to find a way into the sealed vault of his own past, but the combination eluded him. Someone had once known who he was and where he came from, but she had vanished and with her every detail of his story before the night that the beam of the policeman's torch, piercing the dark corners of an alley behind St Pancras, lit on the lost baby.

When my own baby was born I thought that the appearance of the next generation might somehow shore up the rickety structure of my blood ties. The solitary self-invention that felt so rich and expansive when I had only myself to sustain seemed suddenly tawdry and insubstantial. Finding myself a mother, I began for the first time since leaving home to think of myself as a daughter. Cautiously, I began to try on the unfamiliar role.

It didn't fit. I had done too efficient a job of severing myself from my history for any attempt at reattachment to prosper. Over the years I had developed a habit of fostering myself on a series of likely-looking families – rambling, expansive organisms in which an extra person about the place was absorbed as easily as an extra kitten. These had become my prototype of an ideal family: rackety, volatile, resilient, spontaneous, uncritical. My real family – respectable, orderly to the point of rigidity, vulnerable to the unexpected turn of events – struggled with the process of parley and truce over a period of years until the expanse of uncomprehending dead ground became too wide to span with language.

The experience of love starving from lack of language was not unfamiliar. It signalled the ends of love affairs when, in general, I was keen to keep talking, but the object of my discourse was desperate for me to shut up. The handsome medic who took Violet's fancy actually had to disappear in order to escape my voluble efforts to argue him into loving me.

One moment he was there, in the form of a stream of crackling blue airmail letters and occasional, dramatic visits when he would arrive late and urgent in the small hours, smelling of cold, metal and oiled wool, invade my bed in commanding fashion and drive away to Brize Norton at first light. The next he had vanished as completely as if he had slipped through a slit in time. No more letters, no phone number, just an unyielding, adamant absence.

I wrote him long, angry, pleading letters, but there came no answer and eventually I stopped sending them and instead conducted indignant conversations with him in my head, producing in evidence this phrase, and this, and this, from the little heap of creased blue onion-skin love letters that was my only proof that I hadn't imagined the whole affair. There was a violence to the silence, as though I, rather than he, were the one who had vanished – as though by disappearing he had erased me.

At first I suffered from the idea that he wasn't the man I had thought him – that the intimacy and complicity had been all a sort of performance. But then I began to think that it was I who was the impersonator. I had been swaggering about, sleek and glossy in the important certainty of being loved, but that was the illusion. As the triumphant glamour of having been chosen – picked for his team by someone who wanted me – subsided, I retreated into the worlds of the nursery and the office, where words were wholesome and obedient and did what you expected of them, rather than darting about like a glittering shoal of elusive little fish.

Years of working as a newspaper sub-editor had engendered a belief in language as a tractable raw material; a formless mass like clay or dough from which the ordinary person could produce a perfectly serviceable artefact, while expert craftsmen could chivvy it into any shape that took their fancy. I was startled when I failed to talk my lovers into staying with me; felt diminished when my powers of narrative proved insufficient to keep them captivated. But somehow I still believed I could talk into existence the family of my fantasies. When they declined to become figures in my narrative and instead confected an alternative version of our joint story in which they insisted on my appearing in character as their version of me, I was reduced to silence.

I had friends, single women mainly, but a few men as well, with untapped reserves of tenderness who, as middle age advanced and their parents grew old, contrived to invent a different sort of conversation – one in which their own story of family life and their parents' account of the same events merged into an autho-rised version on which everyone could agree.

Immense effort was required from these children (as their parents still thought of them), in editing their own feelings. Prodigies of patience, tact and a kind of resolute self-obliteration sometimes produced a marvellous late flowering of love on a branch that had seemed so dead and withered that the child had wondered for years what on earth the parents had expected when they set about conceiving. Just as often, though, there was no springing of green leaves from the dry stem, just a wiseacre satisfaction from the parents when their wayward child appeared to have repented of its errors and acknowledged (at last!) that the parents had been right all along.

One woman I knew concealed from her mother the existence of her two cats, on the grounds that Mother considered her (aged 68) too irresponsible to own a pet. The cats, like Mother, were ancient and ailing; the logistics of concealing their existence from her convoluted; the emotional contortions involved in leaving them in order to visit her excruciating.

'What would happen, Isabelle,' I asked, as she handed over a sheaf of their complicated dietary needs before leaving, reluctantly, for a weekend stay with her mother, miserably convinced that their death agonies would begin the instant the front door closed behind her, 'if you were to tell her you've got two sick cats who need your attention as well?'

'It would kill her,' said Isabelle. I wondered if she meant that Mother would expire from pure chagrin at having been defied. Another woman, having acquired a couple of rescue cats, told her mother that she planned to call them Lucy and Jeremy. 'You can't call them that,' retorted her parent. 'Those are *people's* names.' She added that on the whole she thought my friend should hurry up and follow my example by having a child on her own. 'We could bring it up for you,' she added, menacingly.

I regarded the limber emotional manoeuvres of the dutiful daughters with the same baffled admiration that I felt when watching gymnastics or showjumping on the telly. I admired the beauty of the performance; its courage and technical polish. I wished I could do it myself.

Sometimes, for a second or two during some particularly dazzling display of altruism I felt a surge of energy so invigorating that it seemed almost possible that I might pull off a similar feat: execute the emotional handstand with perfect balance; clear the tricky double of Christmas and New Year with yards to spare. But the instant I tried to channel that borrowed vigour into some manoeuvre designed to reconnect me with my family, I felt it drain away. My sense of self was too imperious and fragile for me to lead the double life that my friends had mastered so adroitly.

They split their personalities as though separating conjoined twins; sacrificing important aspects of themselves – a kidney here, half a liver there, the odd limb – in order to maintain the integrity of the family. I couldn't do it. The mutilation seemed too extreme, even though I could feel that the consequence of failure would be the strange weightlessness, the drifty lack of attachment that comes in middle age when self-invention falters and there is no anchoring family to hold you steady.

I had an aunt who seemed to have found a way through the emotional labyrinth. Unlike her two siblings she had not married, but had taken her own line – a line that sometimes struck her family as eccentric, perilous, unsuitable. In my childhood she turned up on the occasions when family convention demanded it and gave the impression of someone difficult, questioning, ill at ease.

I remembered her one Christmas in the large, hot, slab-sided, brick-built hutch where my paternal grandparents lived, where the gas fire and the television glowed perpetually in the velvet-lined womb of a living room from which all verbal intercourse had long since been banished by my grandmother's deafness and my grandfather's laryngectomy.

With the sound on the telly turned down in honour of the

season, my mother embarked on a virtuoso display of social juggling, bellowing festive cheer into the stopped ears of my tiny
grandmother, who dabbed her eyes in a corner of her red velvet
armchair and said, 'I wish I could hear you, dear,' and 'This will
be my last Christmas.'

'You'll outlive us all!' shrieked my mother, straining, meanwhile, to catch the drift of my grandfather's mouthed jeremiad,
probably along the lines of how the socialists were bringing the
country to its knees. As though to underline his point the *Goodies
Christmas Special*, flickering silently on the screen in the corner of
the room, showed a rapacious flock of Christmas-tree angels descending on a plump turkey and stripping it of flesh.

My aunt, the spinster daughter of the house, wheeling in the tea
trolley with its burden of tinned-salmon sandwiches, chocolate
biscuits wrapped in holly-sprigged foil, warmed-through mince
pies and a Christmas cake Artexed in royal icing, ready to add its
brooding weight to stomachs already heavy with chipolatas,
stuffing, roast potatoes and a dense, black, suety, brandy-soaked
plum pudding, caught sight of the scene on the television, began
to shed silent tears and left the room. She was a committed
Christian. As were we all, though our side of the family favoured
an urbane Anglo-Catholicism, capable of attending Christmas
Mass in the morning and accommodating the Goodies' secular
satire of Yuletide materialism at teatime.

Perhaps her parents and mine saw in my aunt's untimely
distress the graceless emotional lability of menopause; the sadness
of the middle-aged spinster *sans* husband, children, love or hearth
of her own; the empty, purposeless female about to spend
Christmas night in a narrow, candlewick-covered single bed in
her parents' spare bedroom for want of any more pressing domestic attachment while we returned to our own cheery home, littered
with the bright trash of a successful family Christmas, lights
twinkling, toys strewn, the larder fat with succulent leftovers, a
plaster baby Jesus snug in his crib at the centre of the Nativity

scene arranged on the mantelshelf, the cat stalking the feathered robins perched on the lower branches of the Christmas tree.

I was too young to diagnose hormonal perturbation as the cause of her unhappiness but I picked up the disapproving frisson that trailed her out of the room; sensed the disturbance she'd caused by letting her misery be seen, subverting in the process the intricate mechanism of suppression by means of which everyone else managed to keep up appearances.

For decades after I left home for university I scarcely saw my aunt. The image of her weeping over the tea trolley as the television muttered inaudibly in the corner became a comic shorthand for everything that was wrong with a family Christmas. But by degrees she came to seem to me the heroine of the scene. From the general impression of hot overstuffed dreariness there crystallised a sense of her longing for the chill simplicity of the newborn child, the starlit night, the angels singing, the startled shepherds in the dark fields. Her misery at not finding anything resembling that truth among the red velvet curtains, the unwanted food and the constrained discourse of her family struck me in retrospect as the only authentic emotional response in a roomful of complicated evasions.

Time passed. My aunt and I met at intervals – family occasions mainly, unconducive to all but the most formulaic of conversations, and our paths diverged. In the summer of the year that my son turned 14 she invited us to her eightieth birthday party, a gathering in a church hall to which she wore a pale blue robe embroidered in silver – a souvenir of a trip to Egypt. She seemed surprisingly well travelled, for an aunt.

The hall was filled with a jostling mixture of ages and nationalities. Across the room I caught sight of my own profile, as though glimpsing a reflection of myself at an unexpected angle in a mirror, and recognised with a shock a cousin whom I hadn't seen since we were children. He was an excise man now: tall, handsome, reticent, with an edge of off-duty authority.

Chatting to the babel of friends in the hall, I began to discover things I didn't know, or only half knew, about my aunt. She was an ordained priest. A prison visitor. A campaigner for the rights of refugees, some of whom she had occasionally sheltered in her own house. Without detaching herself from her family (for here we were, some of us, meeting one another for the first time in years at her party – and what a very curious sensation *that* was) she had invented a world for herself, a place of safety, surrounded by these friends.

I would have pursued this line of thought, but music struck up and there appeared a venerable belly dancer in orange drapery and silver anklets, flashing a roguish expanse of naked flesh between breast and haunches that scandalised my prudish son. I hadn't been to an eightieth birthday party before, but this one seemed livelier than I had anticipated.

Some weeks later my aunt asked me if I wanted to take a trip with her to the Isle of Sheppey, where her mother had grown up in her grandparents' farmhouse. Generations of Jarretts and Hinges – her parents' and grandparents' families; my ancestors – lay buried in Iwade churchyard, on the landward side of the Swale.

I knew their names already – they were written in a spidery copperplate hand in a heavy old family bible with thick, rippled pages and a flaking brown leather binding reeking of must and age. As a child I had copied them into the back of my own bible, a handsome little volume printed on fine, gilt-edged India paper with a scarlet leather binding, given me by my aunt as a christening present. I said yes to the trip, but shyly, wondering whether we would find enough conversation to keep us going for a whole day.

Sheppey is an island – or rather a small archipelago silted into a single entity – in the Thames Estuary, the last before the estuary empties into the sea. The island looks north across open water to Essex, and south towards Kent, from which it is separated by a narrow channel, the Swale. Low-lying, marshy, windswept, it is home to sheep, birds, prisoners, caravans, container ships, ancient churches and bungalows. I grew up within sight of the island, in Sittingbourne, but had never been there. Girls from Sheppey attended my school. They arrived by train and had the unruly, raffish air of people who make a daily trip across water to the mainland.

On the mainland side, the charmless Saxon villages straggle at intervals along the straight Roman road, bordered with orchards of cherry and apple, dwindling towards the muddy shoreline into flat marshland, a place of sheep, birds and the rotting hulks of old barges, half sunk in brackish ooze like tarpit mammoths. On the island the homely prettiness of fertile land is absent. Here are no fruit gardens, no undulating slopes, only wind, sky and water that seem ready to overwhelm at any moment the scabbed encrustation of human activity.

My aunt drove across the newly built Sheppey crossing with the defiant expertise of someone who had learned to drive when it was still a bold thing for a girl to do; then turned off the main road towards Harty, where the Ferry House Inn stands above the old ferry slipway. It was a fine blue-grey September day after a sodden summer. The willow leaves were turning yellow; the rosehips scarlet in the hedges. We rounded a sharp corner where high hedges parted on a vista of bleached grassland shading to a flat, watery horizon. Perched on the blasted branch of a dead tree to our right was a curious shape – stout, feathery, head sunk between sloping shoulders. Oh, stop! I said. It's an owl.

It was a barn owl, perching with its back turned towards us – a startling orange-tawny. As we got out of the car and drew near it swivelled its head so that its crisp white doily of a face was turned towards us, and stared through us with blank sloe eyes, then spread its wings and flew driftingly away down the hedge line. Small brown birds haunted the fields as we drove; a weasel looped across the track as we turned into the Ferry House Inn. We ate lunch alone in the empty dining room, looking out over mudflats where the seagulls mewed and the boats lay aslant, waiting for the tide to refloat them.

The farmhouse where my grandmother grew up had gone, my aunt said. From time to time she used to visit it with her mother, but over the years it had declined into a barn, a hay store, then fallen into disrepair and at last into ruin, reabsorbed into the windblown coarse grassland as though pressed into nothingness by the elemental horizontals of the landscape of air, earth and water.

In Iwade churchyard we crouched on the mown grass in the low shadow of the flint church to read the gravestones of the people who had lived in that vanished farmhouse: William Hinge and his wife, Helen, both dead at 58, then a dismal list of dates recording the brief lives of my infant ancestors: William Henry, died 2 June 1864, aged 10 months; Louisa Fanny, born 10 September 1864, died the next day. William Archibald, died 19 August 1873, aged 15 months.

Perhaps the parents of Helen Elizabeth and Florence Emily thought they were safe. They survived the croups and agues, the fits and rashes and inexplicable failures to thrive to which their baby siblings had succumbed. They grew into big girls, old enough to make themselves useful to their parents – help around the house, look after the younger children, tend the sheep that cropped the poor pasture. But death came all the same, in the high summer of 1875 for Helen Elizabeth, who would have been eight in December; in dead of winter for Florence Emily, aged 13 years and 9 months on 22 January 1892.

The churchwarden, a slight woman in a neat blue jacket and owlish glasses, began to toll the pair of twelfth-century bells whose knell had marked the passing of the inhabitants of the churchyard. I wondered if babies got the full funeral service, even day-old Louisa Fanny. There is a shortened form of baptism in the Book of Common Prayer, for urgent use at home in cases where a child is thought unlikely to live, but no form of the burial service specially adapted for infants.

Man that is born of a woman hath but a short time to live, and is full of misery. He cometh up, and is cut down, like a flower; he fleeth as it were a shadow, and never continueth in one stay . . . I wondered how often, as parents bringing child after child to the churchyard, like apples or sheaves of corn to Harvest Festival, you could hear those words without going mad with the pity of it. I tried to think myself inside the minds of these Hinges, some of whose blood, after all, ran in my veins and was even now animating the brain struggling to conjure their shades from the dates neatly cut on their tombstones by the stonemason's chisel.

They weren't a very ambitious family. Didn't do much to better themselves. The census showed them existing for generation after generation as agricultural labourers, farmhands, scratching a living from the same patch of earth already worked over by their fathers and grandfathers. I imagined them cold, sparse, cloddish as the land on which they worked. As shepherds, they were used to the random ease with which the spark of life could be extinguished, by accident of birth, crow, fox, worrying dog, harsh weather, treacherous terrain, disease. Perhaps that farmer's fatalism, that apparent lack of will to do better, own land, prosper, extended to the children they kept doggedly producing, these Williams and Florences and Louisas, so few of whom survived into adulthood.

I thought of my mother's father, whose lack of parents was the great drama of his life. Of these distant relations, who must have had to find a way of edging the death of a child into their peripheral consciousness; of refusing to make it the defining drama of their lives. All those lost histories. All that contradictory longing and detachment dwindled to the exiguous sprig of the family tree – the smallest a family could be and still lay claim to the name – their descendants, my son and me.

I couldn't summon any sense of attachment to the bony clan of ancestors buried some feet below the turf on which we stood. It was the place itself that haunted me. I'd done my best to get away from it; this flat watery landscape of Danish pirates, decayed medieval grandeur and hideous modern decline. I was always trying to graft myself on to prettier, more welcoming places: couldn't visit somewhere new without wondering what it would be like to settle there, to belong; had succeeded in moving myself fifty miles or so upstream to Greenwich.

But to return here was like hearing again faintly the sound of music I'd known a long time ago. Accumulated layers of memory and experience, more recent and more vivid, had almost obliterated it but then something – a chance combination of notes, the mud, the water, the flint church, the owl on the stump, the weasel crossing the dusty track – something woke up that sleeping sense of belonging somewhere so intensely that you are the place, and the place is you.

9
Cracks in the Fabric

I was slow and reluctant to acknowledge the part of myself that was rooted in the North Kent marshes – longing, always, to come from somewhere easier to love. But no such ambiguity clouded my son's attachment to the place where he was born.

When he was small I used to flee London at the weekends, strapping him into his car seat and driving to Oxford where we'd share a picnic in the Parks or the Botanic Garden, walk along the river, wander the pavements, peering in through the open wicket gates of the colleges from where everyone I had known had now vanished. The result was that Alexander developed a lively hatred of food eaten out of doors, botanical gardens, long car journeys, and anything to do with Oxford.

Turning the car away from Crick Road, where my tutor had taught Browning and Tennyson in a garden shed where two rickety chairs and a single-bar electric fire crouched among stalagmite piles of books, thickly powdered with the ash of innumerable chain-smoked Disque Bleu, I would be gripped by an exile's piercing sense of being shut out from the land of lost content.

'Wouldn't it be lovely to live here?' I'd sigh. No, no, Alexander would say urgently. We live in Greenwich. London is our home. Faugh, London, I'd sneer, unable to admit that I wasn't just passing through, though it was twenty years and more since I'd left Kent for Oxford, and Oxford for London. I hadn't realised that if you have a baby in King's College Hospital, Denmark Hill, what you've given birth to is a Londoner. I only really understood when someone gave us a video of *Bedknobs and Broomsticks*, a film in which three cockney children are evacuated to the countryside and lodged with an amateur witch, Miss Price, among whose more successful spells is the ability to make a large brass bed fly. When urgent business calls her to the capital, she and the children mount the bed, which sails off across the night sky like a great four-postered galleon, setting them down moments later in what turns out to be Notting Hill.

Is this London? asks the littlest child. Yes, says his sister, rapt and blissful to be home. Can't he smell the lovely, sooty London air?

This, my son explained, was how he felt about London. He liked the smell of it. And the noise. It was exciting. He didn't want to move, particularly not to the country, which was full of pointless trees, dangerous animals, vile agricultural stinks and no shops, and populated exclusively by people wearing dung-coloured clothes and mumbling incomprehensibly about haylage and worm burdens.

I grumbled, but made no serious plans to move. Instead I planted my resentment of city life in the fertile London earth. There were bluebells in the garden of the Greenwich house when I bought it, and a hawthorn hedge like the one around the playground of my village school. I planted an apple tree, climbing roses, phlox, lupins and nasturtiums. A wild hop self-seeded in the rose bed and swarmed over the Variegata di Bologna. The place began to look as though a modest village house had come to visit a London cousin and decided to stay.

And after a while, though I still threatened to leave the city from time to time – when a lap-dancing club and a gambling arcade opened at the top of our road; when men from the council came and chopped down the lime trees in our street – the thought of leaving the familiar territory, the river, the great chestnut trees in the park, the masts of the *Cutty Sark*, the florid quadrangles of the Naval College, the grocer and butcher who knew me by name, the London Library, the wren in the hawthorn hedge, gave me a feeling as though someone were tugging at the very centre of me – somewhere more elemental than the heart: in the seventeenth century they would have called it the bowels.

The house assumed (or revealed) a personality. Because it was so badly built it felt flighty to me, impermanent, like a beach hut. I was always surprised to find when we came back from holiday that it was still there at the end of the street and hadn't nipped off somewhere while our backs were turned.

It is hard for two people to live together all alone with nothing to mediate the intensity of their relationship and so the house became a character in our domestic life. 'Knock through!' urged friends, folding themselves with difficulty into one or other of the two exiguous downstairs rooms filled with spindly Victorian chairs on which no one heavier than a child could safely sit. But from my desk (which was, at mealtimes, the dining table) I had a view framed by doorways like a Dutch interior, over the book-strewn table, across the narrow hall and into the living room, where tarnished silver lustre jugs and cups stood on top of a cupboard and a white china hand (one of a macabre pair of bookends) pressed against the white-panelled wall as though trying to keep it from toppling over. I liked this vista. The milky pallor of the walls and cupboard was easy for the eye to rest on and the unseen part of the room gave a companionable feeling that at any moment a figure might step into view.

I found myself searching junk shops and charity stalls for things that would echo the spirit of the house: not presents for myself (I rationalised), but propitiatory offerings to the household gods. A pair of carved wooden wall sconces in the shape of a child's plump fists, a bunch of blue jay's feathers, sea glass and shells, and two bronze griffon's claws – the disembodied feet of some long-vanished piece of furniture – which gripped the ground at either side of the hearth. It was like living in a storeroom of cast-off artefacts from the Pitt Rivers museum: crowded, but interesting.

'You'll end up like one of those women in a Molly Keane novel,' said an old friend. 'Living in one room, boiling a kettle over an open fire in the grate, surrounded by the worm-eaten ruins of good furniture and chipped oddments of Royal Doulton.' I was extremely taken aback by this vision of my future. It felt as though I'd visited a fairground fortune teller and instead of the usual comforting predictions of wealth, love and long life, had been told in exchange for my money to expect misery, loneliness and penury.

Cruel, I said. What a cruel thing to say. And of course if you were to take care of me, nothing like that would happen. The friend, who liked a quiet life, backtracked as fast as he could: my little house was lovely, my taste perfect, my fondness for eccentric objects highly original; of course he would never let me dwindle into a solitary madwoman. But it was too late. The sense of fragility, of the contingency of my life as a construct that I had felt during the row with my son in Crete now returned, more menacing than before. Someone who knew me well and cared for me had seen my fate, and it wasn't anything like the version I had been conjuring for myself.

As though his prediction had released some kind of virulent spore into the air, signs of decay began to encroach upon the house. The downstairs rooms were clad in wooden tongue-and-groove on which cushiony black fungus began to bloom. A crack appeared where the bathroom extension met the main house. When it rained, large puddles formed on the floor. After a particularly violent storm it rained down the stairwell too. The walls were all mottled and damp. It was my fault. I had done no maintenance since I'd moved in – hoping always to make enough money to set things right, but never saving enough, always succumbing to the pretty object, the irresistible treat, grasping the possibilities of the present and trusting the future to take care of itself.

The indoor rain dampened my insouciance. I resolved to be sensible from now on. I commissioned a firm of local builders to caulk and make watertight my house. The firm was run by a pair of brothers of whom the elder came to inspect the work that needed to be done. He was an avuncular figure with a comfortingly phlegmatic way of dismissing the various cracks and bulges that I interpreted as signs that the house was about to fall down. I felt reassured that this correction, this bit of making good, would be enough to ensure a change in the psychic weather from foul to fair. The house would be sweet and dry again, and we would be safe.

The builders asked for money in advance. Quite a lot of it. The elder brother was replaced by his less avuncular younger brother. Little progress was made. The back door frame was so badly decayed that the door fell off its hinges. We slept a night in the house with the door frame gaping open to the dark and whatever stirred in it.

The rain continued to fall indoors. The drains became sluggish, unreponsive to the sinister concoctions of syrupy purple vitriol that I poured down them (they went down with a spiteful hiss, sending a wisp of sulphurous white smoke, like a sleeping dragon's breath, coiling up from the plughole).

In the back garden the jasmine and climbing roses grew unchecked and monstrous, swarming up the rotting trellis until the weight of them brought down the panels, which swiftly became engulfed in a mass of tangled stems so dense as to be impervious to my haphazard snipping with shears and secateurs. I knew I should do something, but I felt paralysed, as though the strangling honeysuckle and jasmine had engulfed my spirit as well as my garden. My money was gone. I daren't borrow more. Besides, I had other things to worry about.

While the garden grew unchecked so, suddenly, did my son. Overnight, or so it seemed, he sprang from being half a head shorter than me to half a head taller. A faint shadow marked the still childish curve of his upper lip. In a strong light, fine pale-gold threads of incipient beard could be seen growing from his cheeks and chin like tendrils groping towards the light. When I went into his room in the mornings he would be asleep on his front in the deep abandoned unconsciousness of adolescence, with his newly hairy ankles (and when did that happen? The golden down of childhood replaced by this wiry, greyish pelt that glinted bronze in the morning light?) and huge yellowish feet sticking out beyond the edge of the mattress of his little iron bed.

The sight reminded me of the chapter in *Winnie-the-Pooh* in which the bear gets stuck in the entrance to Rabbit's hole and is obliged to remain there, fasting, with his snout in the open air and his back legs protruding into Rabbit's kitchen until he gets thin enough to emerge. Rabbit, pragmatic, uses the legs as a drying rack for damp tea towels. In a spirit of frivolity one morning I draped clean T-shirts over my son's stuck-out legs. He wasn't amused.

He was unamused in a new, deep-voiced, grown-up way. No, Mother! he said, in the tone of a grown man exercising his authority. This was new, too. Throughout my grown-up life the only will, the only temperament in my household had been mine. I was amused and obscurely pleased. After an adult lifetime of not deferring to anyone, making every decision myself, from what to eat to where to go on holiday, I thought it would make a nice change to have a man about the place, imposing himself.

Walking down a street with this large young man beside me, turning my face up, rather than down, to his as we spoke brought back a feeling that I hadn't had since my twenties. When he was born I felt certain that single motherhood would mean the end of love affairs, partly because no one would want me, encumbered with a child; partly because I couldn't see a way back from the wreckage of the attachment that had produced my son.

About the first assumption I was wrong: All sorts of grown-up Lost Boys, observing me kind but firm with my own child, were keen to attach themselves to me in the hope that I'd take the same line with them. If what I had wanted was a boyfriend, I would have had less trouble finding one after the baby than before. But I had grown wary and cautious now that I had not only myself but my son to think about when allowing someone over the threshold of domestic intimacy. I couldn't afford to be making experiments. The list of necessary qualities seemed too complicated and exigent for one man to embody them all.

'You'll never get a man now,' said a friend's husband. 'You're too much of a perfectionist.' After a couple of cautious skirmishes and the painful entanglement with the doctor – especially painful because he had seemed, miraculously, to possess all the qualities of trustworthiness, kindness, dependability and what-have-you that I had thought it impossible for one man to embody; besides which, my son liked him – I concluded that the friend's husband was right and that protracted, perhaps permanent, solitude would be the price I would have to pay for motherhood.

A distinctive feature of the Greenwich house was that it seemed quite hostile to men. Its dimensions were too small; its rooms too cramped. Over time I had furnished it with furniture constructed, like the house itself, for the less well-nourished generations of the early 1800s. As long as my son was a child, the oddness of the proportions wasn't really apparent. It was only when a farmer friend came to supper and couldn't fit his huge agricultural knees under the table, or when my son was mugged for his phone on the way home from school and several strapping policemen tried to squash themselves and their laptop on to the three-quarter-sized sofa that had always seemed such a cosy fit for the two of us that I suddenly felt the press of the shrunken world we inhabited.

The precipitate growing of my son threw the sense of domestic normality into chaos. It wasn't just the size of him that was disconcerting – the way he filled rooms just by sitting in them – but his sheer physical heft. Entire doors came off in his hand, their brittle old cast-iron hinges snapped like glass as he heaved them open; inexplicable dents appeared in the brass doorknobs; the fixings of the banister rope sprang out of the wall where he touched it; the small, stout, iron key to the Victorian wardrobe in his room bent mysteriously in half. The wooden slats of his metal bed-frame rattled to the floor at the sound of his footsteps, as though they knew they couldn't bear the weight of him as he flung himself down on the mattress.

One dreadful November afternoon I was on the way home when my phone rang and I answered it to the sound of wrenching male sobs: he had been using my laptop (there was a rule forbidding this; naturally he ignored it) and somehow it had fallen to the floor and was broken – the screen a dramatic composition of jagged black slashes with rainbow edges behind which, somewhere, lay this book, imperfectly backed up.

Nothing in the fridge or food cupboards was safe. A trip to the supermarket that used to last us a week began to vanish in a couple of days, with the curious detail that he left behind the empty packaging of what he had consumed – so I would find a multi-pack of crisps filled with a rustling void; a packet of cheese that (moments ago, surely?) had contained a huge slab of Cheddar now vacant but for a few gnawed crumbs; a biscuit tin, the lid ajar, harbouring an airy flock of coloured wrappers.

I couldn't work out if the leaving behind of the wrappings when the food was gone was a sort of joke – like the fresh-air eggs we used to make when he was little, turning the empty shell of the boiled egg upside down in its cup so it looked as though he hadn't begun to eat it. Or whether some kind of magical thinking was at work and he hoped that if he left the packaging I would fail to notice that the food had gone, like the idiot humans in Naomi

Mitchison's children's book, *The Fairy Who Couldn't Tell A Lie*, stupidly unable to tell that the delicious fairy fruit gums and bull's eyes on which they were gorging themselves were knocked up from old sycamore leaves and wood shavings.

Whatever the impulses behind the splintered furnishings and vanished food, I began to share the apprehension of Beatrix Potter's Mrs Tittlemouse, a spinsterish woodmouse who returns one day to her fastidiously kept mousehole to discover an unwelcome male presence – a considerable toad, Mr Jackson, who has made himself very much at home in the parlour, where the mouse finds him 'sitting all over a small rocking-chair, twiddling his thumbs and smiling'.

Spurning a snack of cherry stones with uncouth cries of 'No teeth, no teeth, no teeth!', he wanders the narrow passages in search of honey, leaving large damp footprints everywhere as Mrs Tittlemouse follows him, twittering with distaste. When she finally gets rid of the damp malodorous masculine intruder, she fetches twigs and partly boards up the front door, to prevent his ever entering again. Henceforth he can only peer wistfully in through the window.

There were times when I felt that I should have liked to do the same. Half child, half man, my son roamed the house after his shower, leaving large damp footprints everywhere while I stabbed spitefully at my keyboard and implored him to get dressed.

We had always been tactile, the drama of family life played out in a pantomime of hugs and kisses, smacks and flounces, turned backs and affectionate reconciliatory embraces. Until now my superior size and strength meant that I'd been in control of these exchanges. Now the physical balance had shifted. Often his embraces were more in the nature of an assault – what began as a hug would end with his twisting my wrist or (especially horrible) pinching my Achilles tendons.

Conscious that the feel of him in my arms when we hugged had become almost indistinguishable from an embrace I might bestow on a lover, I grew wary and began to detach, avoid, even fend him off as he blundered hugely after me and I retreated. His nanny, when he was small, used – to my astonishment – to kiss him on the lips. I felt very glad now that I hadn't followed her custom. Absurdly, I found myself still smacking him when I was cross, using my elbows to fend him off as I would have done with some large, disobedient horse.

I was expecting his adolescent rebellion to take the conventional form that I'd read about in books and the family pages of the newspapers: outlandish clothes, horrible music, offensive posters, unsuitable friends, violent rejection of all the values I had tried to teach throughout childhood, heart-stopping excursions to alien destinations (music festivals, the summer beaches where teenagers flocked) and attendant disastrous experiments with sex, drugs, alcohol and reckless tattooing and piercings.

Though pretty well kept down as a teenager, I had nevertheless contrived to get through everything on that list, except the drugs and the tattooing (the latter an omission that I always regretted). I also developed a black, brooding persona of toxic malevolence with which I could poison the household atmosphere or reduce a entire school classroom to a state of silent gloom. When my son showed little inclination to smash, subvert, disrupt or defy in these obvious ways I was rather gratified; I took it partly as a tribute to my success in raising him, and partly as a sign of a kind of grace or luck.

Physically, his transformation from boy to young man was quite gracefully accomplished. His sparse tendrils of gilt beard sprang from a complexion only a little coarser than his child's skin had been. I was astonished by the gruffness of his friends' breaking voices – unmodulated troll's roars emerging from windpipes that used to produce only treble fluting – but his voice just slid down the scale to a pleasant baritone, then stopped. I began to feel stirring the glorious pride of being the mother of a fine-looking, clever young man. I took his academic success for granted. He read books avidly. How could he not do well? ·

It was true that he had some difficulties at school. His handwriting was chaotic, his confusion in maths and science abject, but under the guidance of teachers who relished mild eccentricity he flourished. After years of lonely turbulence, I prepared to relax into the delicious spectacle of watching him succeed, sweeping through GCSEs towards A levels and the glorious rewards beyond.

It was a shock when his school reports began to come home larded with angry complaints: inattentiveness, forgotten books, missing homework, general hopelessness, dumb insolence. His head of year, Mr Jones, a mild young man with the wary expression and nervous hypersensitivity of a small prey animal, began to email and telephone me on a daily basis. This couldn't go on, he said. My feelings precisely, I countered. We were each inclined to blame the other for Alexander's academic collapse but settled instead on blaming him. He was impervious to our efforts to get him to engage with his schoolwork. He wasn't defiant, didn't appear angry, resentful, or especially unhappy at school. Separately and occasionally together, Mr Jones and I renewed our efforts to reason, cajole, persuade, shock or threaten him into understanding the importance of the examinations for which he was now studying.

When that didn't work I took to describing the bleak future that he could expect without qualifications: unemployment, boredom, loneliness and destitution while his friends went on to university, well-paid jobs, sexual fulfilment and starter mortgages. To all our approaches he seemed quite amenable. He agreed that it would be for the best if he were to pass his exams, promised to do better in future. For a day or two, he would appear to be trying. And then he would revert to his old habits of implacable chaos.

'He's a very stubborn lad, Mrs Shilling,' said Mr Jones, who couldn't quite bring himself to call me Miss. 'I've never seen anything like it.' I hadn't myself. We marvelled in joint frustration at his remarkable stubbornness. Often I felt like crying. Sometimes it seemed as though Mr Jones did, too. I had no idea what married life was like, but there was something about the quality of my near-daily conversations with this teacher; some peculiar note of complicit baffled anguish at our joint failure to get a purchase on the smooth impermeable surface of Alexander's quiet anarchy, that made me wonder if this was what marriage was like.

I knew that we ought to leave it alone; or at least, that I ought to, since my professional *amour propre* was not at stake. But somehow I couldn't. The alternatives to the conventional trajectory of exams, more exams, university, graduate job, seemed appalling, largely because I had no idea what they might be. Alexander said he knew what he wanted to do. He was going to be a writer. 'But you can't just *be* a writer,' I heard myself saying. 'You need qualifications . . .'

In the long summer holiday, he took to writing a book. It was a memoir of his life as a West Ham fan and it seemed to be going very well. Whenever I went into his room he was lying on his bed in front of his laptop, the screen filled with text. 'Twenty-five thousand words so far,' he announced. 'How's your book going, Mother?' My book was stuck, as he knew perfectly well.

I realised that it wasn't my son's future success and happiness that I feared would be in jeopardy if he failed his GCSEs, but mine. A horrid spectre formed in my mind, of him looming all over the house for the next fifty years or so, until he was 66 and I was 99, the pair of us still quarrelling bitterly as we tottered around the supermarket on the Friday night Big Shop. It lodged like a maggot in my head. It seemed all too plausible a vision of the future.

At home the discreet rebellion leaked from schoolwork into the intimate fabric of our lives. My son claimed control over the body whose maintenance I had until now regarded at least partly as my responsibility. The daily shower, brushing of teeth and hair, automatic until now, became battlegrounds; the subject of exhausting argument, conflict, suspicion and strategic ambush.

An orthodontist prescribed braces which he refused to wear –
lost, forgot, broke and eventually abandoned. The orthodontist
was politely but palpably furious with me for allowing the waste
of NHS time and money. I was gripped with rage and incomprehension that my son should have refused to comply with the
treatment that he had himself requested, and in doing so made
me seem (I thought) a useless mother. I couldn't quite relinquish
the idea that I had some kind of residual right over his body – the
body that had sprung from mine, and which he was now refusing
to maintain according to my standards.

He wouldn't keep up my standards of housekeeping, either.
His progress through the house was marked, like that of Hansel
and Gretel through the dark wood, by a trail of crumbs and
discarded clothes. The bathroom became a realm for amphibians,
the floor submerged beneath great puddles of soapy water, the
towels sodden, the windows running with condensation as I
followed him about with a mop, tight-lipped and vengeful.

I loathed housework. I loathed the drudgery of it, hated the
way I was always hurting myself in small ways when I did it,
knocking into sharp corners of furniture, banging myself with the
vacuum cleaner, pinching my fingers in cupboard doors, choking
on mists of acrid cleaning fluids. I resented with a burning rage the
endless cycle that meant there was never a moment to sit down in
a clean house, because no sooner was the task completed than it
would begin to unravel again, the dust settling, the synthetic citrus
reek of the pristine bathroom undercut with the ammoniac taint
of yet another mis-aimed male piss. The personality of the house
as a presence in the household it contained began to feel stifling,
more like a cell than a shelter. My life seemed like a maze full of
dead ends: blind alleys and closed passages whichever way I ran.

'Efface yourself,' my father used to demand. Now I felt that my
son's quiet indifference to everything I asked of him was about to
accomplish the absolute obliteration of my personality that my
father's rage had never quite achieved. I began to struggle. Days

and weeks passed in which every word I uttered turned into a complaint. Angry reproaches fell from my lips like the toads and serpents from the mouth of the wicked sister in the Grimms' fairy tale. And I blamed my son for this, as well. I wasn't a harridan by nature, I screamed. It was he who was turning me into one with his contempt for my standards, my wish to live with a degree of grace, to keep our small shared space clean and orderly.

My son said nothing, but shrugged, insolently, I thought, though perhaps he had just run out of language, or didn't choose to engage with me on my home ground of violent, extravagant articulacy. I had run out of language myself. My sense of violent affront, of being simply blotted out of existence by this person, this intimate stranger to whom my life was coupled, was so extreme that it scorched into oblivion any terms in which I might have expressed it. I couldn't speak at all.

One night I locked myself into the rotting bathroom and rang the Samaritans. The person at the other end of the line listened in the distinctive dead flat Samaritan silence as I wept my way through a recital of what ailed me: the terrible loneliness, the gnawing money worries, the decaying house, the sense of impending academic disaster and the concomitant terror for the future, the overwhelming feeling of having failed as a mother, the feeling that I couldn't, couldn't go on with this. And yet that I must, for what else could I do?

At last I sobbed myself into silence. There was a protracted pause. And eventually, 'Yeah, that is bad,' said the Samaritan. I went to see the GP, with roughly similar results, except that, glancing at her watch and agreeing that I certainly was having a frightful time of it, she wrote out a hefty prescription for temazepam, quite enough for me to have offed myself with ease, if I had felt inclined.

I didn't pick up the prescription. I was finding it hard to sleep because my life was intolerable, not finding life intolerable because I couldn't sleep, and I knew perfectly well that she had written out the scrip not for my benefit, but in order to tranquillise herself against the feeling that she had done nothing to help her patient. In another of those rare moments of shocking clarity that my middle age seemed to be throwing up, I saw in an instant that the prison in which I felt myself trapped was one that I had painstakingly constructed for myself.

I had imagined that I was doing the right thing in renouncing a social and sexual life in order to devote myself to my son. Although at first I minded terribly the restriction of rarely being able to go out in the evenings or at weekends, of having, while I was still a young woman, only just out of my twenties, to renounce all opportunities to fall in love again, eventually it became too painful to carry on minding so much.

For several years I ran up and down my cage in a frenzy, frantically trying to think of a childcare arrangement that would let me get away once in a while. But there wasn't one, or not one that I could feel satisfied with, and in the end I stopped struggling and tried to embrace my circumscribed life with as much grace as I could muster.

I was dimly aware of a suppressed accusing bit of my consciousness that thought this was no more than I deserved. I had picked the wrong man, casting off quite brutally along the way plenty of people who had loved me dearly and might have been willing to settle down with me. Instead I had 'got myself', in my GP's startling turn of phrase, pregnant. And now I'd been presented with the bill for my waywardness, my unkindness and lack of regard for other people's feelings.

More rational, as my forties approached, was the feeling that although it was painful to sacrifice a social and cultural life and the possibility of meeting someone, that loss was minor compared with the anguished renunciation felt by half a dozen of my friends who would have loved to have had children and would have been excellent mothers, but never had the opportunity because they didn't meet the right man, or met him too late to bear his children, or thought they'd met him, only to lose him again just as their fertility began to dwindle.

Even at the very worst moments, when I felt like running away from home or shoving my son out of the house and boarding up the entrance so that he couldn't get back in again, I never quite lost my grip on the small hard gem of feeling that the accidental pregnancy had been, above all, an amazing stroke of luck.

Looking through the album of pictures that Linda gave us when she left prompted me to sort out the untidy bundles of photographs that I had taken over the years. As I leafed through them I saw with amazement that we had been happy. At any given moment, if I had been asked how things were going, I should have said, very difficult, a continual exhausting struggle with money, with alienation from my family, with solitariness and the retreat from love, the grim, almost physical, daily sense of grappling with the apprehension of being cared for by no one, of having only myself to reinforce my sense of self – of existing in a constant state of dangerously slippery solipsism.

But looking at the pictures of my son – in the park, on the beach at Dymchurch or in Devon, in the square at St-Florent, at Hampton Court or on the rough little low-goal polo ground at Ham, I saw that it wasn't true; that the glass may have felt fixed for sixteen years on Stormy Weather, but that at the moments caught and preserved in these pictures we had been laughing, lucky, happy and complicit in each other's company; having a lovely time, in fact.

Even now, when I felt myself shrinking and diminished – dwindling into a tiny scolding Mrs Pepperpot as he grew larger, more powerful, more hugely indifferent to my shrill, diminished presence, while still sucking out of me the vital energy I needed to go on, to work, to write, to keep up the momentum of the household – the old love, the comic double act of our attachment somehow remained powerful.

When our joint narrative seemed broken down almost beyond

repair, storytelling at its most basic and melodramatic could get it going again. It was the fundamental element of our relationship. Every night, from the day I brought him home from hospital as a newborn baby, I used to read to him. When he woke in the night or was ill, I would tell him a story. As a child myself, I had peopled my world with characters from the imagination of Beatrix Potter, Mary Norton, E. Nesbit and Anthony Buckeridge. Now I passed on the habit to my son.

His nanny had introduced him to the storytelling of soap operas – *Neighbours, EastEnders* – and now he passed that habit back to me. *Corrie, The Bill, Waterloo Road, The Vicar of Dibley* – anything with a strong narrative offered us a place in which to take temporary refuge from our emotional storms; to watch the consoling spectacle of other people getting their relationships spectacularly wrong, and sometimes chancing upon the archetypes of forgiveness, of the way back from what seemed unforgivable.

'I wrote down those things you said,' said my son one day, during a *Stenders*-brokered truce after a particularly vicious and protracted battle. 'I wrote them all down on a piece of paper to get them out of my head.'

What did you do with the paper then? I asked, full of shame at this evidence that, small and powerless as I felt myself to be, I had succeeded in injuring him so gravely. He said he'd screwed it up and pushed it behind the wardrobe but when I went to look for it, this written testament to my fury and unkindness and failure as a mother, in order to take it away and make it seem as though the words had never been spoken, it was nowhere to be seen.

From the repeated pattern of fight and truce a revelation at last emerged. In a moment of anguish following yet another bloody, pointless skirmish over homework from which we had both retired hurt, I suddenly saw that all my hard-won self-sacrifice had actually been a sort of complicated selfishness. I'd shut out the world as much as I'd been shut out from it. I'd turned my loneliness into a virtue, made a fetish of my independence and ability to cope and now, when I couldn't do it on my own any longer – because what my son needed more than anything was to get away from the *huis clos* that was our life together, and that was the one thing I couldn't do for him – I had no one to turn to.

10

The Retreat from Love

Years had passed: several years and then more than several during which I would have said I was in retreat from love, if only there had been any love to retreat from. I didn't look for it and it didn't seek me out. From time to time someone would take an interest, but I gave them little encouragement and I never fell in love.

One day I found myself crossing the road at the same time as an older man with whom, once we had reached the pavement on the other side, I fell first into conversation and, after a while, into a comfortable habit of weekly lunches. Sometimes I thought this state of mildly flirtatious emotional limbo suited me very well. It provided me with the grown-up conversation of which I had felt starved for years, along with an appreciative male eye and a decorous sexual frisson. There was no risk involved in this charming but essentially tepid relationship; no danger that a storm might blow up and come roaring through my house, sweeping aside all my tidy routines and certainties. If it all came to a sudden end I should be sorry, but not very. There was no chance of my heart being broken again: it had been so long since I had fallen in love that I doubted whether I still had the ability.

Yet sometimes I felt restless; discontented and cross with my old friend, or myself, or with the thin, wine-and-water emotional sustenance that was all the attachment could offer. The gentle, daughterly flirtation was enough to remind me of what I had been missing for so long. I began to feel troubled; cheated; to wonder if I'd love anyone, or be loved, ever again.

If I'd allowed myself to think about it, I should have regretted most bitterly the thing I should never now have, even if I were to fall in love again. Even if I were to find my true love immediately, and marry him, and stay married for the rest of my life, the best of it – the real richness of a partnership – was unattainable. I'd never now know what it was like to build a life with a man I loved: have his children, raise them in the complicity of a successful family. I tried to stifle the thought of it as much as I could. To think about it made me feel as though great caverns of sadness were opening up beneath my feet, into which I might vanish altogether.

To stop myself being engulfed by regret, I sometimes found it helpful to contemplate the marriages of my female acquaintance, some of whom had promised themselves, for better or worse, as long as they both should live, to men who seemed like huge, demanding toddlers, incapable of taking care of their own basic needs, emotionally fragile, at odds with the world around them – always losing things or breaking things or getting upset because their plans had gone wrong.

'But Jane,' said Isabelle over the road, who now lived alone with her two sickly cats, but had been a racy beauty in her day, 'that's just men. It's what they do.' I wasn't altogether convinced that it was. I didn't recall, in any of my handful of serious love affairs, being called upon to act as the mummy or nanny of my lover. Either this was something that overcame men in middle age, or else I just happened to have friends who were quite content to be married to these large male infants.

I thought I would find it difficult to sustain an erotic life with a person who treated me as his housekeeper, weltering in self-pity and leaving his socks and coffee cups all over the house for me to tidy up when I got home from work. Like Mme du Deffand, whose most contented thought in old age was that she wasn't married to a certain M. de Jonzac, I warmed myself with the thought that at least I didn't have to share my bed with a petulant 50-year-old toddler.

Still, I knew there was a mystery there, inside these apparently unenviable marriages, that I should probably never get to the bottom of, and I couldn't help gnawing away at it – sometimes relieved, sometimes with the sensation of having missed something rich and full of vitality; always fascinated.

'The two things I aimed for I failed at,' wrote Martha Gellhorn to her friend Betsy Drake. 'I wanted a great single man-woman love and to write a great book.' I wasn't that ambitious. Just the great love would have done for me.

Three or four times in my life, between my early teens and mid-forties, I thought I had found the magic formula that would admit me to the place where my search for a lasting love would come to an end. But each time the proportions had proved wrong; the product of the alchemy had been at worst a devastating explosion, the air filled with sharp shards of anger, reproach and contempt; at best a corrosive vapour of disillusion or regret. In either case, the door to the place where love was calm and reciprocated remained obstinately shut.

In adolescence, at the beginning of an erotic career, the ideal arc of love and desire seemed marvellously simple, even if the realisation of it remained obscure. At 15, I knew without doubt that I would fall in love: there might be difficulties and dangers along the way but eventually my love would be returned and then I would live happily ever after. The tenacity of this belief was remarkable. Long after all sorts of other ambitions – for academic distinction or worldly success – fell away, the primitive belief in the existence of my true love – out there, somewhere, searching for me – persisted.

Such fantasies feed on the conviction of singularity. It is only when you turn to the lonely hearts columns and see, laid out like a shoal of herrings on the fishmonger's slab, the terrible pathos of the thousands of accumulated 35-to-seventysomethings, all hoping beneath their wistful taglines of 'Better luck this time????' or 'Could you be the one for me?' for 'a gentleman to sweep me off my feet'; convinced that 'life is what you make it'; brightly touting themselves as 'fun to be with', gallantly admitting that they 'need to get out more', or are 'a bit of a weeble really', that doubt begins to grow and the idea of a dignified retreat from the fine old conflict begins to look altogether more desirable than fighting on.

The experience of love was so distant by this time, its disturbances dwindled to a vestigial twinge, like the ghostly intimations of a long-abandoned adolescent talent for tap-dancing or playing the trumpet, that it was hardly necessary for me to make a gesture of renunciation. Love had renounced me.

On the outside, I was still playing the game: still painting and dressing myself each morning in the elaborate armour of attraction. But my bruising clutch of maladroit attachments had made me – too late – wary and farouche, while years of bringing up a child alone had developed my wilful and bossy tendencies to the exclusion of more pliable traits. Fate had neatly fixed it so that the only men who might possibly find me attractive were the kind that wanted a competent maternal figure to take care of them – the very ones, in fact, whom I absolutely couldn't be doing with.

During the summer holidays my son began taking tennis lessons at the court in the nearby park. It was a pleasant walk on a summer's day from our house to the courts: up the hill beneath the avenue of old limes and sweet chestnut trees; past the boating lake and the playground of shrilling toddlers, over the parched grass strewn with the clinging bodies of lovers, around whose static bliss jostling gangs of schoolchildren adroitly swerved. Through the rose garden with its formal beds of orange and knicker-pink hybrid teas, and out at the gate by the putting green where the tennis coach's wooden pavilion looked like a bathing hut at low tide.

The inhabitant of the hut was Luke, a sweet-faced young man with a sparse crop of blond stubble, who dressed like a toddler in baggy three-quarter-length shorts and little white ankle socks. He was a very good teacher: patient, but unforgiving of idleness or fits of temperament. From our desultory weekly conversations as I handed over the cash for the lessons it emerged that the tennis was only a summer job. The rest of the time he was a linguist – a trainee translator with a couple of degrees. He lived with his parents and was quite a lot older than I had guessed – late twenties rather than early.

One sunny afternoon as I lay in the shade of a mulberry tree by the tennis court, half reading a novel, half listening to the pock of racquet on ball and the murmur of Luke's admonitions to Alexander, a shadow fell over the page and I looked up from my book to see the brilliantly polished shoes and elegant pale-grey summer-weight trouser legs of my old friend of the weekly lunches. I was delighted to see him, as one is on meeting a friend in an unexpected setting. Normally I saw him only by appointment, grasping his knife and fork on the other side of an expanse of starched tablecloth. There was something sweetly flighty about this encounter under the mulberry tree – something wayward and suggestive about the setting of artificial pastoral, like the chance meetings in woodland of Shakespeare's comedies or Mozart's operas, from which so much bittersweet confusion results. We chatted for a moment, until the lesson was over. Then he left, kissing me as we parted, and I turned back towards the tennis court, where Alexander was picking up balls while Luke stowed the racquets in his hut.

'Was that Alexander's father?' he asked as I gave him the money for the lesson. The idea was so bizarre that I laughed. 'Only it looked,' he said, rather severely, 'like a secret assignation there, under the tree.'

'But not very secret, in the middle of Greenwich Park. And not an assignation,' I said, still laughing as I uncapped my bottle of water and took a swig. 'Would you mind if I had some of your water?' he asked. I passed him the bottle and he put his mouth to the lip of it, just where my mouth had been a moment before.

It was a gesture at once trivial and fraught with a sort of erotic pique. He was very good-looking, very charming and very sweet – the darling of the tennis mothers. And he evidently hadn't cared for the vignette he'd glimpsed under the tree, of one of his adoring flock being distracted by some old bloke in a city suit. The little pantomime with the water bottle had a quaint air of reproof about it – the young stag chasing off the old chancer.

Ha! I thought, flouncing homeward down the hill, I am an object of desire, this sunny summer's afternoon, to two separate men. Pity one of them's old enough to be my father, and the other one young enough to be my son. But still . . .

And then I was suddenly nailed in the vitals by an appalling stab of desire and an equally terrible stab of shame. Not so much shame at the idea of wanting to be seized and crushed into the corner of the tennis hut by a youth half my age in little white socks (or seized and crushed into the bark of the mulberry tree by a distinguished old party in a pearl-grey business suit, come to that) as by the sheer silliness of that redundant stirring of desire, of which nothing was ever going to come.

It was the last tennis lesson of the summer holidays. There were no more idle sunny afternoons dawdling through the park, but a flurry of joyless last-minute shopping expeditions in pursuit of things with which more prudent mothers had equipped themselves weeks before. Alexander crammed his feet into stiff new shoes, shouldered his schoolbag with its pencil case full of cedar-smelling pencils and pristine rubbers, and set off disconsolately towards days chopped into arbitrary segments of maths, physics, chemistry and the rest, leaving behind an absence that reverberated in the silent house.

After the drifting expanse of summer the year seemed to gather speed as the leaves fell and the last roses were nipped by the first frosts. After Hallowe'en and Guy Fawkes night came Alexander's birthday – a sophisticated affair these days, marked by lunch in a restaurant and a trip to West Ham away at Chelsea. After that Advent and then, always wrong-footing me a little, always arriving just before I had managed to send the last of the cards, or ice the chocolate log still rolled up in a sugar-strewn tea towel, Christmas.

Alexander went to bed late now. Quite often I'd leave him sprawled in the dark living room, watching the homunculi on the television capering or gesticulating to bursts of tinny laughter while I went upstairs to bed. With some difficulty I persuaded him to go to bed before me on Christmas Eve, so that I could put the hidden presents under the tree and wrap the contents of the Christmas stocking on which he still insisted. It was just past midnight and I was working fast, wrapping the last of the stocking trash – a Teenage Decision-Maker die, its faces marked with HOMEWORK, CHILL OUT, WATCH TV, ANNOY YOUR PARENTS and so on – when the letterbox flap was quietly pushed open. A white envelope fell on to the mat before the letterbox slowly closed again with a click.

The lights of the Christmas tree flashed mechanically on and off. The house was silent I hadn't heard footsteps on the path, or the gate latch open. I sat with the half-wrapped die in my hand and my heart thumping, trembling as though someone had tried to break in.

Years of working at a table next to the front door hadn't trained me not to regard the opening of the letterbox as a violation of my domestic security. The night after we moved in, I was woken in the small hours from a dead sleep by a muffled rhythmic banging. Still half asleep, I looked out of the window and saw a man rattling the letterbox, which was loose on its screws, as though he thought he could pull the whole door off. I wondered afterwards if it had really happened, or if it was an eerie bad dream – a companion piece to a recurring nightmare of a gang of jeering children who overran the house. Dream or reality, the incident had left me with a dread of the unexpected opening of that little hatch. Even the sound of the post arriving sometimes made me jump, but what I really hated was people peering in.

It happened surprisingly often. Jehovah's Witnesses, men hoping to persuade you to change your electricity supplier, pushy boys selling expensive oven gloves and dusters door-to-door would advance up the path, bang on the door and, if there was no answer, push open the letterbox and squint in. Occasionally, if I hadn't seen them coming in time to take refuge upstairs, I'd slide out of sight under the table, from which vantage point I once watched as an especially persistent would-be boyfriend manoeuvred a long-stemmed rose, bud-first, through the aperture – the flower on the end of its long stalk wavering about like the questing proboscis of some sightless, attenuated creature.

I finished wrapping the decision-maker die (CHILL OUT, it advised, as I folded the paper over it), and looked at the envelope on the mat which was, now I came to think of it, obviously a late Christmas card from a neighbour. I picked it up. My name was written on it in a familiar hand. It was a Nativity scene with a note inside, from James, the doctor for whose return I had longed so passionately.

For a long time after he had left me without a word, I told myself that one day he would come looking for me. One night there would come the sound of my front gate being unlatched, a footstep on my path, a knock at the door and I would open it and there he would be, standing on the doorstep. I would fall into his arms, and my long wait would be ended. As I stood looking at the card, there was a tap at the door. It was just as I had imagined. My lover had come looking for me. My long wait was over.

I I

The Fork in the Road

After a moment's hesitation I opened the door and there he was, standing in the middle of the path, half turned away, as though he had changed his mind and was on his way towards the gate again, his hands clasped behind his back.

Hallo, I said. What a surprise, would you like to come in? Yes, thank you, he would. A drink, perhaps? No? Some coffee, then? No to that too. Well, do sit down, anyway.

So he sat on the edge of one of my little chairs, with his back wedged against the piano with the Nativity scene on top, and his knees brushed by the bushy branches of the too-large Christmas tree with its tinkling freight of silvery bells and spun-glass birds. And I perched on the sofa and waited for him to speak.

There was a pause. But years of working as a GP had rendered him extremely resourceful in tricky social situations. After a beat of silence he launched into a fluent stream of small talk. In the instant of deciding to open the door (rather than hide under the table until he'd gone away), I had braced myself for all sorts of exhausting drama. But for small talk I was unprepared. I balanced on the arm of the sofa as the flow of talk meandered gracefully from anecdote to anecdote. The central heating shuddered and died. It grew cold around us, but still he spoke.

I looked at the clock. It was almost 2a.m. Suddenly I felt overcome with confusion and misery. Why had he come here? What on earth did he want? I wondered whether, like the Duke of Wellington returning after years away at war to find his old love Kitty Pakenham so pale and altered that he no longer desired her, he was shocked by how much I'd changed. Perhaps he'd knocked at the door intending to make some dramatic declaration and been deflected into small talk by the sight of me. At any rate, I'd had enough.

Goodness, I said, getting up. Is that the time? He rose. Where was he staying? Oh, he was headed for home now. Home, I knew from the address on the card he'd put through the door, was several hundred miles away. It seemed a long trip to be making upon the midnight clear. Goodnight, then, I said.

I thought that was the end. But apparently it wasn't. Postcards began to arrive: graceful, whimsical, affectionate. Occasionally he sent books – old hardbacks of Jennings, paperbacks of P.G. Wodehouse – to Alexander, who liked them and was pleased. From time to time he would take me out for dinner. Afterwards we would return to my house and sit for half an hour or so in awkward proximity by the unlit fireplace in my drawing room before he drove away again into the dark. After a handful of these excursions it occurred to me that he hadn't come to London on other business, but was making a special journey – a round trip of many hundreds of miles – to eat dinner with me and drive home again afterwards.

Each time he came I thought that this must be the evening when he would address directly the thing that lay unspoken between us: that years ago, between one profession of eternal love and the next, he'd vanished without a word. I found its silent, oppressive presence impossible to ignore. It slouched on the hearthrug between us like some terrible old pet as we chatted uneasily in the drawing room. It loomed over the restaurant table, casting its distracting shadow over the plates of *steak frites* and *poulet chasseur*.

Almost anyone whom I'd asked for advice at this point would have said, for goodness' sake, let it go. It's an unsatisfactory ending to an unsatisfactory story. What else did you expect? Move on.

The trouble was that I couldn't, in the brisk, resolute style in which other people seemed to manage their emotional lives, move on. I felt sure that my old love's reappearance presaged one of the last great choices I would have to make: whether to spend the rest of my life alone, or attempt, almost certainly for the last time, the adventure of spending it as half of a couple. For that was what he appeared, in oblique fashion, to be suggesting. And although I was vividly aware of the folly of allowing myself to trust someone who wouldn't, or couldn't, tell me what was in his heart, the fact was that I was now apparently being offered a version of what I had wanted for so many years.

Most of my adult life had been spent in a state of tense anticipation of the moment at which someone would choose me; my completing half would turn up, we would cleave together, neat and inevitable as magnets, and the rest of our lives would be spent growing together into a single entity, like the two old trees into which Baucis and Philemon are changed at the end of their lives in the myth.

Twice I had thought I had found my completing half, and twice I had found that I was mistaken when the completing half wrenched himself free and went off to find completion elsewhere. At last I had come to accept that what I did while I was waiting for my real life to begin – the tending of the house and garden, the small extravagances on self-adornment and objects to decorate the house, the cooking, the books, the writing by which I earned our living, the cherishing of my child, my friends and my animals – all this *was* my real life.

And if it mostly lacked the grandeur, the ideal intimacy, that I imagined was the hidden secret of a great adult love, there were other kinds of happiness: calm, stability, solitude, the intimacy of old, new and rediscovered friendships, the pleasure of the life I had built in my house, my street, my neighbourhood near the Thames, the pride I felt in being able to keep us fed, clothed and housed by my pen, and the even greater pride and pleasure in having raised my son from a helpless infant to a young man.

If they lacked the glamour, the epic quality of love found early and sustained over years, I thought that there was still a kind of small glory in these things. They seemed more solid, less fragile and contingent than love. My sense of myself had been badly damaged twice when men whom I thought I loved turned out not to love me with the same fervour, but it had happened while I was still young and resilient enough to recover.

Now I was arriving at the age at which a long-married wife might one day find herself betrayed or – just as terrible – wake to the realisation that she was married to someone she no longer recognised: an unpleasant boor or bore incapable of intimacy, with whom she no longer had anything in common but some children, a postal address, a dire domestic proximity and – if she were very unlucky – a fatal financial dependence.

From that danger I was safe; and safe, too, from the lesser dangers of love: the misunderstanding and anguish and extremities of rage, remorse, rejection or – worst of all – uncertainty which, even now that they were long past, I recalled with fear and horror. The absence of all that was enough, almost, to console me for never having really known what it felt like to be loved.

Love, I had eventually come to understand (though it took me almost fifty years to work it out), is as much about the ability to *be* loved, to recognise and accept the gift when it is offered, as it is about the active expenditure of feeling on a chosen object. If you don't learn when very young how to be loved, what it looks and feels like when it comes your way, then your chances of recognising the real thing when it arrives later on, unless you chance upon someone exceptionally patient and discerning, are poor.

Linda, the heroine of Nancy Mitford's *Pursuit of Love* is picked up by a short, stocky Frenchman on the *gare du Nord*, where she is sitting on a suitcase, crying, having run away from her second husband. Almost at once she is filled with a strange, wild, unfamiliar happiness, and knows that this is love.

> Twice in her life she had mistaken something else for it; it was like seeing somebody in the street who you think is a friend, you whistle and wave and run after him, and it is not only not the friend, but not even very like him. A few minutes later the real friend appears in view, and then you can't imagine how you ever mistook that other person for him. Linda was now looking upon the authentic face of love, and she knew it, but it frightened her. That it should come so casually, so much by a series of accidents, was frightening . . .

Though not, perhaps, as frightening as the experience of looking back over a life and realising that your authentic love was there, present in your life not fleetingly, but for years and years in clear view and still you managed to miss him, distracted by strangers whom you mistook for the real thing until it was far too late.

I didn't like to think about this. It was the most terrible mistake of my life and entirely irreparable. Arriving at a fork in the road, I had taken the wrong path and in that instant, the landscape of my existence changed for ever. Not everything that sprang from that wrong choice was lamentable – the lovely accident of my son, for one thing.

And for another, the fact that, on the cusp of middle age, a couple of decades (if you accepted Diana Athill's definition of 70 as the beginning of old age) before the shortness of my remaining time might be expected to begin pressing hard upon me, I seemed to have arrived at the state of moderately contented detachment from the struggle and drama of the fertile years, sweetened by friends, animals and gardening, recommended by the grave and judicious philosophers of the menopause as the middle-aged female's state of grace.

Only now my state of grace was all upset and I found myself in just the state of painful uncertainty that I had hoped never to experience again. It wasn't love itself that disturbed me now, but the apprehension of standing once again at a fork in the road, and of the urgent need, this time, to choose the right path. I no longer trusted my instincts or the inclinations of my heart. I'd always followed them before, and each time the consequences had been dire. In any case this situation was so peculiar as to bypass instinct altogether. I had opened the door on Christmas night with apprehension and closed it again with confusion. Now I didn't know what I thought.

What stopped me from retreating at once from this hesitant middle-aged courtship was the feeling that while it was ludicrous, even rather sinister, to imagine that love would have the same quality in one's late forties that it had in one's teens and twenties (wasn't there a line in *Sex and the City* about full-on weddings looking 'a bit Diane Arbus' once you were past your mid-forties? Even that was pushing it, I thought . . .), it wasn't at all stupid to think that the possibility of new love of some kind – great love, even – might survive into middle age and beyond. Not hectic, breathless, sprung-from-nothing romantic love, but something, I imagined, closer to kindness.

'The important thing,' says Nancy Mitford's Linda, not yet middle-aged, but speaking from the pinnacle of her experience of two unsatisfactory marriages and a glamorous but distinctly elusive lover, 'if a marriage is to go well . . . is very great niceness – *gentillesse* – and wonderful good manners.'

This quality of *gentillesse*, unlike charm or beauty, isn't a gift but a decision. You can train yourself to do it, if you wish, and often it provokes an answering echo from other people. Since my grandparents had died there had been little *gentillesse* in my close relationships. Only when my son was born had I discovered some unsuspected reserves of patience and niceness. Though they often failed and there were long, ugly stretches of intense disagreeableness, the periods of niceness were sustained enough for me to feel that I had a capacity for nurturing that wasn't confined to plants and animals, and that when my son left home, I would find the loss of another person with whom to share my life desolating.

Plenty of middle-aged women, if the sprightly volumes on 'second life' were to be believed, found adequate outlets for their caring instincts in their pets, their gardens, their grandchildren, in self-improvement, artistic endeavour and good works. I had, myself, been keeping for quite a while a list of the many things with which I planned to fill the half longed-for, half dreaded, empty time after Alexander left home: an ambitious regime of language learning, travel (to the places where my new languages were spoken), books, concerts, galleries, charitable endeavour and domestic industry (a well stocked store cupboard, an orderly kitchen garden).

All this, plus the fact that I would certainly have to work for a living well into old age, since I had no savings and a negligible pension, meant that I wasn't very afraid of suffering from the attacks of anomie to which mothers left behind in their empty nests were said to be prone. What's more, I loved solitude; craved it, sometimes, with a desire as urgent as thirst. On the very rare occasions when Alexander was elsewhere, I relished it, not as an absence but as something more like a palpable sensation, like music, or poetry.

But that was, after all, as a contrast to the constant company of an entertaining male. I loved my solitude when he was gone because it was so rare and precious. And at the same time I missed his company. I liked the whiff of testosterone about the place. I liked hearing the story of his day and reporting the story of mine;

I liked having someone to go to films with; someone with whom to anatomise the television dramas, soap operas and episodes of *Top Gear* for which he had infected me with his enthusiasm. I even, sometimes, quite liked having someone to cook and iron for.

I was, in a way, grateful for the things I made a fuss about: the barbarous tedium of football; the outrageous sexism of the girly posters on the wall. (Although were they, in fact, sexist? After delivering a stinging feminist lecture on the exploitation of women, I picked up one of his lads' mags and discovered that half these semi-naked girls were enthusiastic volunteers, rather than professional glamour models. So now I wasn't quite so sure of my position on naked breasts, especially not the ones belonging to Readers' Girlfriends, oddly juxtaposed as they were in the lads' mags with Readers' Severed Fingers – blurred or all-too-clear snapshots of ghastly domestic accidents with chainsaws and strimmers.) Anyway, I had come to regard these things as a useful irritant; a means of ensuring that my life didn't dwindle into miniature, enclosed, female preciousness.

Solitude, I noticed, was big in the accounts of how to make the best of a post-menopausal existence. The route to a serene, composed 'second life', according to these manuals, was to be found in a kind of ecstatic renunciation: a sloughing-off of the busy accumulations of the first part of life so as to enter into a mystical communion with yourself and Nature which would prove, if you got it right, much more satisfactory than the muddled and frustrating pre-menopausal courtship dance.

If the fertile years were all about narcissistic perfection of the body and the life, the post-fertile years, so the argument went, should involve a stripping away of the garish intrigues of desire, attraction, self-adornment, a discovery of one's essential nature through a cleaving to the elemental: whether religious or some more inchoate sense of animist spirituality. The reward for the bitter travail endured by the ego in divesting itself of the trappings and stratagems and evasions of allure was to be a kind of innocence regained: a pure permeability to the eloquent, inanimate world of essence; a feeling of communion with the fragrant upturned clod in a ploughed field; the shrill aria of the ascending lark; the haze of green leaves budding beneath a washed spring sky.

Lovely though all this sounded in theory, I was not altogether convinced. The arguments about a relationship with nature as a more satisfying substitute for human attachment tended to be made, I noticed, by writers from an urban background: late converts to the virtues of pastoral. Those who already knew the countryside intimately, having grown up there, generally took a more sceptical view of nature worship.

In her writing on middle age, Colette often represents the experience of sexual passion as a malaise – a kind of fever for which there is no remedy, beyond that of waiting for it to burn itself out. She conflates the idea of the post-menopausal 'convalescence' from the fever of desire with a retreat from the poisoned sophistication of urban life to an asexual Eden, free from the sting of need and longing. But at the same time, the country-bred child in Colette understands that the redemptive power of nature is a wish: a story she tells herself, not a lifeline.

Another country-bred child, Lorna Sage, gives a pithy summary of the downside of ecstatic pastoral in *Bad Blood*, her memoir of a childhood in rural Wales: 'Try as I might to lose myself in the landscape . . . I was still only an apprentice misfit and self-conscious in the part . . . The truth was that often no amount of trudging would get me to the state of dreamy abstraction I craved. Then I was simply lonely. . . .'

The childhood habit of mesmerising oneself with solitude was familiar to me. From my house to my primary school was a walk of about a mile. The route from our road of solid villas bordered with lime trees and flowering cherry dwindled after half a mile into farmland: arable fields smelling in autumn of newly turned earth, cherry and apple orchards, paddocks with sheep and grazing horses.

A quarter of a mile further on you came to the village of Tunstall. At the top of the hill, an ancient church of knapped flint and brick in a yew-shaded churchyard crowded with carious tombstones. Beyond the churchyard, the old rose-brick walls of Tunstall House, sown with toadflax and wallflowers. Through the iron spears of the gate you could just see the diamond shape of the clock, half masking the rectangular window frame into which it was set. A romantic ghost was attached to this house, an apocryphal story of forbidden love between a Puritan girl and a Cavalier soldier that ended with the girl's being walled up in her room. Her shade, grey-clad, was supposed to walk on midsummer's eve.

The thought of the shut-inness of the ghostly girl in the dark room behind the clock, and the shut-outness of me, peering in through the iron-barred gate, disturbed me. I passed the old house with a foreboding sense of love turned dangerous, and was glad to find myself among the quieter dead of the churchyard.

At the end of a cinder path lay my primary school, a Victorian schoolhouse in pointy gingerbread Gothic, surrounded by a slew of mobile classrooms flighty as henhouses, a pungent block of spider-haunted outside lavatories overgrown by an enormous lilac tree, and a low, dank concrete building, once a wartime bomb shelter, now a store for wooden hoops, skipping ropes, bristly coir mats and the school maypole with its tangle of coloured ribbons. Beyond the classrooms, a hawthorn hedge; beyond the hedge, orchards as far as a child could see.

At school the flimsiness of our temporal existence was impressed on us early and often. We were always being reminded, on our frequent trips to church, of the cloud of witnesses, composed of the souls of the faithful departed, that invisibly surrounded us. It seemed likely that we were breathing them in with every lungful of air, splashing in puddles of them every time it rained. And there, in the churchyard, was further evidence of the promiscuous mingling of animate and inanimate nature: all those defunct

Jacobs and Hannahs and their dearly beloved children, resting in their beds of earth, patiently waiting for the glorious Day of Judgment while worms fed on the dust that once had been their talking, laughing, loving, quarrelling, embracing flesh and trees sprang from the earth where the worms tunnelled.

At some point on the dawdling, solitary daily journey home I discovered that if I repeated inside my head, 'Who am I?' over and over until the words lost their meaning, I could induce in myself a state, simultaneously thrilling and alarming, in which I seemed not to be me any more, as though my body belonged to someone else altogether and I (whoever 'I' was, if not the inhabitant of the body in which I usually dwelt) took on a separate, incorporeal being as part of the landscape that I knew so intimately.

I was the powdery rose-brick wall; the yellow-lipped purple flowers of the toadflax that grew on it; the sound of the cracked church bell as it struck the quarter, the scent of pee and lilac that rose from the primitive playground *pissoir*, the curve of the road as it crossed the invisible frontier that separated the ghost stories and apple orchards of school from its neighbouring realm, the place of flowering cherries, *Belle et Sébastien* on the television, and shepherd's pie for tea, that was home.

It became easier and easier to think myself into this state of giddy detachment, but then I became frightened that a moment might come when I wouldn't be able (or, even more frightening, wouldn't want) to get back into my body and carry on with my normal life. So I stopped doing it, and once I began the journey through the examination system that would eventually take me away from home and out into the world, I lost the knack of absenting my inside self from my everyday carapace, though I kept the habit of identifying with certain places and things.

The return to them made me feel more myself. For all the years of my grown-up life during which I lived in places that I had not chosen, or in which I was unhappy, I felt as though the substance of me, worn threadbare by the abrasive surface of living, could have its liveliness restored by haunting the places where I had once felt that I belonged.

When I took to riding in my late thirties, after almost twenty years of city life, the feeling I had as a child, of becoming my surroundings, came back as though it had never subsided. The stillness that haunts hunting in wooded country, the long passages of gazing, poised between boredom and concentration, into the same narrow expanse of covert, revived the sensation – like feeling under my fingers the notes of some once-familiar piece of music – of looking with such intentness that I seemed to grasp the withheld qualities of the landscape.

Looking across the stubble fields towards the long, low, animal curve of the great greensand ridge that rises and dips like the body of a sleeping creature beside the road that leads to Charing and on to the brickish skirts of Ashford, I felt an intimacy with the lie of the land that must be something like the deep, calm affection that people harbour for their cherished old spouses or lovers of many decades.

It is easier to maintain a relationship with a landscape or an animal than it is with one's fellow human. At the yards where I kept my mare I noticed there were often women whose capacity for love seemed perfectly fulfilled by the care they took of their horse (although some of them had partners – shadowy, taciturn figures, occasionally summoned to hitch a stubborn trailer or help chivvy a reluctant loader up the ramp before being briskly dismissed back to the golf course or the pub).

Often the horse women were so absorbed by the maintenance of their animal – the mucking out, grooming and worming, the accumulation of equine kit and the obsessive pulling of mane and tail – that they hardly had time to ride. When they did, the management of the animal's quirks with different combinations of bit and noseband, massage and diet, afforded endless opportunities for delicious speculation, and the seductive possibility of eliminating altogether the communication gap between two individuals that is such a baffling obstacle to contentment in human relationships.

With such an imperfect record in my human love affairs, I felt keenly the attraction of perfectibility in these less complicated attachments. But although I valued whatever self-possession I had learned from the sentimental mistakes of my twenties and thirties, and didn't mean to relinquish it carelessly now, I saw as much danger in a retreat from the battleground of love as I did in letting down my guard.

I recalled my frustration, as a haughty adolescent, with what seemed to me to be the smallness and incuriousness of my parents' world; their contempt (born, I thought, of a narrow timidity) for what was new and strange, their disinclination to experiment with what lay beyond their established boundaries of habit and respectability.

At a certain point (I thought) they seemed to have stopped imagining themselves, to have decided that enough was enough, that their reservoirs of experience were now full enough not to need further replenishing; that they need discover no more of the world than they knew already.

In thinking this I was doubtless mistaken: they were beleaguered, at the time I was observing them with my unforgiving teenaged eye, by all sorts of strains of which I knew nothing. No wonder they clung to the known and didn't appear to crave strangeness or adventure.

But although I, too, longed for a life of stability and calm, I thought now that I might be in less danger from the disruption of my composure than from a certain cold contraction of the heart: a narrow prudence, a cautious indisposition to love, an absence of daring, an inability to be delighted. A calcified heart is undoubtedly well protected from predators, but it is well protected from the rest of human experience as well.

In *A Time to Keep Silence*, his short, brilliant book on the monastic life, Patrick Leigh Fermor described the anguish of enduring what might now be called a process of detoxification from his ordinary life. Seeking somewhere quiet and cheap to stay while he completed a book, he followed the advice of a friend and sought refuge in the Benedictine Abbey of St Wandrille in Normandy.

Welcomed by the monks, with nothing to do but get on with his book, Leigh Fermor sat at his desk in a state of overwhelming gloom, imagining 'the temperature of life falling to zero, the blood running every second thinner and slower as if the heart might in the end imperceptibly stop beating'.

Anguish gave way to restlessness, insomnia and nightmare, followed by an extreme lassitude. After which there came an onset of pure, vigorous, creative energy: the beauty and calm of the monastic way of life lost their strange austerity and became familiar, loved, enviable.

When the time came for Leigh Fermor to return to secular life, the shock of transition was even greater than that of the initial detoxification: 'The world seemed an inferno of noise and vulgarity entirely populated by bounders and sluts and crooks. This state of mind, I saw, was, perhaps, as false as my first reactions to monastic life; but the admission did nothing to decrease its unpleasantness.'

Leigh Fermor makes the point that prayer is the defining quality of the monastic life. Without faith, a withdrawal from the world is, essentially, narcissistic. Without a purpose wider than the refinement of one's own interior life, an absorption, however rapturous, in landscape, music, art or poetry is doomed to a reductive solipsism: what one adores in these things turns out to be, essentially, a grandiose reflection of the inside of one's own mind.

This is the note of foreboding sounded by Colette and Lorna Sage in their descriptions of their childhood nature worship: both child-selves were aware of a self-consciousness, a lack of fulfilment, a taint of boredom underlying their pastoral reveries. If trees and fields and skies are easier to love than people – less disappointing and potentially dangerous – they also have their ways of wrong-footing you, reflecting back joke-grotesque images of yourself like the distorting hall of mirrors at the fairground.

I longed to be good, but I associated goodness with emotional generosity rather than solitude. My imaginary alter ego, the calm matriarch inhabiting the ancient house on the edge of the wood, didn't live there alone, sequestered among her plants and animals, but presided over a large household of children and friends and, somewhere about the place (though I hadn't endowed him with any particular characteristics, beyond a certain shadowy bookish-ness and, to be sure, a serene competence in the hitching of tricky trailers and chivvying of reluctant loaders), a husband – an extended family, in fact.

Although I had read *Middlemarch* and *The Portrait of a Lady*, and knew, in theory, about the fatal silliness of idealising marriage, I was not convinced that it was any sillier or more dangerous than Gloria Steinem's cute vision of the post-fertile woman as a sort of wrinkly Héloïse – the 'clear-eyed, shit-free, I-know-what-I-want, I-know-what-I-think, nine- or ten-year-old girl . . . with her own apartment', of which the accounts of the ecstatically detached self-possessed menopausal woman seemed like a more sophisticated version with a richer inner life.

Martin Amis wrote in his autobiography, *Experience*, of the early, successful years of his father's marriage to Elizabeth Jane Howard: 'For a long time, the household had the confidence and humorous liberality that gathers itself around a dynamic marriage.'

That seemed to me an interesting ideal, perhaps achievable even in middle age – given kindness and patience. It is true that the confident dynamism of that marriage came to a bitter end – and even while it lasted, Elizabeth Jane Howard's description of the domestic arrangements in her memoir, *Slipstream*, makes the marriage sound very much less benign than her stepson's depiction of it: the fearful demands of the housekeeping on a generous scale, for which she somehow became solely responsible, had a lamentable effect on her writing life, and after being discovered weeping by her doctor one Sunday morning as she peeled innumerable potatoes (everyone else had gone to the pub), she ended up on Tryptosil and Valium, which stopped the crying, but were equally inimical to creativity.

But that (I told myself), was in the unenlightened Sixties, when men still entertained the delusion that it was acceptable to push off down the pub and leave a very brilliant and beautiful female writer (or even a woman with perfectly ordinary looks and no special talents) weeping into a pile of half-peeled potatoes. In my fantasy household there would be ground rules about this sort of thing. Burdensome tasks would be shared. Many hands would make light work (for the purposes of this reverie I chose not to recall the frequent bitter scenes between my son and me, when he trod mud or spilt food on my newly cleaned house, and I cursed and wept tears of impotent rage).

'Certainly,' wrote George Eliot of Dorothea Brooke, in the closing passage of *Middlemarch*, 'these determining acts of her life were not ideally beautiful.' The sententiousness of this used to make my university English tutor, herself a noble beauty with a fine, passionate nature, much beleaguered by domestic concerns, spit with rage. But rereading that passage in the context of my own life, the determining events of which were far from ideally beautiful, I found it hopeful.

Then I came across another passage, by the American scholar and feminist, Carolyn Heilbrun, who wrote, 'We women have lived too much with closure – there always seems to loom the possibility of something being over, settled, sweeping clear the way for contentment. This is the delusion of a passive life. When the hope for closure is abandoned, when there is an end to fantasy, adventure for women will begin.'

Juxtaposed, these scraps from a larger, more complicated pattern – the abandonment of the perpetually deferred fantasy of a life of 'ideal beauty' and settling instead for affectionate imperfection – gave me a glimmer of hope that a muddled past need not necessarily mean a muddled future. With a little effort of will, I thought, I might yet free myself from the unchosen solitude of my thirties and forties. But still I stood at the fork in the road and hesitated, unable to decide what to do.

12

The Change

While I was absorbed in this reverie of the future, something more dangerous was happening (more dangerous than love? Perhaps). There was a change of editor at the newspaper where I had a freelance contract. It had happened once before during the years I had been at the paper, but that transition had been so quietly accomplished, with so few casualties, that this time I felt at first no particular heightening of the anxiety that is the habitual state of mind of a freelance journalist.

The new editor was said to be brilliant and cultivated: a fine linguist with 'a hinterland', as one of my colleagues put it (meaning that he read books). That sounded almost reassuring. In the absence of any instructions to the contrary I carried on writing, hoping that if his eye fell on the section of the paper in which my work appeared he might read and approve.

But soon there came from the direction of the newspaper office a sound of crashing and toppling, as of a considerable earthquake with many falling buildings and quantities of bodies buried beneath the rubble. My section editor of twelve years was removed from her job, along with several of her senior colleagues, and her place taken by her deputy. This was not altogether unexpected. The unexpected bit came with the redeployment.

From my listening post on the other side of the river, picking up fragments of rumour, whispered phone calls on people's mobiles abruptly terminated as they were summoned to yet another meeting, I thought there seemed to be a whiff of cultural revolution about the process; the devising of ingenious humiliations for the old ruling cadres – making them skip a bit for the amusement of the new regime. But after a while I thought it wasn't really personal – just the natural instinct of the newspaper industry to toy a little with those whose moment is past, as it is the instinct of a cat to toy with a mouse. Still, it is an unusually philosophical mouse that finds much consolation in that thought.

Through it all I wrote on, waiting for something to happen. I didn't know what else to do, and writing took my mind off the gnawing worry that was the alternative. Soon enough, my turn came. I was invited into the office for coffee with the new section editor. Coffee, I thought, sounded ominous. Lunch would have been more encouraging. But no, I was told by various friends who had managed to hold on to their jobs, coffee was the new lunch. It didn't necessarily presage anything bad.

What shall I wear? I asked, thinking of the terrible ideas meetings with me in my bag-lady chic among the sharp ambitious girls in their tight skirts. 'At this stage,' said a friend who was an editor on a different paper, 'I really don't suppose it matters.' On second thoughts, she added, 'Don't wear jewellery. It looks old-fashioned.'

Jewel-free, I turned up and was shown into the section editor's office. She was a woman about a decade younger than me, dressed (I observed from force of habit) in a flirty skirt, a little cardigan and a pair of lace-trimmed leggings, the hems of which stopped at her bare mid-calves. I had worn footless tights when they were fashionable first time around, during the dancewear craze of the Eighties, but in those days we used to wear them like ballerinas at practice class, pulled down around our ankles.

Come in, come in, said the editor with great energy. Coffee? Tea? Biscuit? Really? A glass of water, then? I was writing a book about middle age, wasn't I? Such a great subject; they would definitely want to consider it for extract. Such a fascinating time of life, middle age – so full of opportunity and change, didn't I think? That was it. I was doomed.

I sat silently as she spoke on – time for change, don't want you to vanish from our pages, always admired your writing, freelance opportunity, say ten pieces a year? I wonder, she said suddenly, if I ought to introduce you to Jonathan (the new overall editor and author of all this stimulating change). You're such a good writer, I'm sure he'd love you.

For a moment, I thought I was saved. A painful sensation of relief began to break in my chest, like something tearing. But after a pause, she flapped the idea away with a graceful dismissing movement of her hand – maybe later, he's so busy at the moment – and resumed the flow of talk: regular features meetings – do come! – three months' notice . . .

I think my contract says a month, I said.

Really? Well, for goodness' sake don't tell the managing editor's office that, she said with a complicit giggle. She got up. The meeting was over. She moved towards me, clasped me in her arms and kissed me. Afterwards the thing I really minded was that kiss. I wished I'd had the presence of mind to step away from it and flee with that scrap of my dignity intact. But I didn't.

I emerged from the slab glass office with its chill artificial atmosphere of air conditioning into the spring sunlight and the roar of the city traffic. Towards Tower Bridge a blackbird was singing, perched among the sticky pale-green buds of a lime tree. I wanted very urgently to get home, to see my child, my garden, my cat; to be safe inside my front door, among my books.

It wasn't until I was on the Docklands Railway, rattling over the flimsy concrete track that soared past the blackened brick slums and bald patches of waste ground of Shadwell and Deptford, past the glinting granite and steel of Canada Water and Canary Wharf, past Heron Quays (where no heron, I bet, had ever been seen), before plunging beneath the river to emerge at the safe familiarity of Cutty Sark, that it occurred to me that I wasn't travelling away from danger towards safety.

Nowhere was safe now, for safety cost money and in three months from now (or one month, if the managing editor's office took a glance at the relevant clause in my contract) I would have none. My home wasn't mine unless I had the money to pay for it. There would be no food in the cupboard, no heat, no light, no water, no petrol in the car, for all these things cost money and suddenly I was earning none.

For twelve years I had written 1,000 words a week, 46 weeks a year. For all that time the shape of my week had been the same – the lovely empty expanse of Monday and Tuesday, filled with book reviews or other scraps of freelance writing; the pressure beginning to gather on Wednesday, a day spent sitting on the floor, scissors in hand, searching the crackling dross of four days' worth of newspapers for the seed of an idea that would grow on Thursday morning into an essay. The horror of the conviction each Thursday that the magic wouldn't work, the page would be blank, or that I'd write something, send it through to the subs, but that it would turn out to be gibberish, not thoughts arranged into an argument, just paragraphs of fragmentary nonsense, like dummy copy. Then the curious shame of Friday, when I could never bear to read what I had written, unless someone happened to say it was all right. After that, the breaking of the wave, the flat calm of the weekend, and the start of the process all over again.

I had grown to love the essay form; the diligent, schoolgirl satisfaction of pursuing an argument through three paragraphs of development to a sweet, ringing conclusion. I kept volumes of essays by my bed, studied Bacon and Montaigne, Johnson and Hazlitt, tried to copy their muscular concision, marvelling at the fact that there was no subject so inconsequential – Leigh Hunt on

'Getting Up on Cold Mornings' – that it could not be put to work in an essay; no experience whose anguish could not be assuaged by writing 1,000 words about it and filing them by midday on a Thursday. Until now.

Above all, I said to myself as the train trundled towards Greenwich, I must not frighten Alexander. I must tell him what has happened, and that life may be hard from now on, but I must tell him that we will be all right in the end, and I must believe it myself.

I managed it well enough until he went to bed that first evening, but then I was overcome with a sense of pure, scalding shame at my fecklessness, my failure to protect us against this (easily foreseeable, in fact inevitable, I now saw) disaster.

I started to call and text my friends to tell them what had happened, scribbled down their advice, phone numbers, emails of editors who might be willing to give me work, then mechanically prepared something to eat, drank several glasses of wine and eventually, with a curious, loose, rattling feeling inside, as though my chain had slipped its gears, went to bed and lay awake, dry-eyed and terrified, trying to think sensibly about what to do now.

At about 1.30 in the morning, the phone buzzed. It was a text from a friend, quoting Julian of Norwich: *All shall be well, and all shall be well, and all manner of things shall be well.* I felt as though I wanted to cry, but couldn't.

The next day was a Saturday, when normally I would go to the stableyard to ride. There seemed no reason not to, although I knew that I shouldn't be able to keep the mare for much longer. The whole of life had taken on a provisional quality, the limbo feeling of having left school and not yet started at college, or the selvedge of time between selling one house and moving into the next one.

It was a fine April day, a fuzz of green buds on the woods either side of the road, a robin hopping on the gatepost as I turned into the yard. I went up to the field where the mare was grazing and leaned against her for a long time, scratching her withers and breathing in the sweet, calm smell of her neck until she got bored and bit me. Then I brought her in and went over to the tack room for her saddle.

They had been working on the yard over the winter. The old wooden stables had gone and been replaced by smart, white-washed breeze block. At the angle of the stable block there was a new tack room, almost finished, just waiting for the electric light to be connected. In front of the door was a tiny step. As I opened the door and stepped inside from the light to the dark, I tripped and half fell, catching the side of my brow on the breeze block. It didn't hurt much, but as I stood up, blood started to pour from a cut above my eye.

I leaned against the whitewashed wall with blood dripping through my cupped hands and splashing on the whitewashed concrete at my feet, with a confused sense that this blow to the head was in some way connected to my lost job; that the blood pouring into my hands was my life, leaking away.

'Are you all right?' said someone, but I couldn't put a coherent sentence together; I gazed stupidly at the crimson splashes of blood on the white breeze block and the ground and the little puddle of it in my hands, thinking dully that if only I could stop the bleeding, my life would be put back together, mended some-how, and then everything would be all right again.

'All right' was an expression much repeated by my consoling friends in the following days. 'You'll be all right,' they said. 'You'll be picked up by the *Brute*, the *Beast*, one of the Sundays. X is bound to look after you, or Y. What about Z, have you sent him an email?' I must not panic, they said. I needed to get my name out there. I should tap up everyone I had ever worked with. Above all, I must keep my nerve. Everything would be all right.

I wanted very much to believe this, and managed to some of the time. I had been sacked several times in my twenties, mostly from dull clerical jobs that I didn't much mind losing. I'd only minded the last of those sackings, from a job I loved, as assistant to a man I had thought of as a friend. 'In time,' he said, giving me the bad news, 'you will come to see this as a good thing.'

'Sanctimonious old idiot,' said I, furiously ignoring the half-apology hidden in this unappetising bit of cold consolation and scuttling the friendship with the superb recklessness of the very young, who think that friendship is an infinitely renewable resource. He was right, though. After the end of that job I shifted from publishing to journalism, from dealing with other people's writing to writing myself; and felt, for the first time in my working life, as though I knew what I was doing.

Early in my writing career I was sent to interview a Frenchwoman, a designer who had had the idea – commonplace now, but original twenty years ago – of using the hoardings outside buildings undergoing renovation as giant canvases for artwork. In 1991, when I visited her studio on the outskirts of Paris, she had covered the hoardings outside the church of the Madeleine with a *trompe l'oeil* image of the Madeleine itself. Earlier she had wrapped the Arc de Triomphe in a French flag. When the restoration projects were finished, so was the life of her artwork: it was unwrapped, dismantled, photographs the only proof that it had ever existed.

I was newly pregnant when I interviewed her, and newly parted from the child's father and some of my disturbance of mind must have communicated itself to her, for when the interview seemed to have ended and I was putting away my tape recorder she said, in the very clear, rather formal French in which she had given the interview – slowly, so that I would understand properly what she meant – that she had found that life changed, completely, every seven years or so and that although change was painful – *pénible* – and hard the thing was to embrace it, not to resist but to go with it, see where it took you. She wished me good luck with what I undertook in the future.

It was so kindly said, and with such infectious serenity that it silenced the voice that had been shrilling inside my head since I'd discovered that I was pregnant: 'What am I going to do? Whatever am I going to do?' And although the borrowed stillness and composure lasted only as long as the trip to Paris and dissolved again into panic and disorder as soon as I got home, the memory of them left a permanent impression.

I thought now that I should try to live this crisis more gracefully than I had that one. I had spoiled my pregnancy – my only chance at pregnancy – with panic and hysteria, made myself very unhappy, transferred goodness knew what stress hormones to my unborn child – and for what?

In the end everything had turned out well enough. I had not gone entirely mad, or died of loneliness, or been unable to cope with the baby. A marvellous stroke of good fortune – the arrival of Linda – and a lot of accumulated acts of everyday kindness from my neighbours and friends had kept us safe at the beginning, and as the early danger passed our life had grown into something of which I felt proud. I was a writer, and a good-enough mother. That was not nothing.

Except that now I wasn't a writer, and if I couldn't keep a roof over our heads, I wouldn't be a good-enough mother, either. 'Not very secure, is it, a contract?' more solidly employed friends would sometimes say. 'Aren't you scared?' Terrified, I'd say, and I would trot out a little anecdote about the goldfish in Sellar and Yeatman's comic gardening manual, *Garden Rubbish*, who lives in a lavatory cistern in a sordid bit at the bottom of the garden known as the Unpleasaunce, swimming about in a state of permanent terror that someone will come along and pull the chain. I am that goldfish, I would say, and whoever I was saying it to would laugh merrily and so would I.

I was guilty, I saw now, of what Joan Didion calls Magical Thinking: the delusion that one can bargain with fate, or deflect it by sheer force of will. In my rational mind I knew my job couldn't last for ever. Columnists' lives are generally short, and at twelve years I'd already outlasted the average life expectancy by many years. But in my magical mind I believed that fate would take into account my personal difficulties – the fact that I was a hard-working single mother, doing her best to keep a home together and raise a happy, well-educated child – and pick its moment before administering any kind of serious blow.

I knew one couldn't live a life without setbacks – that was how one grew as a person, after all – but I felt that it would be only fair if mine came singly. My plan, insofar as I had a plan, was to hope that my luck held until Alexander had finished his education, then sell up in London and retreat to an even smaller house in the country. I had not allowed myself to think what might happen if fate chose not to play by my rules.

On that first dreadful white night after losing my job, and on many sleepless nights afterwards, I tried to hold myself together by thinking of my foundling grandfather – the resourcefulness with which he had steadily resisted his own blows of fate (so much more numerous and dangerous and discouraging than this of mine. A hard, bitter fight all his life to survive, yet he'd never made it look hard.)

As a child and a teenager I remembered him always engaged, always charging at life, always amused, interested, always trying to shape the random muddle of happenstance into a story, to use words to impose a meaning and a form on chaotic accident. His own mother had had to give up the struggle to take care of him; I thought he would think less of me if I were not to fight now for my own small household. All the same, I wasn't sanguine about where fighting would get me.

As my notice came to an end I received a letter from the managing editor's office, confirming that my contract had been terminated and thanking me for my 'contribution over the past few years'. I wasn't an employee, so there was no question of redundancy pay. The following month, for the first time since leaving university, there would be no income. I visited my financial adviser, to see if he had any counsel to offer. He was a kind man, but it was a short, bleak meeting. 'Your best bet,' he said, 'is to educate your son as well as you can, and hope to God he looks after you.' Outside in the high summer sunshine I turned my face to the hot brick wall of his office and, for almost the first time since it had happened, I wept.

It was strange to walk through the park with the sun on my back. For whole minutes at a time I would feel perfectly happy; absorbed in the animal contentment of the sunshine, the smell of the hot grass, the hum of London in midsummer.Then with a shock I would remember that my life was in freefall, nothing belonged to me: even the half-pound of sausages in my basket had been bought with borrowed money.

The excursions I made into London social life were odder still. Even after my son was old enough to be left alone in the evenings, I had never much liked going out. I was afraid of parties and would rather stay at home, cook supper, hear about the school day, oversee the homework (it was, of course, this fatal lack of networking that had done for my career).

Now I began to accept the invitations that I had been accustomed to avoid: launch parties for magazines, book publication parties, a PEN charity quiz, celebrity-packed and compèred by a fashionable comedian at the Café Royal. Night after night I got dressed up in the least eccentric clothes I could find and set off for clamorous gatherings in the prosperous West End: champagne and smoked salmon at the Wallace Collection; more champagne at the Natural History Museum; an exquisite dinner of tiny plates of spiced doll's-house food at a smart Indian restaurant; yet more champagne at the Polish Hearth Club, a party from which I had to sprint to yet another party on the same evening. The latter, I learned from the gossip columns the following morning, had been the Party of the Year.

There was a fine line to be struck at these gatherings: on the one hand, my purpose in attending them was in the hope of meeting someone who might feel inclined to give me some work. On the other, I was well aware that misfortune repels. People don't like bad luck: they think it's catching. It was important not to look desperate. Sometimes, as the parties thinned out and people went on to their other engagements, I would run into another middle-aged journalist who was having similar difficulties with work. Garrulous, resentful, a little shabby, she terrified me. I thought that if I wasn't like her already, I surely soon would be.

Not all the parties I went to were alienating. Sometimes I found myself, to my astonishment, having a nice time, even talking happily to strangers – the thing I most dreaded about going out. A capacity for sociability, dormant for years, put out a cautious shoot. At a dinner party to celebrate the publication of a very good novel by an Albanian novelist I found myself sitting next to the novelist, who spoke almost no English, but kept up a lively conversation alternately in Albanian to his left-hand neighbour, the Albanian Ambassador, and in strongly Albanian-flavoured French to me.

On my other side was a young woman who worked on the Foreign Desk of the paper that had just terminated my contract. She had no idea that we had once been colleagues. She was at the beginning of her career, excited about her job with a grand overwhelming passion, as though it were a new love affair. The Foreign Desk had allowed her to save up all her leave, she said, and to take some additional time off so that she could attend an intensive Arabic course at Damascus University. After that she hoped to become a Middle East correspondent.

A fierce and terrible pang of envy shot through me when she said this, like the one that used to grip me in my late twenties when one of my friends announced that she was getting married. Earlier that year I had cut out a newspaper article about a three-month intensive Arabic course run by Tunis University during its summer vacations. I had been to Tunis once and liked it very much: the pale Roman mosaics in the museum, redolent of a life of cultivated ease, the dark and fascinating market where I bought a pair of blue-and-gold leather slippers and a silver bracelet embossed with roses, the flower stalls selling bunches of jasmine bound on to little sticks, which I later saw being gracefully twiddled by men strolling and talking in the cool of the evening, the francophone sensibility, so familiar and so entirely strange.

When I saw that newspaper article I thought that I should like nothing more than to spend three months at Tunis University, learning Arabic. I was used to seeing things that I thought I'd like to do and having to dismiss them because of the tyranny of school terms, but as I began to do the same with this idea, it occurred to me that in a couple of years' time, Alexander would have left school. Whatever he chose to do afterwards, he would certainly not be needing me around. If I wanted, I could let the house and go for three months to Tunis, there to learn the hard language that I wished I had studied when I was younger.

I had been hugging this idea like the promise of a reward – my pay-off for accomplishing eighteen years of motherhood; the first act of my new future of freedom. But something about my conversation with this very bright and sensible girl, whose career path stretched ahead of her in orderly stages, the route clearly marked, not all haphazard and chaotic as mine had been, made me feel suddenly silly, with the particular silliness of a middle-aged woman caught out in fancying herself still capable of doing at 50 the same things that she had done at 20.

Suppose I did go to Tunis for the summer, suppose my ageing brain proved capable of mastering the rudiments of Arabic – what on earth would be the point? It was hardly likely that I could reinvent myself as an Arabist at this stage of my career. It would be a vanity project, of the sort that people take up in their retirement to kill time: petit point, watercolour painting, wood turning. Amateur accomplishments; conversation pieces, ugly and pointless as mantelpiece ornaments.

In the luxurious gloom of adolescence I had counted the careers already closed to me at 14 or 15 – dancer, pianist, vet: proper, demanding vocations, I thought, measured against which writing, which I knew I could do, seemed a negligible, frivolous skill. Now, looking back over the succession (as it seemed to me) of missteps by which I had inexorably closed down the opportunities life had offered me, I was gripped first by a piercing regret for my 20-year-old self, so clever, so unhappy, so stupidly blind to the riches at my disposal; and then by a sort of terror for this young woman, so unlike my younger self in her composure and certainty: a feeling almost like a prayer, of wanting her always to be as safe and certain as she was now, for hateful middle age never to come and blight the confidence, the conviction that she was in charge of her own destiny, that presently shone from her like virtue.

It was only a mood, and by the morning it had changed again; the idea of a trip to Tunis to learn Arabic – not for any particular purpose, just for the sake of the journey and the pure exhilaration of learning something new – seemed once again a bold, interesting, enchanting project. The principal symptom, I was finding, of unemployment was the violently opposed perspectives of the future that it dangled before the mind's eye. I had most of the time a sharp physical sense of cracking open, as though I were an egg from which something damp and bedraggled was struggling to emerge into a future that seemed alternately appalling or exhilarating.

I was haunted by a sense of the extreme fragility of our domestic life, the terrifying speed with which it could unravel. All it would take would be a few months of failing to pay the mortgage, and the carefully arranged stage set on which the past sixteen years of our life together had been played out would vanish: the house repossessed and sold to someone else, the spindly chairs, the pretty woodcuts and bits of chipped china dispersed and just us left, two bare forked animals, stripped of all the accumulated narrative of our lives.

Then again, I had observed in myself over decades a timid tendency to cling to situations – lovers, jobs, places – long after someone braver would have got out. There were a few sunny mornings when the world seemed not poised to disintegrate, but full of possibility for self reinvention, even so late, even as the arc of life was curving away from its apex. But the feeling was elusive and as no work came it visited me less frequently.

'Debt,' wrote Merryn Somerset Webb in *Love is Not Enough*, her admirable manual for women on how to manage money, 'erases freedom more surely than anything else. Once you are in real debt your quality of life disappears.'

We were not – yet – in really serious debt. The one prudent financial decision I had made in my life was to buy a fairly cheap house on a sensible mortgage and overpay steadily. What I had not done was to save. I had not, in newspaper terms, ever been particularly well paid. At the height of my prosperity I was irritated to learn that I was earning slightly less than the starting salary of a friend's 23-year-old daughter at a firm of city solicitors. We had lived comfortably – a week's nice holiday a year, the middle-class flourishes of piano and tennis lessons, a well developed junk shop and second-hand book habit – but not very extravagantly; no dishwasher, no freezer, no widescreen telly, an ancient car. Apart from the baroque folly of keeping a horse in livery.

If I had saved all the money it had cost to buy and keep my mare, I would have had a calamity fund sufficient to keep us going for about six months. How to balance what she had given me – the passport into a new world and all that I had learned there about her, about myself, and about the landscape into which she had taken me – against what I had lost by keeping her: the tormenting anxiety that now assailed me, the real prospect that we would have to relinquish everything I had worked for and begin again? The accounting was too hard, and in any case pointless. I gave it up.

But I could not shake off the vertigo of not having an income; the feeling of plunging dread each time I handed over my debit card to pay the grocery bill. Reading the letters of the novelist

Penelope Fitzgerald, who struggled for much of her life with money, I recognised the panicky disorder of tiny, mad economies that I had begun to adopt. Fitzgerald saved Green Shield Stamps, mended her sandals with plastic wood from Woolworths ('unfortunately they only had "antique walnut" . . .') and resorted to dyeing her hair with a used tea bag ('but it did not make much difference').

I took to rinsing Alexander's discarded drinks bottles and refilling them with squash for the next day's packed lunch. Root vegetables began to feature prominently in our diet; I became ingenious with mince, experimented with home-made yoghurt. As a small girl I had been taught by my grandmother to darn. Now, after a gap of forty-odd years, I resurrected this useful skill. When my linen bed sheets (bought from a fashionable supplier of bed linen at what now seemed ludicrous expense a shockingly short time before) grew threadbare and began to disintegrate, I turned the sides to middle as I had seen my grandmother do with her own worn-out sheets. It was fiddly work, and the result rather lumpy to sleep on, but it gave me the illusion of doing something.

My son put up with most of this quite stoically. He liked some of the home cooking (the cakes, not the root vegetables), and the fact that the piles of darning meant I would sometimes sit through *Match of the Day* with him, stitching, when before I had always claimed to be too busy. When I said that we couldn't afford a summer holiday, he said furiously, '*Why* can't you be successful?' but that was his only reproach to me.

He was to take his GCSEs soon after I lost my job. His grades were borderline and I was afraid our trouble would distract him from his work. On the day the results came out we arranged to meet in a café near his school. Privately, I had already resigned myself to bad news. I was trying to train myself not to care about anything that didn't involve mortal illness or actual homelessness. He arrived looking pink and flustered, holding a scrap of paper. He had got into the Sixth Form quite handsomely, with marks to spare. I felt as though we'd stolen something back from fate; caught hold of something useful and solid in the slithering freefall of our circumstances.

It was the solidity that I missed; the fat chink of money in exchange for goods; the swift progression from desire to ownership of a book or a picture glimpsed on a market stall; the ability to give in to a generous impulse to buy a present or go out for a treat, to lunch or a film. Now we breathed a thin air of renunciation; wrung every drop of value out of each coin of the week's budget.

About the house, things were becoming frayed and shabby: the matting on the stairs was trodden into treacherous holes that caught at our feet as we went up and down; the cane bottoms of the dining-room chairs had worn through and hung down in a bristle of loose ends on which we perched precariously. A tri-angular breach appeared in the lining paper of the stairwell, and behind it a disturbing, dusty looseness where the plaster had rotted. A trickle of plaster dust and clots of ancient disintegrating horsehair bled constantly from the hole, as though the house were haemorrhaging. Alexander complained of something sharp in his bed and when I looked I saw that the coil of a metal spring had worked its way through the wadding and was sticking out. I turned the mattress over and promised that we would buy a new one as soon as I could afford it, whenever that might be.

With a synchronicity too perfect not to seem malevolent, all the appliances in the house began to break down: the oven gave a faint pop and died, halfway through cooking a cake. The washing machine began to emit grinding sounds of struggle during the spin cycle until, with a grievous clank and a terrible expiring shudder it, too, gave up. Sick at heart, I replaced them both on credit. I'd never worried about things being shabby before, but that was in the days when I knew the trick of how to turn words into money – like the girl in the fairy tale, spinning straw into gold, I used to think – and it seemed that as long as the words didn't run out, neither would the money. But now the knack had gone and the fate maliciously predicted for me by my friend, of becoming a mad old woman living in a decaying house full of ruined bibelots, seemed all too plausible.

It was late December. I had been unemployed for six months. Despite everything, I said, we will have a lovely Christmas. Better things will come in the New Year. We bought a huge, bushy Christmas tree in Blackheath and wrestled it into the drawing room. I went to an Advent service at the Naval College chapel and sang carols of peace and renewal. It was very cold, with a biting north-easterly wind, but clear and sunny. Indoors it was warm and the smell of pine resin and baking filled the house. But on the night before Christmas Eve, as I stood in the shower, the water ran cold. The boiler had stopped working. In the morning an engineer came and said that it was too old to repair. There was nothing to be done. We would have to wait until the New Year for a new one to be installed. It would cost a couple of thousand pounds. In the meantime we had no heat, and no hot water.

It was freezing indoors and out. The bathroom was so cold that it was almost unbearable to get undressed for long enough to wash in a kettleful of boiled water. I thought of my grandmother's stories of being sewn into her vest for the winter as a child. In bed at night, with two jumpers over my nightgown, clutching a hot-water bottle and the cat for warmth, I couldn't sleep for cold. Yet I had grown up in a house without central heating, warmed only by open coal fires, with hot water intermittently supplied by a sullen and filthy coke-fired furnace. I remembered waking to find a hard glittering tracery of icy leaves and flowers and star shapes etched on the inside of my bedroom windows. How odd, I thought now, that I should remember only the fantastical prettiness of the ice patterns, and not the savage chill that must have accompanied them.

The radio, fascinated by the unaccustomed freeze, broadcast programmes about frost fairs on the Thames, the reminiscences of Seamus Heaney of washing in biting cold water drawn from the outside pump, packed with straw to keep it from freezing solid. They had a frosty glamour, these tales of chilly revelry, that seemed absent from our present squalid experience. The refrigerator, presumably in a spirit of sympathy, stopped working. Not that it mattered, since we could keep our food cold simply by placing it on the gelid stone floor by the back door. 'Inside the fridge is the only warm place in the house,' I said to friends as we exchanged bulletins on our Christmases, trying as usual to control the uncontrollable messiness of life by turning it into a story.

What I can't get over, I said to my friend Prudence Entwhistle, who was dividing her Christmas in orderly fashion between family, friends and her elegant flat among the silent turrets and quadrangles of her deserted school, is the random spitefulness of all this. The lost job *or* the expensive series of domestic disasters, surely? Not both at the same time. Not that I expect to be exempt from bad things, you know? But I wish they'd form an orderly queue . . .

You must have noticed, said Prudence, that this is what life is like at our age. Just when you think you've got a grip on one thing, something else goes wrong. Like dragon's teeth: you sort out an intractable problem and another three spring up to take its place. It was true. Even during the past year, while I had been preoccupied with shoring up the breaches in the walls of my own existence, I had noticed that a wave of change had broken over my contemporaries, swelling silently behind us as we paddled about in the calm waters of our daily lives, the undertow catching us off balance and dragging us away over a bruising series of hidden rocks: divorce, bereavement, illness, debt.

With an abrupt shift of perspective, like a blurred image seen through a telescope coming into focus, I understood that all of us, in different ways, were being forced to learn the art of losing. The sense we had of ourselves when young as invulnerable, immortals with a superb mastery over our own destinies, was still recent enough for our instinctive reaction when things went wrong to remain that of astonished resentment. 'The timing is *terrible*,' said a friend taken unexpectedly, outrageously, seriously ill. 'It's *so inconvenient*. In another couple of years, perhaps, when things were quieter, it wouldn't have mattered so much. But at the moment. It's just . . . *not me*.'

'So many things seem filled with the intent/to be lost that their loss is no disaster,' wrote Elizabeth Bishop in a poem cataloguing a series of wrenching losses survived – door keys, an ill-spent hour, houses, a lover, a continent, her mother's watch . . . 'Lose something every day,' she wrote. That, I knew, we were all doing already without even trying. Time, in particular, but other things as well.

Soon after Christmas I saw my neighbour's daughter come up the garden path. She was holding a black bundle. 'Mum wanted you to have this,' she said when I opened the door. 'She's getting rid of her bits.' The bundle was a doll: one of the elaborately costumed tribe with which Violet's front room was filled, like silent guests at a party. This one stared fixedly from green glass eyes with a silky fringe of eyelashes, an infinitesimal spattering of russet freckles across her china nose. She was dressed in a black velvet riding habit, laced black boots, a black veiled hat perched on a mass of reddish ringlets. From her china hand dangled a black whip, silk-bound. 'Mum thought you'd like her because she's dressed in riding clothes,' said Sylvia.

'But why is Violet giving away her dolls?' I asked.

'She says she don't want them no more,' said Sylvia.

While I was considering what to do with this macabre and infinitely touching souvenir the telephone rang. My sturdy, adventurous, redoubtable aunt, not long returned from a strenuous road trip around the Shetland Isles with a friend, had got tangled up with a small dog in a park and fallen, breaking her leg.

The hospital where she was being treated did not conform to the dire image of NHS hospitals often described in the press. The ward was clean, the nurses mostly kind and attentive. Yet it seemed to me a fearful place, filled with hulks of humanity, beached on their metal cots in the hot rooms like the decayed sail barges whose forlorn ruins, half sunk in the mud-flats around Oare and Milton Creek, I used to visit as a child with my grandfather.

Once all these old people had been babies; their tender fingers and the perfect curve of their cheeks piercing their mothers' hearts with love as sharp as pain. They had skipped ropes and kicked footballs, learned grammar and fractions, made friends and enemies, kissed and fought and danced and made love, had children of their own, watched their parents and grandparents decay with pity and perhaps with impatience. Now they lay in their beds, toothless mouths agape, moaning a little in their dreams, or propelled themselves gallantly in wheeled chairs to the bleak common room, where a little black television perched high on a corner bracket chittered irritably to itself like a sick monkey.

What unnerved me was how quickly my proud and contrary aunt had learned to live by the rules of this place: her larger world contracted to the limits of her shared room with its cramped storage space and hard fluorescent strip light, the rhythm of her days marked by the oddly early hours of her mealtimes with their nursery names – breakfast, dinner, tea – her individuality sub-sumed into the role of a good patient: ungendered, trusting, compliant. The things that had made her distinctively herself – her intelligence, her questioning spirit, her scepticism of authority, even her femaleness – now represented impediments to the smooth running of the machine in which she was being processed. She must suppress them, or be thought difficult and suffer the consequences of that ominous adjective.

The realisation gave me a shock like a slice with a knife. I had thought, abstractly, of old age as involving a loss of independence, of advancing ugliness and feebleness – the chagrin of lost allure and the humiliation of physical decline. Perhaps, too, a certain blurring of affect (though the old people I had known well – all four grandparents, Violet and half a dozen more who had become close friends in one way or another – had all remained very sharply themselves). I had not, until now, considered that such basic instincts as modesty, curiosity or an opinion about the functioning of one's own body might become luxuries as one approached the end of the journey.

I had thought of the term 'second childhood' as describing a personal medical disaster: a catastrophic decline in individual cognitive function. I had not considered that at 80, with one's wits intact and nothing wrong beyond a broken tib and fib, one might be urged into that state of sexless, opinionless dependence by professionals for whom the combination of sound minds with unsound bodies is incompatible with efficient systems management.

Emerging from the stifling heat and wilful ugliness of the hospital, with its sickly pastel draperies and linoleum the colour of highly polished dung, into the compromised tenderness of a spring twilight in the Medway towns, the grind of traffic fighting with a late, lyrical blackbird as the sun set over the sluggish river and the metallic grey torrent of the motorway in a sky of pure violet, I was filled with a sense not of *timor mortis* but of a life not yet lived. The rise and fall of my breathing, the ache in my thighs where I had been gripping the saddle at the weekend, the shape of the crescent moon growing sharper in the darkening sky above the lurid glow of headlights and street lights all gave me an urgent sense of what remains as things fall away.

There are thirty years between my 80-year-old-aunt and myself; thirty years between my present self and the 20-year-old self that leaned against the honey stone of the sash window in the Oxford college, listening to the Four Last Songs and thinking about love. Thirty years since I was young, and thirty years more before I am old, if I should live so long.

'I don't think of the future, or the past, I feast on the moment,' wrote Virginia Woolf in her diary. 'This is the secret of happiness;

but only reached now in middle age.' Is that the secret? To eschew regret and apprehension alike? Perhaps.

There came a telephone call, asking me to attend the funeral of my old Latin teacher and, a month later, of her husband: Baucis and Philemon, the two old trees withering together. They had taken me in as a furious teenager, given me a home when I had lost one, tried to show me that hard work would give me a way out of the small-town dead end in which I was angrily struggling.

Twice in a month I drove the fifty miles from London, turned off the motorway on to the tree-lined street, unvisited in decades, where I grew up; retraced the route I walked every day to school and back. Woodstock Road, Park Avenue, Tunstall Road – the map of the suburban streets scratched on my heart, all but obliterated now by later superimpositions: St Giles, the Broad, the King's Road, Peckham Rye, the Trafalgar Road and who knew where next.

At the top of the hill by the church I turned into the rectory and parked the car. Crossed the road, tottering in flash London mourning of high heels, tight black skirt and diamonds, hefting on my hip a tray of cheese scones and fairy cakes for the funeral tea. Opened the heavy church door of blackened oak with its familiar creak and there rose the scent, instantly recognisable though I had not smelt it in three decades, of cold stone, damp carpet, wood polish, candle smoke, hymn books and incense.

Twice in a month we, the assembled family and friends of the departed, considered the intelligence, resolution and high spirits that took my Latin teacher and her husband from families in small Welsh villages, unaccustomed to educating their children at university, to colleges in Oxford and Cambridge and minds stocked with mediaeval French and Latin. Twice in a month we sang 'Cwm Rhondda' in their honour. Twice in a month the passing bell was tolled in the bell tower whose quarterly chimes marked out the hours of my childhood; and I looked round at the congregation – my old headmistress, dark and glittering as she was 40 years ago when I used to skip a rope in the shade of the lilac trees in the school playground; a scattering of my old schoolfriends, the lineaments of our childish faces visible in our middle-aged faces only to each other, like secret runes – and I thought, these are the only people who remember me as a child. When they are gone, my childhood will have vanished.

After the first funeral I drove back to London in tears, gripped with bitter regret for the love that my teacher and her husband had given so freely, and I had absorbed so greedily but never repaid; never said thank you, or tried to reciprocate later, when I could easily have afforded to. I said some of this to their children, who said, But they were proud of you. They read everything you wrote. As though that were good enough.

The second time, I followed the path round to where they both now lay buried in new graves, side by side in the shadow of the ancient church and the young yew tree planted to mark the millennium. And then, in the gathering dusk, I walked up the narrow path between the church and the school that I had travelled every schoolday between the ages of five and 11. Past the dark thicket of trees behind a wooden paling fence; along the cinder alley between the orchard and the blackthorn hedge, and out at the school gate.

Changed, now, a little, from my memory of it: a post-and-rail fence instead of the hawthorn hedge that used to enclose the asphalt playground where we rolled our marbles and fought with conkers. The Nissen hut full of wooden hoops and coiled skipping ropes vanished and replaced with airy brick-and-glass classrooms.

But the pointed Victorian Gothic façade of the old schoolhouse was there still, and so was the orchard at the back of the classrooms where I used to gaze out from my desk on early summer after- noons, chewing my pencil, watching the sparrows quarrelling among the apple blossom and thinking, thinking, about time and words and what might happen next.

Envoi

'My concern is not to depict the individual as he exists,' wrote Montaigne, 'but to show him in the act of becoming. I paint the passing of time – not from one age to another, in seven-year stages, as people say – but from day to day and minute to minute. My story changes with the passing hour.'

A story such as this of mine changes, like Montaigne's, with each passing day and minute. One has to find a convenient place at which to stop – and inevitably ends are left dangling.

Some I can tidy up. I did, in the end, decide to try what life might be like as part of a couple. But I made up my mind too late. My lover found that he liked the idea of me better than the reality and, with a certain symmetry, told me so one New Year's Eve.

Towards midnight I made a small package of the things he'd given me and the letters he'd sent over the years, and walked down to the Thames, intending to throw it in. But I'd forgotten a crucial detail. The tide was out. Instead of a satisfying splash as I hurled the packet into the stream, there would have been only a little squelch as it landed on the muddy foreshore. So I took it home again. In matters of the heart, my timing had always been lamentable.

A year after losing my newspaper job I was offered another, just in time to avert real disaster. It wasn't the same sort of job, but it meant that we could stay living in the same house, and even that I could keep my old mare, who was ageing, as animals grieve their owners by doing, even faster than me. An injury ended her jumping career. But I tried a side saddle on her, and she took to it with verve.

My son turned out to have the knack, which I have always admired in other people and never mastered myself, of working quite hard while appearing to make no effort at all. After banishing me firmly from his academic life, he passed his A levels and got a place at an excellent university, a very long way from home.

It was so far away that it took us two days to drive there, and on the way a strange thing happened. The panicky anxiety about the future that had poisoned the past two years vanished as we got into the car laden with the brand-new domestic impedimenta of his life away from home. And on the long drive northwards the old loving complicity of his childhood returned as though it had never gone. Except that it wasn't quite the same, for he was a grown man now, and my job of bringing him up was done. As I unpacked his stuff in his new room, one of his flatmates stuck his head round the door. 'Are you moving in?' he asked, not seeing Alexander, who was bringing up the last of the boxes.

'No,' I said. 'He is. I'm just a mother.'

My own ageing has surprised me a little by its swiftness. 'Each day in the mirror I watch death at work,' wrote Cocteau. And that is what I feel every morning as the lineaments of my face swim into focus in the glass and I see reflected there not the face I still think of as mine – the face to which I became accustomed during the first three decades of my adult life – but a version of those features that I can't quite connect with the person I still feel myself to be.

Of course this process is troubling, especially after a sleepless night, or too much to drink, or on a fine spring morning when I jump out of bed feeling 20 years old again, and see my 50-year-old self peering back at me. Time passes no more swiftly than it did when I was young, but I am haunted by the sense of how little of it is left.

It is a melancholy calculation, but not, in its way, uninteresting. I have had to learn once, at the end of my childhood, to inhabit a set of changing features, and now I am having to do so again. Like the narrator of Marguerite Duras's novel, *The Lover*, I watch the process 'with the same sort of interest I might have taken in the reading of a book . . .' This is my life story, written here on my face, and who knows what the next chapter may bring.

Bibliography

While writing *The Stranger in the Mirror*, I found the following books helpful:

Athill, Diana, *Somewhere Towards the End* (Granta Books, 2008)
Barnes, Julian, *Nothing to Be Frightened Of* (Jonathan Cape, 2008)
de Beauvoir, Simone, *Force of Circumstance*, translated by Richard
    Howard (André Deutsch and Weidenfeld and Nicolson,
    1965)
    —*All Said and Done*, translated by Patrick O'Brian (André
      Deutsch and Weidenfeld and Nicolson, 1974)
    —*The Second Sex*, translated and edited by H. M. Parshley
      (Penguin, 1974)
Braun Levine, Suzanne, *The Woman's Guide to Second Adulthood*
    —*Inventing the Rest of Our Lives* (Bloomsbury, 2006)
Byatt, A. S., *The Djinn in the Nightingale's Eye, Five Fairy Stories*
    (Chatto & Windus, 1994)
Chaucer, Geoffrey, *The Complete Works*, edited by Walter W.
    Skeat (Oxford University Press, 1973)
Colette, *Chéri, The Last of Chéri*, translated by Roger Senhouse
    (Penguin, 1979)

—*Claudine At School*, translated by Antonia White (Penguin, 1972)

—*Earthly Paradise*, edited by Robert Phelps (Penguin, 1974)

—*The Evening Star*, translated by David Le Vay (Peter Owen, 1973)

—*La Naissance du Jour* (Flammarion, 1984)

Didion, Joan, *The Year of Magical Thinking* (Fourth Estate, 2005)

Drabble, Margaret, *The Millstone* (Weidenfeld and Nicolson, 1965)

Eliot, George, *Middlemarch* (Wordsworth Editions, 1994)

Foxcroft, Louise, *Hot Flushes, Cold Science, A History of the Modern Menopause* (Granta Books, 2009)

Goldsworthy, Joanna (ed.), *A Certain Age, Reflecting on the Menopause* (Virago Press, 1993)

Greer, Germaine, *The Change, Women, Ageing and the Menopause* (Penguin, 1992)

Hamilton, Christopher, *Middle Age* (Acumen, 2009)

Harvey, John, *Clothes* (Acumen, 2008)

Heilbrun, Carolyn G., *The Last Gift of Time, Life Beyond Sixty* (Ballantine, 1997)

Holder, Judith, *Grumpy Old Women* (BBC Books, 2006)

Jakobson Ramin, Cathryn, *That Memory Book – How to Deal with Distractibility, Forgetfulness and Other Unnerving High Jinks of the Middle-Aged Brain* (Virago Press, 2007)

James, Henry, *The Portrait of a Lady* (Penguin, 1986)

Jones, Dr Hilary, *A Change for the Better, How to survive – and thrive – during the menopause* (Hodder & Stoughton, 2000)

Jouve, Marie-Andrée, *Balenciaga*, translated by Jane Brenton (Thames and Hudson, 1997)

Lee, Hermione, *Virginia Woolf* (Vintage, 1997)

Leigh Fermor, Patrick, *A Time to Keep Silence* (Penguin, 1988)

MacGregor, Dr Anne, *Understanding the Menopause & HRT* (Family Doctor Publications, 2005–6)

Maitland, Sara, *A Book of Silence* (Granta Books, 2008)

Bibliography

—*On Becoming A Fairy Godmother* (Maia Press, 2003)

Mitford, Nancy, *The Best Novels of Nancy Mitford* (Hamish Hamilton, 1974)

Montaigne, Michel de, *The Complete Essays*, translated and edited by M. A. Screech (Penguin, 1993)

Murray, Jenni, *Is It Me, Or Is It Hot In Here?* (Vermilion, 2001)

Oakley, Ann, *Fracture, Adventures of a Broken Body* (The Policy Press, 2007)

Opie, Iona and Peter (eds.), *The Oxford Dictionary of Nursery Rhymes*, (Oxford University Press, 1997)

Paloge, Helen, *The Silent Echo, The Middle-Aged Female Body in Contemporary Women's Fiction* (Lexington Books, 2007)

Sage, Lorna, *Bad Blood* (Fourth Estate, 2001)

Sheehy, Gail, *The Silent Passage, Menopause* (Random House, 1991)

Simpson, Helen, *Constitutional* (Jonathan Cape, 2005)

—*Hey Yeah Right Get a Life* (Jonathan Cape, 2000)

Thurman, Judith, *Secrets of the Flesh, A Life of Colette* (Bloomsbury, 2000)

Tyler, Anne, *Back When We Were Grown-ups* (Chatto & Windus, 2001)

Webb, Merryn Somerset, *Love is Not Enough, A Smart Woman's Guide to Making (& Keeping) Money* (Harper Press, 2007)

Wilson, Angus, *The Middle Age of Mrs Eliot* (Penguin, 1961)

Woolf, Virginia, *The Diary of Virginia Woolf,* Volume III: 1925–1930, edited by Anne Olivier Bell (The Hogarth Press, 1980)

—The Diary of Virginia Woolf Volume IV: 1831–1935, edited by Anne Olivier Bell (The Hogarth Press, 1982)

—*Mrs Dalloway* (The Hogarth Press, 1929)

—'On Being Ill', from *The Moment and Other Essays*, (The Hogarth Press, 1947)

—*To the Lighthouse* (The Hogarth Press, 1927)

—*The Waves* (The Hogarth Press, 1931)

Acknowledgements

The author's name on the title page gives the impression that writing a book is an individual enterprise, but of course it is not. I should like to thank my agent, Ed Victor, and my editors, Alison Samuel, Becky Hardie and Clara Farmer, for their encouragement and patience. I am grateful to Beth Humphries for her perceptive copy-editing, Parisa Ebrahimi for her calm and meticulous help with the final details and Audrey Bardou for her eloquent photography. Juliet Brooke kept me company on the photoshoot – a task well beyond the ordinary call of editorial duty. The London Library was indispensable, both as a resource and a sanctuary. It is hard to imagine a writing life without it.

I am very grateful to Brian MacArthur, Sandra Parsons, Michael Prodger, David Sexton, Gaby Wood and, especially, Sarah Sands, for keeping me afloat financially during the eventful gestation of this book.

My love and thanks to Sarah Crompton, Andrew Hayward, Sarah Lock, Colonel John Mennell, Pip Moon, the Selby family, Audrey Shilling and Helen Williams, all of whom at various times encouraged me – sometimes quite forcefully – to kick on. Several people not mentioned by name here played heroic roles in helping me to get started and, having started, to continue. you know who you are and how much I owe you. Molly, Nico and Caspar make everything seem better. My dear son Alexander tolerates with patience and generosity the trials of having a writing mother. He is the point of it all.